W9-BEM-943

Copyright @ 2011 Carol Scudere
All rights reserved.

Cover design by eCover Makers
Edited by Nichole Haschke, Mark Zacek, and Shannon Seyer
Recipes tested by Carol Scudere and Tammy Anders

First Printing by:

Budget Meals, Inc.
67 Clairedan Drive
Powell, Ohio 43065
614.505.6431
www.Budget-Meals.org

No part of this book may be reproduced, stored in a retrieval system, or transmitted in any form or by any means—electronic, mechanical, photocopying, recording, or otherwise-without prior permission in writing from the copyright holder except as provided by USA copyright law.

ISBN-13: 978-0-9839390-5-4   Paperback 8 ½ x 11 inches

SAN Number 920-0657

Dedication

This book is dedicated to all of the schools that I attended that taught Home Economics, and gave me skills in sewing, cooking, and caring for a home; for all the friends that allowed me to practice my cooking skills on them; and for all those who wish to improve the quality of food they consume, and the meals offered to their families, at the lowest possible cost.

Introduction

My name is Carol Scudere. For over twenty years, I have spent my professional career building a prominent national employment service agency and state-certified school, Professional Domestic Services & Institute. In this business, I have been helping the wealthy in the efficient management of their households and training individuals who wish to enter this profession.

Today, we are suffering through the worst economy in over eighty years, for which there is no end in sight. I feel compelled now to help another demographic in the management of their households: those families who face a radical loss of income due to job loss or the replacement of a well-paying job with one where the ends no longer meet, or anyone who wishes to stretch their food dollar while improving their nutrition and the quality of their food.

It is for these families that I founded Budget Meals, Inc., a non-profit organization based in Ohio and dedicated to teaching others through local classes on how to budget, plan menus, cook, shop, and "make do with less." Through this education, local food pantries as well as state and federal agencies can become less strained as families learn to improve their self-sufficiency. Budget Meals takes to heart the ancient proverb, "Give a man a fish and you feed him for a day. Teach a man to fish and you feed him for a lifetime."

Teaching families these life skills through Budget Meals' classes is highly rewarding for all involved. However, teaching through classes will always be limited in its reach. I realized that the lessons Budget Meals teaches and the knowledge that I have acquired in a lifetime of helping others could reach a greater number of people if the lessons were available in book form. That is why I have written and published this book. May it reach all those who have need of these life skills and those who wish to teach the lessons of this book to families in need.

It came as a surprise to me how much a poor economy affected our way of living. Everything has been touched by things happening in the world around us.

Our way of life has changed so much:

Gasoline prices reaching extreme highs

Food prices exceeding everyone's expectations

Home foreclosures

High unemployment

Multiple families sharing homes

More families than ever seeking food assistance from churches, food pantries, friends and family members, and so on.

This book, like the classes offered by Budget Meals, was designed to help families so that they could provide more food for their families at the lowest possible cost. The methods described in this book came about from years of research and practice to help prevent hunger in families.

During this recession many individuals have called me seeking employment, and I have been unable to help. This recession has affected not only the employment situation of my own business, but also almost every other business known to mankind. I asked myself, what could be done? Since cooking is a passion of mine, and everyone needs to eat, developing a way to save money on groceries seemed to be a way to help. My goal was to be able to feed a family of four (4) for approximately $300.00 a month, with food that is well-balanced nutritionally as well as tasty and enjoyable. However, with the current economic situation, some adjustments may have to be made.

In 2009, I formed Budget Meals to provide educational classes to teach a system I developed for myself and others. This process has enabled me to save up to 60% off my groceries on almost every shopping trip.

When I provide costs/prices in this book, remember that it is for the area that I am currently residing (Columbus, Ohio), and based on sale prices for the food I purchased during the year of 2011. Your own area and shopping habits might influence how much it would cost you to prepare similar foods. However, if you are willing to change of your shopping habits, you should also be able to achieve similar savings.

I owe many thanks of gratitude to Shannon Seyer, Nicole Haschke, Mark Zacek, Tammy Anders and others for their contributions, suggestions, testing of recipes, hard work, and the thousands of hours of research, to make this book a valuable asset for every home.

Part I

Chapter 1

Save up to 60% on

Your Groceries

One way to save money is to prepare meals at home rather than eating out. Grocery shopping can take a large chunk out of your budget every week, and the price of food continues to rise every year.

Not all food products are inflated equally. Prices for grains products, such as cereals and baked goods have risen as much as 9% while the cost of fresh fruits and vegetables are up 10%. Depending on how high the cost of gasoline goes, expect everything you purchase to go up in cost.

As of the date of this publication, beef has gone up almost 40% for some cuts. However, the price of chicken has remained relatively low, followed by pork and fish.

Fortunately, there are many ways you can reduce the amount you spend on food while still making delicious and nutritious meals for your family. Here are some guidelines to follow.

First, *plan ahead.* The best way to spend too much on food is to go shopping without a list or without having planned a menu for the week. You will spend a lot more on impulse and convenience food purchases that way. Before you go shopping, sit down and write a week's worth of menus.

- While you make these menus, <u>look in your pantry, refrigerator and freezer</u>. You

Learn to Save
Save 30 to 60%
on your Grocery
Shopping

Free Class

Budget-Meals, Inc.
614.505.6431

Details: www.budget-meals.org
Email: carol@budget-meals.org

may find some forgotten-but-still good items that you can incorporate into a meal. The more you use the food you have on hand, the more money you save on food you will not have to buy.

- If a recipe calls for a certain convenience food, <u>read the ingredients</u> list on the convenience food packaging and see if you have the key ingredients. You can then use your own ingredients instead of purchasing the convenience food, which may have additional ingredients (preservatives and excessive salt, for instance) that you will not want to use.

- Another step in making your menus and lists is to <u>read grocery store ads</u>. See what is on sale, then incorporate the sale-priced foods into your menus. I personally never purchase anything that <u>is not on sale</u> and if I need something will then go to my pantry or freezer to make a selection.

- Once you have finished preparing your menus, <u>make a shopping list and organize it by department</u> (for instance, produce, meats, dairy, canned goods, pasta). This will not only save shopping time, but it will also prevent you from entering aisles you do not have to, which in turn will help prevent impulse purchases.

- <u>Shop no more than once a week</u>, if possible. This saves gas and time and prevents impulse purchases.

- If you have more than one grocery store nearby, <u>compare prices</u>. It is common for the same items to be priced differently at different stores. Do not neglect thrift bakery stores. In addition to bread, they often sell other food items such as dairy and canned goods. However, if you are driving to many different places to save on your grocery shopping, you will spend more in gasoline and time away from your family or work.

- <u>Purchase in bulk</u> whenever possible, but make sure you are getting a savings by doing this. Also be certain you store these items in insect/rodent proof containers.

Second, *shop smartly.*

- If you can <u>shop alone</u>, do so. Children may pressure you into purchasing items not on the list. If it is not possible to shop alone, explain to your children before you go that you will buy only what is on your list. Or if you can afford it, you may allow them to select one item not on the list as a special treat for their good behavior.

- <u>Never shop hungry</u>. You have probably heard this advice before, but it bears repeating. When you are hungry, everything is a temptation, and you are more likely to buy more than you need.

- <u>Stick to your list</u> unless you are substituting. For instance, if you were planning to buy a particular vegetable or cut of meat, but discover a special discount on another, consider substituting the sale item. Many times stores will offer specials that are not shown in their store flyer.

- Shop by unit price. Price tags on store shelves contain a notation for "unit price," meaning the price per specific unit of measure, such as ounce or quart. You will identify the bargains by comparing unit prices rather than item prices.

- Do not be reluctant to purchase store brands. These are often bargains (not always, though—compare prices carefully), low in price and high in quality. When purchasing a store brand for the first time, purchase only one item to be certain that it meets your quality standards. There will be disappointments. For instance, I have yet to find a store brand that I like as well as Dawn liquid dishwashing detergent.

- Purchase convenience foods sparingly. Do not purchase higher-priced convenience foods that are easily prepared at home. Canned or frozen beans are an example of a convenience food that may be worth purchasing. Frozen dinners are definitely not. You can prepare your own frozen dinner equivalents that are not only less expensive, but will have maintained the nutrients otherwise lost in commercial processing and will have avoided chemical additives.

- If they are a better bargain, purchase whole chickens rather than pieces. Roast a chicken for one meal, and then use the leftovers for additional meals, such as soups, sandwiches, and casseroles. Currently, I can purchase chicken thighs in my area for 89 cents per pound when they are on sale. For less than $2.00 I can purchase 8 chicken thighs, which will provide four adult meals (2 thighs per adult). Pork loin is another good economical choice that you can use in many ways; as a roast, pork chops (even stuffed ones), pulled pork, sandwiches, or in a stir fry.

- Be very selective when purchasing snack and junk foods. Junk foods should be strictly limited, as they are a prime contributor to obesity and have a terrible nutritional value and a high price.

- Snack foods are acceptable if they are priced low and are nutritious; however this is a difficult combination to find! You may want to stick to raw fruits and vegetables for snack options, which may require training of your children as well as yourself. One snack food that we have found to be relatively high on both the economic and nutrition scales is popcorn. Steer clear of the microwave pouches, though; instead, get jars or bags of popcorn kernels. You can air-pop them (if you have an air popper) or pop them on the stove with some oil in a large pot. When I purchase snack foods I purchase the most economical bag, then I break it down by serving size and put them into baggies. This way I do not overeat the snacks. I can usually get one bag of snacks to last me a whole month. I also got out of the habit of purchasing soda by making a fresh pitcher of iced tea (approximately 2 ½ quarts) each morning. Then I either drink either that or water. On the occasion when I have to have a soda, I limit myself to one can per day; usually do not drink all of that unless I am eating pizza or spaghetti.

- Know some of the tactics stores use to encourage you to spend more.
  - **Endcaps:** stores often advertise sales on endcaps. This may lead you to believe that this brand carries the lowest price on a particular product. But that is not always the case. In general, avoid endcaps and focus your shopping within the aisles where you can compare prices.
  - **Location:** The most commonly purchased staples are placed in areas that force shoppers to walk past other items that will tempt them to make impulse purchases. Stick to your list and do not give in to temptation!
  - **Checkout aisles:** These are full of budget-wreckers like gossip magazines and dreadful-for-you single-serving bottles of soda, candies, and gum. Stick to your list and avoid temptation. (This is another good reason to leave the children at home if you can!)
  - **Loss leaders**: these are items the store is willing to take a monetary loss on, in order to get you into the store to make high profit purchases. If you go into the store just for a loss leader item, be sure not to fall into the temptation of buying other, more costly items. Of course, it is best if you never go to the grocery store for only one or two items. Careful planning of your menu and your shopping list will largely prevent such trips. This will also save you time and gasoline.
- Take your time. Time spent checking for bargains and comparison shopping will be worth the money saved. If you can avoid shopping at times when the stores are crowded, you can save time waiting in lines or maneuvering the aisles.
- Some stores will offer damaged or bruised fruits and vegetables at a lower price that can save you up to 75%. Find out what time they put these items out and try to do your grocery shopping then so that you can take advantage of these great bargains. Beware that not all stores offer these discounts.
- Be sure to check shelves high and low for the best prices. The most profitable items for the store tend to be placed at eye-level.
- Double-check sale prices. Buy "3 for $10" or even "10 for $10" sales; you usually do not need to buy the quantity specified to get the sale price.
- Take a calculator. This will help you determine the unit price of each item.

Third, *make the most of your food.* You have a lot of options when cooking to make your food not only more economical, but also more convenient. Here are a few ways to do this:

- Use "filler" foods. These include beans, pasta, and rice. These stretch the size of your meals with less expensive ingredients while adding flavor and, particularly with beans, nutrition to your meal.
- Cook more than you need for your meal. Use the leftovers to pack in lunches for your family or put in the freezer to provide a quick meal for another day.
- Use fresh, whole potatoes rather than frozen French fries or tater tots. Both sweet and white potatoes are cost-effective and make delicious oven-baked fries, scalloped, mashed or roasted potatoes. You can purchase a small bag of frozen potatoes for around $1.75, whereas you can purchase a 10-pound bag of potatoes for under $4.00. I still remember the good-old-days of just last year when I could buy 10 pounds of fresh potatoes for $2.99 any week.   This has now translated into a 33% increase in just the past year!
- Hate the dinner food-prep rush? Instead of taking time every night to do prep work, take one night a week to do the work for all your meals. Chop vegetables, grate cheese, cut up meat, and then store in plastic bags. Have your children help you. It can be great family time as well as a great way to pass on life skills to your children. Of course you must have your week's menu planned for this strategy.
- Every now and then, examine the contents of your refrigerator for any foods that are nearing their expiration date and work those foods into the following day's menu.
- Rather than dumping leftovers into one enormous bag or plastic container, divide them into single-sized portions. This makes them easier to pack as a lunch.
- Teach your children to eat healthy snacks instead of junk food. If they can peel carrots and cut up celery or make a peanut butter sandwich, they will often take more of an interest in fresh, wholesome foods.
- If you run out of something you need in a recipe, before dashing to the store to replenish that item, consider whether you can creatively substitute. Out of a seasoning? See what spices you have that you could use together to recreate the taste, or even try something new. Run out of brown sugar? Try adding molasses to white sugar. Not enough barbeque sauce? See what you can put together with ketchup, mustard, brown sugar, and some spices. Run out of butter? If you are not using it for baking, try olive oil – it is healthier.   There are charts, later in the book, that will provide you with substitutions.

- <u>Make more than one meal at a time.</u> The other day I cooked rice with my dinner, so I made some rice pudding at the same time. I did the same thing when I was using oats. I also made a meat loaf and no-bake cookies. While I was making a hamburger and pasta casserole, I also made a hamburger and cheesy pasta casserole; they contain the same ingredients except for the cheese. It saved me a lot of time from pulling out and putting away the same or similar ingredients. I put all of the extras into my freezer for another time.
- <u>Inventory your freezer</u> and laminate a chart to put on the outside of your freezer. Then you can make changes as you purchase or use items, and you will always know what you have on hand.

Economical and nutritious choices:

1. **Orange juice.** To get the best value, buy cans of frozen concentrate rather than cartons of fresh or reconstituted juice.
2. **Whole potatoes.** In multi-pound bags, these are economical and great meal stretchers. 10 pound bags are your most economical choice.
3. **Thrift-store bread.** You can save a lot on bread when you purchase loaves from a thrift store rather than from the grocery. If you freeze them it does add some "life" to them. You can also use day-old bread for making bread crumbs, bread pudding, croutons, French toast, or strata.
4. **"Generic"/store brands.** You can save up to 30% by purchasing store brands rather than name-brand products. Before you stock up on any one item, try one item first to see how it compares to what you are used to.
5. **Bulk cereal.** Larger boxes of cereal usually cost less per ounce than smaller sizes. However, be sure to watch the store sales on name brands, and then utilize your coupons after you have compared the store bulk cereal's price.
6. **Instant pancakes.** If you don't want to make pancakes from scratch, a package of instant pancake mix is far preferable to frozen pancakes or ready-made batter, which can cost almost twice as much for the same amount. Making pancakes from scratch, though, is less time-consuming and easier than you may think. You can also cut your time more by packaging up 4 or 5 homemade mixes in separate plastic bags.
7. **Cheese.** Buy blocks and grate them yourself. This is more cost effective than buying pre-shredded cheese and can be done very quickly in a food processor with a shredding blade. However, don't do this too far in advance as the cheese will start to stick together.
8. **Chicken.** Whole chickens are more economical than cuts, and they tend to go further too. The carcass, skin, and other "leftovers" make a great soup base. When on sale,

there is not much difference from getting chicken breasts with or without the bone in. If you purchase with the rib bone and skin, save these for making chicken broth. Thighs and legs can still be had at $.89/lb. when on sale, which is a great value.

9. **Vegetables.** Buy vegetables whole, in prepackaged bags when they are available, and then divide them into smaller bags and/or chop or peel them. You will spend far less money than if you buy pre-cut vegetables, such as peeled baby carrots. Be sure to purchase when in season for the lowest price and the best flavor, and watch for your 10 for $10 sales. The other day I was able to get 3 pounds of carrots for $1. I purchased 9 pounds, and I will be putting carrots into everything for the next month!

10. **Fruit.** Bags of fruit usually cost less than individually purchased fruit. Purchase fruit that is in season for the best quality, flavor, and value. Purchasing smaller apples rather than the larger ones will not only save you money, but also calories.

11. **Rice.** Rice can be a source of protein and is a staple food in many parts of the world, but it is not a complete protein and should be combined with other sources of protein. I enjoy rice more than pasta and can use it anywhere that you might use pasta. I love rice pudding especially with raisins and cinnamon!

12. **Pasta.** Pasta is often served with a sauce, butter or cheese to make a delicious and very economical main course. Whole wheat pasta contains more fiber and more nutrients than refined pasta. Pasta can also be added to soups, stews, and casseroles to stretch a meal.

13. **Oats.** Oats are one of the most versatile grains in the food chain. You can use them to make cookies, pancakes, cakes, bread, meatloaf, breakfast oatmeal, protein bars, and granola.

14. **Eggs.** You can make so many meals around eggs that it would take a whole page to list them. Eggs are inexpensive, delicious, and high in protein and Omega 3. Who could ask for more?

15. **Dairy Products.** Dairy products such as milk, cheese, sour cream, evaporated milk, and yogurt add flavor and nutrition (protein, vitamin D) to many meals. They also make meals more filling.

16. **Bread.** If you enjoy using a bread machine but hate to measure out every ingredient each time, prepare ingredients for ten loaves and measure into ten plastic bags. Then all you have to do for your next ten batches is add liquid and yeast.

The Best Times to Purchase Fruits & Vegetables

Whenever possible, you should buy fruits and vegetables when they are in season. Below is a chart that shows the months that various fruits and vegetables are in season. Note that bananas, potatoes, carrots, cucumbers, onions, and celery are usually well priced year-round.

January	February	March	April	May	June
Broccoli	Broccoli	Broccoli	Asparagus	Asparagus	Apricots
Cauliflower	Cauliflower	Lettuce	Broccoli	Broccoli	Cantaloupe
Grapefruit	Grapefruit	Mangoes	Lettuce	Cherries	Cherries
Leeks	Lemons	Pineapples	Mangoes	Lettuce	Corn
Lemons	Oranges		Pineapples	Pineapple	Lettuce
Oranges	Papayas		Rhubarb	Rhubarb	Peaches
			Spring peas	Spring peas	Strawberries
					Watermelon

July	August	September	October	November	December
Apricots	Apricots	Apples	Apples	Apples	Broccoli
Blueberries	Cantaloupe	Grapes	Broccoli	Broccoli	Cauliflower
Cantaloupe	Corn	Lettuce	Cranberries	Cranberries	Grapefruit
Green beans	Peaches	Pumpkins	Grapes	Mushrooms	Oranges
Peaches	Plums	Spinach	Lettuce	Oranges	Pears
Raspberries	Raspberries	Tomatoes	Pumpkins	Pears	Sweet potatoes
Strawberries	Strawberries		Spinach	Pumpkins	Tangerines
Watermelon	Summer squash		Sweet potatoes	Spinach	
	Tomatoes		Winter squash	Tangerines	
	Watermelon			Winter squash	

Tips for Saving Money When Grocery Shopping

1. Purchase fresh fruit and vegetables in season when you can. Farmer's markets are not always cheaper and do not offer as many choices as the grocery store, but they are a lot of fun and a way to support local agriculture. When fruits and vegetables are out of season, watch for specials.

2. Buying frozen fruits and vegetables is often more economical and just as nutritious as fresh, any time of year.

3. Pick-it yourself farms are cheaper if you need a large quantity for canning or freezing fruits and vegetables. Make sure you have the time to pick and process the produce the same day. I made a case of strawberry jam last week that will last me a whole year and tastes better than any store-bought jam.

4. <u>Another way of saving money is to join a co-op.</u> Fresh wholesale vendors will sell to anyone who wants to purchase in the large quantities that they offer. However, most people do not need 25 pounds of turnips or onions. So many families join together to form a co-op, which then purchases all the food the families selected at greatly reduced prices.

5. If you are concerned about <u>avoiding pesticides</u>, you have options other than buying only organic fruits and vegetables. These options include growing your own; washing fruits and vegetables with cold running water, a small amount of soap, and a scrub brush (on hard-skinned produce); and buying organic only those fruits and vegetables that tend to have the highest concentrations of pesticides. These are apples, bell peppers, celery, cherries, imported grapes, lettuce, nectarines, peaches, pears, potatoes, spinach, and strawberries. Most families do not eat all of these foods regularly; if you buy only the ones your family eats, you will save money over buying all organic produce.

6. When you buy <u>large bags of fruits or vegetables</u>, weigh them. By law, prepackaged produce must contain at *least* the amount printed on the bag. Often food manufacturers will put a little bit more than that amount in the bag to make sure they are in compliance. By weighing the bags before you buy them, you can find the heaviest bag, which will give you the more food for the same price.

7. Sometimes <u>you do not have to pay more for convenience</u>.
   - Whole mushrooms cost the same as pre-sliced mushrooms (watch unit prices, though, as sometimes packages of sliced mushrooms are smaller).
   - Boxed pound cake costs less than making it from scratch because of the amount of butter required.
   - Jarred salsas and spaghetti sauces are often more economical than preparing your own.

8. Try to <u>purchase only those items on your list that you have coupons for *and* that are on sale</u>. For example: you have 5 coupons for Jell-O at 50 cents off on two boxes. The grocery store is running a sale on Jell-O for 50 cents a box. If you purchase 10 boxes using your coupons, all of those boxes will now be free, if your store doubles coupons. This is one way of building up your pantry. Another example would be, to purchase toilet paper when it is 50% off and then use your coupon, the store doubles it, and you save up to 70%.

9. <u>Name brand products are usually sale at the beginning of the month</u> (when families have just received their assistance checks) <u>and private store brands usually go on sale at the end of the month</u> (when families may have less cash available).

10. Not all <u>store brands are the same quality as brand name items</u>. You may want to get friendly with the store clerks. They usually know who manufactured the store brand

item. Or, as mentioned earlier, just try 1 item of the store brand to see if it meets your expectations.

11. In our area <u>at the beginning of the month</u>, one of our stores has a lot of items that are 10 for $10, and if you purchase all ten items (or a variety of 10 items on sale) you receive the 11th free. You are allowed to mix and match. Your items are then the equivalent of 91 cents each. However, make sure that the items you are purchasing are a good price for the 91 cents. In order to do that, you need to know what the regular price is for that item. If you choose an item that is on sale for 10 for $10, and it is normally 94 cents, you are not saving very much on that item. Select the items that you will save the most on when using this practice. This is another way of stocking up your pantry and making your food dollar stretch.

12. <u>A word of warning</u>: you may have a problem with your children wanting to eat everything in the pantry the first week or two just because it's there, and then it will not last to the end of the month. For example: say that you buy 11 two-liter bottles of soda that are on sale for 90 cents each. The children are allowed to have soda only on the weekends. Explain to them that they are not allowed more soda just because there is more on the shelf. The same holds true with snack foods and other goodies. You may have to consider hiding them--especially from your spouse!

13. When you <u>purchase in bulk</u>, be sure to buy food that you know the family will eat during the month. Food must be properly stored to keep it safe to eat. One way of storing food safely is to use a vacuum sealer. If you watch for sales, you can save enough money to purchase one. Using one will help keep you from wasting food that has been stored improperly. I use pint, quart, and 2 quart jars for vacuum-sealing food. If you plan to use canning jars for food storage, make sure you use "wide-mouth" jars. They will provide you with more room to put into and out of the jars. As an added bonus, the clear glass jars look really nice on my cupboard shelves. (See Chapter 10 for more information about using a vacuum sealer.) My friend Tammy (who is helping me test some of the recipes in the book) was here the other day, and she was telling me that after using the advanced vacuum-seal model in my home she was going to throw her cheaper one away. I have always found it beneficial to purchase the best quality kitchen appliances that I could afford. It makes a difference.

14. Try <u>not to purchase ready-made frozen items unless they are simple fruits and vegetables</u>. Highly processed frozen foods can contribute to childhood obesity and increase your food budget. They also have a lot of ingredients and/or preservatives that you would not normally want to cook with, eat, or feed to your children.

15. Watch <u>expiration dates</u>. You usually will not have to throw away food until 5 days after that date, except for meats. Let your nose be your guide for meat and dairy. If

it smells bad, do not use it. Sometimes stores want to stretch the date as far as they can on meat, so be careful. Or they might offer daily products marked way down. It is up to you to check the expiration date, which could be tomorrow!

16. Check food carefully as you shop. Be sure you do not buy food that is already partially spoiled or rotted. Buy meat that looks fresh (not discolored around the edges) and does not smell bad. Examine bags of fruits and vegetables carefully and look out for mold or soft spots. Packaged berries may have mold that you cannot see. If you can, open the package and examine the insides. If you cannot, you may be better off not buying the berries. Before you buy a carton of eggs, open the carton and check every egg. Do not just look at the tops; pick up each egg to make sure it is not cracked on the bottom. Many times though, I will purchase items that just have a bruise on it, or just has one item in a bag spoiled. I will often save up to 75% on such item, if not more, so it will be worth it. Also, if I see something of a poor quality in a bag, I will ask the manager to mark it down in price.

17. Purchase cheaper cuts of meat, which tend to be tough, but will cook up tender and flavorful in a slow cooker or stew. Purchase chicken with the bone in and skin on. Meat cooked with the bone-in will have more flavor. Alternatively, you could remove the bone and skin and use them to make your own chicken broth, which can then be frozen or canned for later use.

18. Avoid purchasing pre-packaged lunch meats or pre-sliced meat from a deli. These are expensive, and there are more economical ways to buy lunch meat. One is to take a well-priced large slab of pre-packaged meat (something that doesn't require cooking, like ham) and request either the butcher at the meat counter or the deli to slice it for you. Usually they will do it, especially if you ask politely (something like "I know it is a lot of work, but could you slice this for me?"). Another option is to buy raw meat on sale, cook it, and then slice it to use as lunch meat.

19. Do not "check out" when you are checking out. At the end of a long shopping trip, you may want to just daydream or scan the covers of the tabloids once you reach the registers. But even though store registers and scanners are more accurate now than they have ever been, human beings are still responsible for coding items and ringing them up. And human beings make mistakes! So pay attention and make sure every item scanned is being rung up at the price you expect. If there is a mistake, let the cashier know about it immediately.

Once your groceries have all been purchased and you have your receipt, check it before leaving the store. You may find more errors there that you did not catch at the register.

20. If you <u>do not know how to cook</u> or do not think you would enjoy it, consider taking a cooking class or watching cooking shows on TV. You can save a lot of money cooking for yourself and your family, and you will really enjoy the compliments you receive! Two of my favorite TV shows that are currently on the Food Network can help you to learn and enjoy cooking. They are "5 Ingredient Fix" and "Semi-Homemade Cooking." Both of these shows also publish magazines and books that are enjoyable and informative, and available at your local bookstore or library.

21. The most <u>effective habits require repetition to perfect</u>. In order to change your shopping habits you must practice self-restraint. You will make some mistakes, but recognize them and strive to improve on your next shopping trip. After shopping to save for many years, I still make mistakes and continually try to improve. Many times you will feel too tired to make out your menu for shopping list for the week. But in order to save a lot of money at the grocery store, you must do this, even when you don't feel like it.

22. <u>Practice patience</u>. You can change old habits into new routines, but it takes time. Remember the old saying, "one step at a time?" That is how you must do it. It will take practice, persistence, and patience, but the payoff could be thousands of dollars a year in savings. That should be enough motivation for you to remember what you need to do.

23. <u>Remember the glow of savings</u>. I remember how I felt when I bragged that I got $120 worth of cat food free; 40 cans of chicken broth free; $150 worth of canned tomato products free; 20 boxes of Jell-O free; 20 bottles organic juice free; 10 boxes of Brillo pads free; 30 deodorants free; 10 bottles of hot sauce free; 8 bars of cream cheese free; name brand cereal for 25 cents a box, and multiple savings on cheese, plastic wrap, Tylenol, Aspirin, and many more. That provides me with the motivation to keep it up.

24. If you <u>live a distance from the grocery store</u> or you need to make another stop before you get home, you might want to consider taking a cooler with you to keep your perishables fresh.

Chapter 2

Creating and Developing Your Budget

When it comes to food, no two people have identical likes and dislikes. You and your family have developed your habits and food choices over many years. In order to save money and expand your eating habits and choices, you will need to develop some new habits that will require you to practice and enforce these objectives. It is just like dieting. You have to stick with it in order to accomplish your goals. And sometimes it is very hard, but you can do it. It just takes practice and determination. Remember what you want to accomplish.

Consider making it a game and see what each family member can do to help you save more money. You could save money with the goal to do something special with the whole family, or purchase something special all of you will enjoy.

First, I would suggest that you call a family meeting. Sit down together and make a list:

- Meals you enjoy, including main dishes and sides
- How often you eat together
- Who does most of the cooking
- Who does most of the cleaning up
- Who does the grocery shopping
- How often you eat out each month. This would include lunches out and take-out meals (including any drive-thru) -- any time you spend money on food that did not come from the grocery store and was not prepared at home.
- How much money you spend eating out each month
- How much you spend on cleaning supplies each month
- How much you spend on pet food and supplies each month
- How much you spend on any miscellaneous items you buy at the grocery store each month, for example books, magazines, children's toys, beer, wine, etc.

Sometimes you may have to make guesses at these expenditures. It is important to nail down exact amounts, however, so you should make a practice of saving your receipts and writing down how much you spend.

You may find, after comparing your guesses to your written expenditures, that you underestimated just how much you actually spend. This is nothing to be ashamed of. Now you can find ways to cut back! Seeing your actual spending written in black and white can be a tremendous motivation toward change.

Now let us try to develop a menu/budget where you spend just $100 a month per person (statistics show that the average is $35 per person/per week). Of course a small child will not eat this much, and teenagers will eat a lot more. Once again, all families are different, and adjustments will have to be made. Even people who live in different parts of the country have varying food preferences. For example, if you have 2 adults and 2 children in your family, you will try and create a monthly budget of $300.00 for your basic menus. If this is not realistic for your family, then you might need to make some adjustments. However, the more food you can prepare for yourself, combined with the savings you will make at the grocery store, the more money you can now save. You will be utterly amazed at just how much! I know of a family in Ohio that has 12 children and they spend only $100 a month on extras as they grow and raise most of their own food. Same thing for another family in California that only spends $200 a month for their 12 children. So it can be done.

Try and shop on a weekly basis in order to get the best sales. Be prepared to stock up on items that are practical. These would include items on sale or clearance that have a long shelf life and/or that you use a lot of. For example, I went to the store the other day, and they had my favorite body wash on clearance for $1.98 when it is regularly $8.99. This was a sale that I could not pass up. So I spent an additional $19.80 on 10 items that will probably last me a year and a half. If I had put that money in my savings account, I would not have earned that much in interest.

If you can afford to spend an extra $50 or more a month, use this money to stock up on items that are on sale. But watch expiration dates. When you put items into your pantry, be sure to put them in order of the expiration date, with the first to be used in the front, within easy reach.

I remember once I stocked up on Miracle Whip. I was able to get the large jars that normally sell for $3.99 for $1.00 each. So I purchased 8 of them and felt real smart. Unfortunately, I did not check the expiration dates, and I normally use just 1 every 3 months. As a result, a few of them expired by the "use by best date." So I ended up throwing 5 of the jars into the trash. I learned a good lesson that day!

Another possibility to consider is occasionally <u>using extra money toward purchasing a small luxury or two</u>. Even luxury food items go on sale from time to time, and if you allow yourself to buy such items at these times, you can keep you and your family from feeling deprived. Luxury food items include things such as gourmet cheeses, specialty nuts, and more expensive cuts of meat.

When you set your weekly budget, you will know your limits, which can be a relief. You do not have to worry about running out of money or going into debt. You *will* have to learn how to delay gratification; you cannot always buy just what you want right when you want it. This also means you will be able to live within your means, which is a worthy goal. The savings will add up, and you can learn to look forward to the rewarding feeling of reaching a savings goal.

Many Ways to save money on food:

- ✓ Watching store sales
- ✓ Purchasing store-brand products
- ✓ Using coupons
- ✓ Shopping at stores that double coupons
- ✓ Shopping at stores when they offer more sales at different times of the month
- ✓ Visiting manufacturer/company web sites to get coupons

- ✓ Shopping at stores that price-match name brand products
- ✓ Bulk purchasing (be careful, this does not always offer savings)
- ✓ Growing food in a garden/containers
- ✓ Making your own versions of convenience foods
- ✓ Purchasing wholesale or through a co-op
- ✓ Purchasing direct from a farmer/co-op

- ✓ Preparing meals at home instead of eating out
- ✓ Eating fewer snacks and junk foods
- ✓ Drinking iced tea instead of soda
- ✓ Stocking up on sale items
- ✓ Not purchasing items just because they are on sale if you do not normally use them

When you start putting these strategies into practice, you will find yourself saving more and more money every week. Keep track of your grocery bills and watch as they gradually decrease. Seeing the savings on that register tape will motivate you to continue using smart shopping strategies!

This week my favorite local grocery store is offering Cottonelle Toilet Paper at half-price. It is normally $7.50 for the large double rolled package. Half price is $3.75. Now I also have a lot of 75 cent coupons which when doubled gives me another $1.50 off. So $3.75 less $1.50 is $2.25. I will be saving $5.25 per package or 70%. I don't know of any bank that will give me that kind of return!

I will be saving $262.50 just in toilet paper...which should be enough to last me the whole year. If you do that with most of the non-perishable items you normally use, you can save a tremendous amount of money. Last week I purchased enough toilet bowl cleaner and the large bottles of Dawn Dishwashing soap for $1.00 a bottle (saving over $1.50 per bottle) to last me a year, and laundry softener for $2.50 a bottle that is normally $5.99 a bottle. Whenever I can save 50% I am a happy shopper. Stocking up when an item is offered at a very good sale price is a very important factor in saving money.

Chapter 3

Coupons & Other Shopping Habits

Can Make a Difference

On Sunday morning I get up early so I can read the Sunday paper and critique the coupons and grocery store sale flyers. The Sunday paper usually contains at least $250 in coupons. I have also started calling on my neighbors to see if I can have any coupons that they are not using. Or if there are some really fantastic sales that day, I will purchase extra newspapers in order to get more coupons. The money I save from the additional coupons will more than make up for the cost of the extra papers.

However, be sure to check the newspaper to see that the coupons are in it before purchasing. Sometimes not-so-nice-shoppers remove the coupons from the newspapers (without buying the newspapers) for their own use.

Then I check the store sales flyer(s) to see what specials they are offering. Hopefully I have coupons for the items they have on sale. If not, I check the websites I purchase coupons from and see if they have anything that I will need this week or in the near future. Of course, all of this will take a lot of extra time, and if I do not have it, I will just use the coupons I get in the paper.

If I do not need the item that I have a coupon for (and it is for an item I use), and the item is not on sale, I save the coupon until a later date, when the item does go on sale.

Many times I purchase coupons from the following web sites if there are some really good savings that I can take advantage of:

www.coupondede.com

www.thecouponclippers.com

Each has different restrictions and policies, so be sure you understand everything before purchasing coupons. One of the above websites has lower purchase requirements, but it does not ship as quickly as the other. Be sure to check the internet often for new companies that offer this service, and other coupon services.

Today someone asked me why I would *purchase* coupons. I gave the following example: One day the web site offered $3.00 coupons on a cat food I was not familiar with. Since I did not know how much the cat food normally sold for, I took a small chance by purchasing only 10 coupons at 20 cents each. When I got to the store, I found that the cat food sold for $3.00 a box, and with my coupons, I got 10 boxes free. I then went home to see if my cats liked the cat food, which they did. I then went back on-line to see if I could get some more of the same coupons. They were sold out; however, they did have some $2.00 coupons, I figured that saving $2.00 a box was better than nothing and purchased 50 coupons. So the following week I returned to the store and they had the cat food on sale for 2 for $4.00. I could not believe my luck: 50 more boxes free! So I got $180.00 worth of cat food for $12.00, plus shipping and handling of the coupons. In other words, I saved $160.00. Was it worth it? Of course! I just wish I had the foresight to get all of the $3.00 coupons I could have.

Now that does not happen every day or week. But it sure feels good when it does!

This would have also proven valuable if the coupon had been in my local paper. Even with the cost of the newspaper, I would have still saved $2.00 per box on cat food. However, by purchasing the coupons, I got them for 20 cents each (instead of paying $1 for a newspaper). Although this does presume that there were not a large amount of other worthwhile coupons in the paper.

I have also gotten the following other items for *free* with this method:

- 40 cans of Swanson chicken broth
- 20 boxes of Jell-O
- 40 pads of post-it notes
- 150 cans of Glen Muir tomato products
- 20 boxes of *Brillo* pads
- 100 boxes of cat food

Many times you can normally save 30% or more by purchasing a store-brand. However, I strongly suggest not to stock up on these or any new products without first trying it a few times. I hate to purchase 10 items of something just because I got them at a good price, and then find I do not like how it performs or tastes.

Two weeks ago my favorite store offered a new laundry detergent. The box had enough soap for 56 loads for a sale price of $2.99. Quite a deal! However, in order not to be stuck with something that I might not like, I purchased one box with my other items, then went home and tried it out with a load of laundry.

The next day I returned and purchased six more boxes. That was fortunate, because the following week the price went up to $5.99 per box. In this day and age, I appreciate saving 50% or more on any item.

Make sure that you read the fine print on coupons carefully and are familiar with the store's policy. Some stores will allow you to use their coupons along with the manufacturer's coupon, but some will not. Some stores will double any number of the same coupon that you present, but others will not. Some stores will double only the first two coupons you present, but others will not.

Imagine you are purchasing 10 of the same items, and you have a coupon for each one -- a total of 10 coupons. Some stores that double coupons will allow only the first two coupons to be doubled. In order to have the remainder of the coupons doubled, you have to purchase the items separately -- in other words, the cashier must ring up every two items as a separate purchase. (Not all stores do this; again, know your store's policy!)

Go through your coupons at least once a month to check for expired ones. I usually go through mine a week before the end of the month and pull out all the coupons that will expire soon. I put them into two piles: ones that I want to use, and ones that I do not think I will use. These could be coupons for items that might have once interested me, but since I did not get any additional store coupons, or the store did not offer a sale, I was not really interested in purchasing them after all.

When using the coupon, make sure that the item you purchase matches the coupon exactly -- for instance, the specific size and brand must be identical. Otherwise the cashier will not honor it.

Be judicious in your use of coupons. Do not spend money on something you will not use just because you have a coupon for it. Coupons can be seductive; manufacturers know this full well, and this is a big reason they offer them. Just remember that you are not saving money if you never use what you have purchased.

Many stores run promotions offering a discount for buying multiple items in one product line. You may have seen them on the store shelves: buy 10 participating products and receive $5 (or more) off today's grocery bill. This is a fantastic promotion to participate in, particularly if you have coupons for these items as well. The items themselves will be on sale, plus you will get the additional savings provided by the promotion itself, *plus* discounts from your coupons. This is one of many instances where saving coupons until an item goes on sale can really pay off!

If a store runs out of an item on sale or that you have a coupon for, ask for a raincheck. Normally they will allow you only a month to purchase it, once they have restocked it. And if the item is on a very special sale and you need to stock up, be sure to ask for multiple rain checks. But then again some stores will not offer any rainchecks on special or promotional items.

However, if they don't have as many as you need, be sure to ask for new rainchecks.

I love buy-one, get-one-free sales that I can also use my coupons on. I save 50% immediately, and then get a discount using my manufacturer's coupons. Remember that you can usually use (depending on store policy) only one store coupon and one manufacturer's coupon per item.

A month ago one of the major grocery stores in our area announced that they would no longer accept a store coupon and a manufacturer's coupon on the same item. I think they will find that this will be their loss! However, each store will set its own policy, and it is up to you to decide where you will spend your grocery dollar.

Over a year ago manufacturers started requiring a purchase of 2 items instead of 1 in order to use their coupon. I suppose they figured they could make more money that way. This bothers me enough that I refuse to use such coupons unless absolutely necessary. You can save more money using coupons if you use them on only one item in the smallest size possible.

Bargains online

Food manufacturers like loyal customers, so they want you to visit their websites to learn more about their products. Many will provide you with wonderful recipes as well as coupons. Make a list of your favorite products and either e-mail or phone them and express your appreciation. Often they will then provide you with free coupons.

Machine store coupons

Have you ever walked down a grocery store aisle and seen the little machines projecting out from the food shelves? They often dispense coupons you can use immediately, right at the register. Just be sure they are already on your list to purchase; if not, take a few coupons home to use later. Remember to check the coupon for the expiration date.

Coupons on product packaging

Many times companies will put coupons that apply immediately at the checkout right on their products' packaging. Be sure to remove them and hand them to the cashier when checking out. It is not kind to remove the coupon and save it to use later rather than purchasing the item that day; be a polite shopper!

Store loyalty Cards

Another way of saving money is to use store loyalty cards. Many stores will allow you to use them with your manufacturer coupons. Loyalty Cards allow you to download coupons from either the retailer's website, or other websites to your card. Instead of sorting through coupons at checkout, you need only swipe your loyalty card. Loyalty cards also help retailers track your spending habits, information they use to gauge which coupons and deals to offer. Not all stores offer this convenience, and some stores will not allow you to use a manufacturer's coupon with the Store Loyalty Card.   Kroger stopped this saving policy in May of 2011. You must choose which discount to apply to your purchase; either the manufacturer's coupon or Kroger's Store Loyalty Card.

Meijer has (as of this writing) 3 ways in which to save extra money. (This is in addition to their policy of doubling coupons up to 99 cents.) They offer a store loyalty card called *Mperks* (which is not really a card, but rather your mobile phone number and a pin number). Then you can print out the items you selected, and input your code when you check out, and the cashier will give you credit for those sale items. Your coupons will also be doubled, if you also have them for those items.

You can also click on the top select bar of the Meijer.com website and select the *Meijer Mealbox*. Click on the Featured Coupons and select as many coupons as you need for additional savings. Before you print out your coupons under Shopping List, go to Specials and select any additional coupons you want.

If you visit Walmart' s website at Walmart.com and then scroll down to "In Stores Now" on the left side of the window, you'll find a link for Free Coupons.

Be sure to check with your favorite store to see what their policy is.

eCoupons

eCoupons are coupons that you can load to your store loyalty card. They can be used with paper coupons so you can receive even greater savings. All eCoupons (except Upromise) are taken directly off your bill at the register. Upromise coupons load to an account that can be used to save for your children's education (or for someone else's children). Not all grocery stores use these companies. My advice is to check the companies out and see if your store is listed, or if this is something that you really want to invest in.

Stocking up

Another way to save money on your grocery shopping is to stock up when food items or home care necessities go on sale and you have lots of coupons to save more money with.

At this time I have enough cleaning supplies to last me for 3 years, enough food staples to last almost 1 year and enough pet food for 9 months. I can do this because I have the space. If you do not have enough space to do this, you can still stock up on food or cleaning products when they are on sale and get enough to last you until they go on sale again.

Bargain buddy

A bargain buddy is someone you can share larger purchases/quantities with, share coupons with, or can help with research.

Coupon Abbreviations

Abbreviations	Description
$1/1	Save $1.00 off one item
$1/2	Save $1.00 off two items
AC	After Coupon
AR	After Rebate
B&M	Brick & Mortar (a physical store – not online)
B1G1 or BOGO	Buy one get one free
B2G1	Buy two get one free
Blinkie	Coupon dispensed in store from a box by the product
BTFE	Box tops for education
CAT or Catalina	Coupon that prints after purchase; usually at a grocery store
Coupon Trains	A way to trade coupons with a group of people
CPN	Coupon
CRT	Cash register tap
DND	Do not double
EBay	If you can't find coupons anywhere, you might be able to find it here
ECB	Extra Care bucks – CVE "money" printed on receipts to be used as cash
E-coupon	Coupons put on your store loyalty card
ESR	Easy Saver Rebate – found at Walgreens
ETS	Excludes trial size
FAR	Free after rebate
GC	Gift card
GM	General Mills
IP or IPQ	Internet printed coupon
MIR	Mail in rebate
MQ or MFR	Manufacturer's coupon
NED	No expiration date

Abbreviations	Description
PG	Proctor & Gamble
Peelie	A coupon found on a product that can be peeled off
Q	Coupon
RP	Red Plum – coupon provider
RR	Register Rewards: Rewards earned at Walgreens
SCR	Single Check Rebate – rebates earned at Rite Aid
SS	Smart Source – coupon provider
Stacking	Using a store coupon with a manufacturer coupon
Tear Pad	A coupon found in a store that can be torn off a pad
TMF	Try Me Free
UN	UniLever
WT or Wine Tag	A coupon found around the neck of a product
Wyb	When you buy
YMMV	Your mileage might vary

Store Policies

It is important to be aware of each store's coupon policy. Once you are armed with that information, you can politely inform your cashier and store manager of how the coupon is supposed to be accepted at their store. I suggest printing out the policy and taking it with you to the store. I am always amazed at the lack of training that some stores give to their employees. Often we (the shoppers) are the ones that have to educate them.

You can get all the information you need on grocery stores/chains by visiting:

http://en.wikipedia.org/wiki/List_of_supermarket_chains_in_the_United_States

This web site will provide you with the stores addresses, phone numbers, web sites, contact information, coupon policy, and almost anything else you would like to know about them. For some reason, some stores have failed to publish or even have a corporate coupon policy, and it is left up to store manager to determine it. This can cause confusion and quite frequently disgruntled shoppers, as there is no uniformity across the chain.

Price Book

It is difficult to know if a deal is really a deal if you do not know what the regular price is for an item in your area. My suggestion is to start a price book. A price book is simply a log of what you pay for items in your area. Once you have recorded your prices for a while, you will know what the item normally sells for or what you are willing to pay for an item. A price book can simply be a small notebook that can fit in your pocket or purse. Take it to the store with you and write down the prices of items you frequently purchase. Another option is to use a binder. Get a small spiral tablet that will fit in the palm of your hand. Then on the top of each page, write the name of a product that you normally purchase. Then on the lines under that product write:

Date   Store Purchased From   Price of Item

This way you can keep track of prices.

If you want to be really organized, you can use a small binder, with an alphabetical index. Or, if you really want to get organized (and sophisticated), a small hand-held computer or smartphone will do the trick!

Organizing Your Coupons

One of the first things you need to do is to purchase a Coupon Organizer. I tried many different systems before I settled on the one I use now. Ones I did not like included the following:

- A recipe box---too small.
- A 6"x 8" plastic box, with plastic dividers—the paper coupons stuck on the dividers and were hard to remove.
- #10 envelopes—I had an envelope for almost everything. I inserted the dividers, then used a 10" box to hold them all. But this was all too much work and too cumbersome to take to the store.
- A filing box with hanging file folders--too large.
- A photo album--the photo area was not made to withstand the constant opening and closing to insert and withdraw coupons, and the plastic started to rip.
- A box purchased from a clipper services for $38.00--it was worse than all of the above.
- I then went to an office supply store and purchased a flexible notebook that you can build anyway you want—perfect.

Things to consider when purchasing a coupon organizer:

Size

Do you need a handle for easy carrying?

Zipper for keeping everything inside

Pockets for a calculator, pen/pencil, scissors, rain checks, rebate forms, and so on.

Be sure to clean out your system every month so that you do not have expired coupons.

You may also want to put your name and phone number on your system, just in case you misplace it and it is recovered by a Good Samaritan!

Coupon Web Sites

Because web sites continuously change, we can't be responsible for the correctness of this list.

Stores offering their own coupons:
www.CVS.com
www.DollarGeneral.com   (coupon.com)
www.GiantEagle.com
www.Meijer.com
www.Walmart.com
www.Kroger.com

Free grocery coupons:
www.bettycrocker.com
www.cellfire.com
www.couponbug.com
www.coupons.com   (many websites are powered by this one, which allows you to only print 2 of the same coupons from the same computer)
www.couponnetwork.com
www.lildailydeals.com
www.lozo.com   (coupons.com)
www.meijer.com
www.ppgazette.com
www.SavingStar.com
www.SelectCouponProgram.com   (coupons.com)
www.shortcuts.com
www.shopathome.com
www.wholefoodsmarket.com/coupons/

Clipper Services:
www.Coupondede.com
www.MyCouponHunter.com
www.SelectCouponProgram.com
www.TheClipperCoupons.com

Coupon Organizers:
www.CouponClutch.com
www.CouponSense.com

Different items/events/groceries:
www.afewshortcuts.com
www.CincinnatiCoupons.net
www.coolsavings.com
www.coupons.com
www.currentcodes.com
www.dealcatcher.com
www.eversave.com
www.fatwallet.com
www.frugalfabulousfinds.com
www.Groupon.com
www.afewshortcuts.com
www.LivingSocial.com
www.lozo.com
www.MotherhoodonaDime.com
www.savingmore.com
www.SlickHouseWives.com
www.Smartsource.com
www.StockpilingMoms.com
www.StretchingaBuckBlog.com
www.RetailMeNot.com
www.Upromise.com (college savings)

Meal Planners:
www.e-mealz.com

How Coupons Work

I used to wonder how coupons work. How could stores afford to accept them? Did it cut into their sales? I have since learned this and other valuable information about coupons, and it has offered me vital confidence in using them as I shop.

Here is how coupons work.

- For every coupon used, stores are reimbursed the face value plus an additional 8 to 12 cents per coupon.
- Any coupon that begins with the number 5 is a manufacturer coupon and can be redeemed anywhere, regardless of what kind of logo it may have on it.
- If a coupon bar code begins with the number 5, it can be doubled. If it starts with the number 9, it cannot.
- If a coupon begins with a number other than a 5 or a 9, it is a store coupon.
- After a coupon expires, stores have about 6 months to submit the coupon for reimbursement.

Redemption:

- Once a coupon is used, the store sends it to a clearinghouse, where it is scanned.
- The clearinghouse creates an invoice for the manufacture based on all scanned coupons.
- The clearinghouse pays the stores, and the manufacturer in turn pays the clearinghouse.
- Coupons that are unable to be scanned by the clearinghouse are referred to as hard to handle (HTH) coupons, and they require more work. Sometimes stores charge a larger handling fee to the manufacturer because of a bad coupon design.

Price Matching

Another way of saving money is through price matching. Many stores nowadays will match prices of their competitors if you offer proof that another store is offering the same product for less money. This is just another way a store can make a sale off you and keep you as a customer. Think of the money you will save by not having to drive to another store -- at today's gas prices, the less you have to drive, the better! Just be sure you take the other store's ad circular with you when you shop, and know your store's price-matching policy.

While most stores will not match products such as meat, dairy, eggs, and produce (only brand-name, packaged products), it never hurts to ask!

Coupon Fraud

We know that you are reading this book because you want to save money honestly. I personally am horrified at the thought of coupon fraud. It costs stores about $300 million a year, and of course this is passed on to us in the form of higher prices for groceries.

Here are some important things to know:

- Do not photocopy, scan, or fax coupons. It is illegal to do so. If the coupon is not legitimate and you receive the discount (amount of the coupon) the store will not receive reimbursement for the amount of the coupon.
- Read the fine print on the coupon and follow it.
- Don't use expired coupons.
- Be suspicious of coupons that are in a PDF format. They are often fraudulent.
- If you think a coupon is too good to be true, it probably is a fraudulent coupon.

http://www.couponinformationcenter.com/ is a great source of information on this topic.

There are severe penalties for coupon fraud:

- Longest prison sentence: 17 years
- Highest financial penalty: $5 million
- Prison sentences of three to five years are not uncommon.
- Financial penalties generally vary, but have often been in excess of $200,000.

Counterfeit notifications:

The CIC has an extensive listing of known counterfeit coupons at their website, under a link called "Counterfeit Notifications." This listing is primarily offered for the benefit of retailers, who might otherwise be unaware that a coupon that they have been offered is a counterfeit coupon.

If you purchase coupons or print them from the Internet, however, it might be a good idea to check this listing yourself, just to be on the safe side, especially if you have never seen such a good deal on a coupon before. The last thing you want to do is add to the problem of coupon fraud by attempting to use a fraudulent coupon -- or, worse, be penalized yourself.

Extreme Couponing

The CIC has a special notice on their website regarding The Learning Channel (TLC)'s show "Extreme Couponing." This notice states that many of the practices shown on the show are illegal, as they violate or attempt to violate the terms of the coupons, particularly in using them in large quantities or in using them for products other than those stated on the coupons.

We mention this because those of you reading this book may have also watched this show and wondered if the tactics represented on the show were good ones to use. According to the CIC, they may not be. So bear this in mind in the event you watch "Extreme Couponing" and be on the lookout for any coupon usage that could be illegal.

Refunding

Are you familiar with refunding? If not, be sure to read on, because refunding can be a major aspect of your shopping and saving plan. You can easily receive refunds from your purchases totaling $2,500 to $5,000 a year.

Refunding is a simple process:

1. Manufacturers issue a refund offer to purchases of their product(s).
2. The consumer follows the terms of the refund; this usually involves filling out a form and sending it to the address specified by the manufacturer with a receipt and/or a proof of purchase (usually the product's bar code), or set limitations.
3. The manufacturer processes the refund and mails a check to your house.

Where can you find refund offers?

Nearly everywhere! You can find refund offers in the following places:

- In stores on store forms, often attached to tear-off pads located near displays
- On the product packaging, either printed directly onto the packaging or in the form of peel-off labels or hang-tags on bottles
- In newspapers or magazines
- In home mailers
- On the Internet

Something similar to refunds is called "premiums." They work the same way, only instead of receiving cash back, you receive free samples or gifts.

Like all shopping savings, one of the best things about refunds and premiums is that they are tax-free income!

When checking-out at the grocery store

It is impossible to unload your groceries and watch the cash register at the same time. I always ask the clerk (very nicely) if they will wait until I have unloaded everything before they begin to ring up your order.

This way I can watch and see if anything is rung up improperly. You would be surprised at the mistakes that computers sometimes make.

It is especially important that you watch and listen to the scanner beeps when they are scanning your coupons. Watch the display as the cashier scans each item to make sure it rings up properly. And listen to the beeps because today's scanners are so powerful that with a simple miscue of the wrist, an item can be rung up two or three times.

We definitely recommend you give refunding a try, if you have not already. Just be sure that you are careful to fill out your refund forms to the letter. Do not skip or overlook anything. If a processing center finds even one error, your form will be returned to you -- without a refund.

Giving Back

Giving back is not always easy to do, especially in tough financial times. However, by using coupons, stocking up, and getting great deals at retailers, we can often get items for *free* (or even be paid to buy items). My challenge for you is to think about how you can give back. Here are my thoughts on possible ways:

- Collect *freebies* (both food items and non-food items) and donate them to a local charity.
- Send coupons you do not need or expired coupons (maximum 2 months past the expiration date) to our troops through the Overseas Coupon Program. Go to www.ocpnet.org for addresses and valuable information on clipping, sorting, totaling and sending. This is a fantastic program that helps soldiers with very small budgets stretch their dollars to support their families.
- Leave an expiring coupon by a product in a store.
- Share your enthusiasm about couponing with your family, co-workers, and neighbors.

Price Comparing

To make sure that you are getting the best prices, you might want to price compare all the stores in your area. Make a form up similar to this one and write down the items that you purchase the most of. Then visit all the stores that you have chosen, in the same week, and compare prices.

Description (examples below)	Meijer	Walmart	Kroger	Aldi	Other
Wheat Thins Flatbread Crackers					
Aunt Millie's Italian Bread					
Hunts Spaghetti Sauce					
Kraft Cheddar Cheese 12 oz					
Ground Chuck 80/20 per pound					
Bob Evans Pork Sausage 1 per pound					
1 gal 2% milk					

Chapter 4

Planning Your Weekly Menu

There are two reasons why it is important to plan your menu every week.

One: without careful menu planning, it is too easy to fall into the "what's for dinner?" trap. What happens is someone says, "what's for dinner?", you look in the refrigerator, realize you have no idea what to make, and you wind up ordering take-out or saying, "oh, let's just go out tonight." You may have appeased your family's hunger, but you certainly have not saved any money.

Two: you must plan your menu to get the most out of your shopping savings program. When you plan your menu before you go shopping, you can take advantage of sales and coupons with the help of the most recent advertisements from your store(s).

Breakfast

During the week, most of us do not have time to make elaborate breakfasts. Fortunately there are many quick and easy breakfast options that are also nutritious and filling. These include:

- cold or hot cereal
- homemade granola mixes or bars
- yogurt
- slice of banana bread
- bagel
- eggs
- fruit

On the weekends, you can plan and prepare more elaborate breakfasts and make something your family (especially your children) will look forward to. This is a great time to make homemade pancakes, waffles, or French toast; omelets; breakfast casseroles or strata; or homemade biscuits or muffins. Making weekend breakfasts something special is also a way to create memories for your children.

Lunch

To most of us, lunch is the forgotten meal. It can also be a huge money drain, especially if you have children. Too often the typical lunch for both children and adults is a sandwich – which is fine – and expensive convenience food snacks – not so fine. Worse, you may choose to buy food from a convenience store or a fast-food restaurant, choices that tend to be equally poor from an economic as well as a health standpoint.

One way to avoid this is to make your own convenience food snacks. Instead of buying a bag of baby carrots, buy a bag of whole carrots and spend a few minutes peeling and cutting them into carrot sticks. You could save 50 percent right there. Rather than small boxes of raisins, buy a large container, divide them up into smaller containers or snack sized bags, and save about 25 percent. Do not buy Jell-O pre-made in cups; instead buy boxes of Jell-O mix, make it yourself, and allow it to set into small individual containers. (Add some small or cut-up pieces of fruit to make it even more nutritious.) Instead of pre-packaged cheese and crackers, buy a large box of crackers, and a block of cheese, and divide snack-sized portions into individual bags. Make up your own trail mix rather than buy extraordinarily expensive pre-packaged bags. Skip the chips, cookies, snack cakes, and other high-calorie, processed snack foods altogether.

If your family gets tired of sandwiches, consider some alternatives:

- A hot lunch. Get a thermos and fill it with soup, stew, macaroni and cheese, spaghetti, or pork and beans, just to name a few examples. Or you could fill it with taco meat mixed with cheese, pack a tortilla and any other items you or your family members enjoy with tacos, and let them assemble their own.
- Leftovers: Some foods can be enjoyed cold, while others will need to be reheated (these can be packed in a thermos). Pack some plastic utensils and encourage everyone to bring them back home so they can be washed and reused. Others will be envious of what you took the time to prepare, not knowing it is last night's leftovers!
- Make a "grab bag" lunch - fill snack-sized plastic bags with various sides like pieces of fruit or veggies, crackers, cheese, trail mix, or pretzels. You could add small containers of yogurt to this selection too. Then in the morning when you pack lunches, you can give them two or three bags or small containers each and they will be ready to go.
- Make more interesting sandwiches by alternating the bread. You can use regular sandwich bread one day, pita bread another day, mini bagels or English muffins another day, and tortillas to make a wrap another day. Or to make a sandwich more fun for children, you could use a cookie cutter to give it a cute shape.

Children like small things. So be sure to cut up carrots, celery, cauliflower, and broccoli into small pieces. If you cut up fruit that turns brown after it is cut, for example, apples or pears, you want to sprinkle them with lemon juice. You may also want to add a dip, like caramel, fruit dip, or peanut butter.

Kids like to help. If your children are school-age, let them help in preparing their own lunches. Or if they complain about their lunches, encourage them to help you. In the long run they will probably brag to their friends that they made their own lunch.

Make lunches healthier and save a lot of money with just a little planning and prep work every week. Then lunch will no longer be the forgotten meal.

Dinner

I plan my dinner menu based on what protein items are on sale. Popular dinner proteins include meat, eggs, beans, and cheese. I try to have at least 2 dinners a week based on eggs to cut costs, since meat is the most expensive item in a meal. If nothing you want is on sale this week, you can pull items from your freezer that you purchased on sale previously. (This is when you will find that stocking up will save you money.)

I usually use a lot of ground meat/beef when it is on sale at $2.29 or less a pound. I use ground beef to make stroganoff, spaghetti sauce, stuffed peppers, and many different casseroles.

Another meat I like to cook with is pork loin which, when on sale, is often around $1.86 per pound. I slice it into chops ¾-inch thick and then cut each chop in half.   The recipe I enjoy using most for pork chops is one that my mother taught me many years ago, for Spanish rice. I use 1 to 2 chops per person in this recipe. It consists of:

one 10 ¾ ounce can of tomato soup
one 24 ounce can of diced tomatoes
one 24 ounce can of tomato sauce.

You can adjust those based on the amount of rice you use (I use approximately 4 cups of cooked rice). I also use onions, bell pepper, oregano, basil, parsley, and salt and pepper in the recipe.

I then fry the pork chops. After they have cooked, I sauté the onions and the chopped up green bell pepper. Then I mix the rice, the canned tomatoes in a bowl with the seasonings, onions and peppers. I then pour it into a casserole dish with the pork chops on the bottom and slowly cook it at 325 degrees until done or bubbly. Remember that when it bakes in the oven, the sauce will thicken, and you don't want it to become dry.

This is a recipe that you can adjust anyway you want to meet your own tastes. The cost of this Spanish rice dish is approximately $7.00; if you add a side of broccoli, that is approximately an additional $1.50. You can make brownies for dessert, using a brownie mix on sale for 50 cents plus eggs for a total of 65 cents. By using sale items and coupons, I can provide a very good meal for $9.15 for 6 people, or $1.52 per person. Of course you could serve just the Spanish rice alone as a dinner and save more money. That's the best part of the dinner anyway.

Another way to save is to prepare 1 or 2 meatless dinners a week. Your menu could consist of pancakes/waffles, omelets, strata, vegetable soup, macaroni and cheese, grilled cheese sandwiches, pasta, any recipe with beans, or a salad.

During the week I try to make simpler meals because I do not have much time or energy to cook after working 8 to 10 hours each day. I might pull something out of the freezer or use something that I have vacuum sealed earlier in the week or last month.

On the weekend I often do more involved cooking. Some people like to cook many meals on the weekend so that they do not have to do as much cooking during the week. That is great if you have the time and space. For example, when you make spaghetti sauce, you might make extra for another meal that could include lasagna, pizza, or stuffed peppers. It does not usually take much additional effort to make another meal at the same time. What you do need is sufficient freezer space and a vacuum sealer to prevent freezer burn.

Some people do all their food prep work on the weekends for the week. They may chop vegetables, make salads, or cook hard boiled eggs, for example. Weekends are also when I have time to bake special treats: cookies, cupcakes, cheesecakes, and three-layer brownies are some of my favorites.

Another trick is to bake cookies using half a batch of dough that you have created, then place the other half in the freezer for another time. Or you can make your own baking mixes, which makes baking quicker and easier. Take a few gallon-size food storage bags, gather all the dry ingredients you need for a particular recipe, and put one recipe's worth each into separate bags. Seal the bags and label with the name of the recipe, the liquid ingredients you need to add, the amount of yeast required (if any), and the oven temperature and baking time. Then place each bag into the refrigerator or freezer. Now all you have to do when you are ready to bake is grab a bag, mix in the liquid ingredients, pour, and bake. This makes baking from scratch fun and easy – and it is far more economical (and better for you, without all those preservatives and processed ingredients) than boxed mixes. Just make sure that before you use a refrigerated or frozen mix, you allow it to come to room temperature.

By the way, I *highly* recommend investing in a bread machine. Using a bread machine for bread baking is far easier, more convenient, and less time-consuming than baking in the oven. You can save a lot of money on buying bread, too. See Chapter 12 for more information on bread machines. However, I sometimes find it more practical to purchase a loaf of bread when I can get it for $1.00 per loaf and it is already sliced.

You can apply this same concept to oatmeal. This is a more economical way of giving yourself "instant" oatmeal (as opposed to the pre-packaged instant oatmeal packets you find at the grocery store). You can make either individual snack-sized bags of oatmeal (say, if the members of your household all leave at different times of day, or if there are only one or two of you), or larger bags for the whole family (if you all eat breakfast at the same time). Add oatmeal and any flavorings and then seal the bag, and label with the amount of liquid you need to add along with the amount of cooking time required.

Quick and/or Thrifty Tips to Help You in the Kitchen

- Find a great price on tomatoes? If you normally use a lot of canned tomatoes in your cooking, try this: wash and freeze those fresh tomatoes in containers or plastic bags. When you want to use them, just thaw the tomatoes. The skins will slip off easily, and you can then use them for cooking!
- Lemons on sale? Stock up and make batches of lemon juice. Lemon juice is found in many recipes, and it is great for homemade cleaners, too! After juicing the lemons, you can freeze the juice for use later. A few ways to freeze juice include measuring ¼ cup amounts, placing in containers or freezer bags, and popping into the freezer; pour juice in muffin tins, freeze, then remove from the tins and place in plastic bags; or pour juice into ice cube trays, freeze, and remove from trays and place in plastic bags.
- Homemade meatballs are delicious and far more nutritious than pre-made. To make them more easily, roll the meat mixture into a log shape, then cut into evenly-sized slices. Then roll the slices into balls.
- Want to make tiny meatballs, like for an Italian wedding soup? Use a melon baller. Each meatball will be perfectly spherical *and* identically-sized.
- Anytime you want to freeze chicken pieces (breasts, legs, thighs, or wings), wrap each piece individually before placing in a bag or vacuum-sealing. This will prevent the chicken from freezing together, and you can remove the exact number of pieces you need without having to pry them apart. Or just package the number of pieces that you would need for a meal in one bag.

- Painter's tape is excellent for labeling bags and containers for the freezer. Even when frozen, the tape will stay in place.
- Keep fresh herbs fresher longer by wrapping them in slightly damp paper towels, then placing in plastic bags before storing in the refrigerator.
- Add more flavor to vegetables by cooking them in chicken or beef broth.
- Did you buy more lemons or limes than you can use? Wash the extras, cut them into wedges, freeze them, and then use them to flavor glasses of water or iced tea. Or make lemon or lime curd.
- Baked potatoes can take a long time to cook. Save time by cooking them in the microwave for 7 minutes, then place them in a pre-heated oven and allow them to finish baking.
- Seasonings can be purchased at more reasonable prices at restaurant food suppliers or bulk food stores. If you do not need such a large amount, share with a friend.
- When you plan your menu, be sure to plan a meal around a protein, a vegetable/fruit, and a starch.
- Make sure that you plan each meal the days/nights that you have other activities planned or you just need to rest. Try and plan/make a meal in 30 minutes, or take a meal out of the freezer and use it.
- The same applies to breakfast. Make pancakes/waffles or strata on the weekend when you can spend more time cooking with the family or having friends over.
- Put all of your favorite recipes on your computer, copied and in a notebook, or on fantastic software by DVO.com. This way whenever you cannot think of something special to fix, you will have lots of recipes at your fingertips.
- Also, keep all of your previous menus in a folder so that you have them to refer to.
- Are your children picky eaters? If so, get them involved in meal preparations.
- The same way you make up a menu for dinner or weekends, you might also want to make up a menu for lunches.
- Be sure to always have someone's favorite meal planned each month.

Choices You Make

The choices you make, when preparing your menu, also determine the cost of your meal. When you are planning your menu or substituting an item in your recipe, you are in control of what you are spending. Are you going to make stroganoff with filet mignon or ground chuck? Are you going to serve shrimp fried rice or sea bass? Osso buco at $14 per serving or Beef Daube Provencal (same wonderful flavors) at $2.50 per serving? When you are making 2 different choices for a meal or a snack you can be miles apart on cost, but if you make a better choice you can be just as satisfied but not break the bank. The same for snacks…popcorn & nuts for a snack is $3.50 for a large bowl or pizza $9? Or pizza flavored popcorn would only be $1.50 for a large bowl. The same applies to desserts or anything else you purpose. Learn to make more economical choices that will satisfy your cravings and help your budget.

Week 1   Sample Dinner Menu

Sunday	Spanish rice w/pork medallions Broccoli or green beans Iced tea Brownie Mix	Approx. $9.15/6
Monday	Chicken piccata Knorr creamy chicken rice Steamed carrots Iced tea	Approx. $6.00/4
Tuesday	Meatloaf Mashed potatoes Sautéed squash or another vegetable Iced tea	Approx. $7.00/6
Wednesday	Omelets w/cheddar cheese, onion, bell pepper (and/or other veggies) Sausage patties Iced tea	Approx. $5.00/4
Thursday	Crock-pot Roasted Chicken Baked potato Small salad Iced tea	Approx. $8.00/4
Friday	Waffles Bacon Iced tea Snack: Popcorn & soda	Approx. $5.60/4
Saturday	Lunch – Grilled cheese sandwiches Tomato soup Dinner -- Spaghetti w/meatballs Broccoli Garlic bread	Approx. $14.00/4

This menu cost us $54.75. This left $20.25 for breakfast and some lunches (based at $75.00 week/4).

Suggestions:

Breakfast during the week should consist of toast, cereal, eggs, or a piece of fruit.

Lunches during the week should consist of leftovers, soup, or a simple sandwich.

Drinks for adults should consist of water, iced tea or coffee.

Drinks for children should consist of milk, Kool-Aid, or fruit juice; if they are allowed soda they can have one glass each on Friday evening, Saturday, and/or Sunday.

Remember to plan your menus around the store's sale prices for the week.

On the next page is an extra form that you can make copies of and use to plan your menus.

Dinner Menu

Sunday	
Monday	
Tuesday	
Wednesday	
Thursday	
Friday	
Saturday	

Chapter 5

Creating a Shopping List

After you plan your menu for the week, you then need to make a grocery list. This will include items that you will need for the week, and any special sale items that you want to use to stock up on. You can also use this form to put items on that you have run out of on a day-to-day basis.

What follows is a comprehensive grocery list that you can use to construct your own shopping list. Because every store is different, we have included some spaces where you can fill in other items as necessary.

Preparation For Shopping

- ❏ Compare store flyers
    - ❏ Newspaper ads
    - ❏ Internet websites
- ❏ Make up a weekly menu from best sales offered
- ❏ Check your coupons
- ❏ Check your pantry
- ❏ Watch expiration dates
- ❏ Make a list of items you still need

10

Basic Grocery List

Packaged Staples

- [ ] Applesauce
- [ ] Artichokes Hearts
- [ ] Beans, *Baked*
- [ ] Beans, *Black*
- [ ] Beans, *Kidney*
- [ ] Beans, *Refried*
- [ ] Beans _____
- [ ] Cereal _____
- [ ] Chocolate Syrup
- [ ] Coffee
- [ ] Condensed Soup, *Cheese*
- [ ] Condensed Soup, *Cream of Mushroom*
- [ ] Condensed Soup, *Tomato*
- [ ] Condensed Soup _____
- [ ] Fruit _____
- [ ] Fruit Pie Filling _____
- [ ] Jam/Jelly _____
- [ ] Lentils
- [ ] Macaroni and Cheese, Boxed
- [ ] Mandarin Oranges
- [ ] Marshmallow Fluff
- [ ] Marshmallows _____
- [ ] Mexicorn
- [ ] Noodles, *Egg*
- [ ] Olives, *Black*
- [ ] Olives, *Green*
- [ ] Pasta, *Macaroni*
- [ ] Pasta, *Spaghetti*
- [ ] Pasta _____
- [ ] Peanut Butter
- [ ] Pesto _____
- [ ] Pickles _____
- [ ] Pumpkin
- [ ] Relish
- [ ] Rice, *Converted*
- [ ] Rice, *Flavored*
- [ ] Rice, *Instant*
- [ ] Rice _____
- [ ] Roasted Red Peppers
- [ ] Salmon
- [ ] Sauces, *Alfredo*
- [ ] Sauces, *Spaghetti*

- [ ] Sauerkraut
- [ ] Sweet Potatoes/Yams
- [ ] Tea
- [ ] Tomato Paste
- [ ] Tomato Sauce
- [ ] Tomato _____
- [ ] Tomatoes, Crushed
- [ ] Tomatoes, Diced
- [ ] Tuna
- [ ] Vegetables
- [ ] _____

Refrigerated

- [ ] Butter
- [ ] Buttermilk
- [ ] Cheese, *Cheddar*
- [ ] Cheese, *Cottage*
- [ ] Cheese, *Grated*
- [ ] Cheese, *Monterey Jack*
- [ ] Cheese, *Mozzarella*
- [ ] Cheese, *Ricotta*
- [ ] Cheese, *Swiss*
- [ ] Cheese _____
- [ ] Cream
- [ ] Cream Cheese
- [ ] Deli Meats _____
- [ ] Dough
- [ ] Eggs
- [ ] Juices, *Apple*
- [ ] Juices, *Cranberry*
- [ ] Juices, *Grape*
- [ ] Juices, *Grapefruit*
- [ ] Juices, *Orange*
- [ ] Margarine
- [ ] Milk _____
- [ ] Pie Crust
- [ ] Pizza Dough
- [ ] Sour Cream
- [ ] Yogurt
- [ ] _____

Produce

- [ ] Apples
- [ ] Apricots
- [ ] Asparagus
- [ ] Avocado
- [ ] Bananas

Produce (Cont'd)

- Beets
- Berries, *Blueberries*
- Berries, *Cranberries*
- Berries, *Strawberries*
- Broccoli
- Cabbage
- Cantaloupe
- Carrots
- Cauliflower
- Celery
- Cherries
- Corn
- Cucumbers _____
- Garlic
- Garlic Cloves, Jarred
- Grapes _____
- Grapefruit
- Green Beans
- Greens
- Lemons
- Lettuce _____
- Limes
- Mangos
- Melons
- Mushrooms _____
- Nectarines
- Onions, *Green*
- Onions, *Red*
- Onions, *Sweet*
- Onions, *White*
- Oranges _____
- Papaya
- Parsnips
- Peaches
- Pears
- Peppers _____
- Pineapple
- Plums
- Potatoes _____
- Radishes
- Raisins
- Rutabagas
- Spinach
- Squash
- Strawberries
- Tomatoes
- Turnips

- Watermelon
- Zucchini
- _____

Baking

- Baking Powder
- Baking Soda
- Bisquick Mix
- Brownie Mixes
- Cake Mixes, Boxed
- Corn Bread Mix
- Corn Starch
- Evaporated Milk
- Flour _____
- Frosting/ Icing
- Sugar, *Brown*
- Sugar, *Powdered*
- Sugar, *White*
- Sweetened Condensed Milk
- Yeast, *Dry*
- _____

Frozen

- Bread Dough
- Desserts
- Dinners
- Fish
- Fruits and Berries _____
- Ice Cream _____
- Juice Concentrate, *Fruit Punch*
- Juice Concentrate, *Lemonade*
- Juice Concentrate, *Limeade*
- Juice Concentrate, *Pink Lemonade*
- Juice Concentrate _____
- Meat Items
- Onions, *Pearl*
- Pizza
- Potatoes, *French Fries*
- Potatoes, *Hash Browns*
- Potatoes, *Mashed*
- Potatoes, *Sweet Potatoes*
- Potatoes, *Tater Tots*
- Shrimp
- Vegetables, *Carrots*
- Vegetables, *Green Beans*
- Vegetables, *Green Peppers*
- Vegetables, *Mixed Vegetables*
- Vegetables, *Stir-Fry Mix*
- Vegetables _____
- Whipped Topping, Ready-Made

□ _____

Condiments, Fats & Seasonings

- ☐ **Bouillon or Soup Base**
- ☐ **Broth**, *Beef*
- ☐ **Broth**, *Chicken*
- ☐ **Broth**, *Vegetable*
- ☐ **Broth** _____
- ☐ **Canola Oil**
- ☐ **Corn Syrup**
- ☐ **Dried Italian Seasoning**
- ☐ **Gelatin**
- ☐ **Ketchup**
- ☐ **Mayonnaise**
- ☐ **Molasses**
- ☐ **Montreal Steak Seasoning**
- ☐ **Mustard**, *Brown*
- ☐ **Mustard**, *Dijon*
- ☐ **Mustard**, *Yellow*
- ☐ **Nonstick Cooking Spray**
- ☐ **Old Bay Seasoning**
- ☐ **Olive Oil** _____
- ☐ **Pepper** _____
- ☐ **Poultry Seasoning**
- ☐ **Powdered Milk**
- ☐ **Pumpkin Pie Spice**
- ☐ **Red Pepper Flakes**
- ☐ **Salad Dressing** _____
- ☐ **Salsa**
- ☐ **Salt**, *Kosher*
- ☐ **Salt** _____
- ☐ **Seasoning**, *Chili*
- ☐ **Seasoning**, *McCormick Grill Mates*
- ☐ **Seasoning**, *Pot Roast*
- ☐ **Seasoning**, *Taco*
- ☐ **Seasoning**, *Teriyaki*
- ☐ **Seasoning** _____
- ☐ **Shortening, Solid, Butter Flavored**
- ☐ **Shortening, Solid, Original Flavored**
- ☐ **Soy Sauce**
- ☐ **Syrup** _____
- ☐ **Tartar Sauce**
- ☐ **Vegetable Oil** _____
- ☐ **Vinegar** _____
- ☐ **Worcestershire Sauce**

□ _____

Meats

- ☐ **Bacon**
- ☐ **Beef**, *Chuck Roast*
- ☐ **Beef**, *Ground, 80% Lean*
- ☐ **Beef** _____
- ☐ **Chicken**, *Breast, Skinless/Boneless*
- ☐ **Chicken**, *Legs*
- ☐ **Chicken**, *Thighs*
- ☐ **Chicken**, *Whole*
- ☐ **Chicken**, *Wings*
- ☐ **Chicken** _____
- ☐ **Cubed Steak**
- ☐ **Fish** _____
- ☐ **Ham** _____
- ☐ **Hot Dogs**
- ☐ **Italian Sweet Sausage**
- ☐ **Lamb Chops**
- ☐ **Lamb** _____
- ☐ **Luncheon Meat**
- ☐ **Pork Chops**
- ☐ **Pork Loin**
- ☐ **Pork Shoulder**
- ☐ **Prosciutto**
- ☐ **Sausage**
- ☐ **Stew Meat** _____
- ☐ **Turkey**
- □ _____

Baked Goods

- ☐ **Bagels**
- ☐ **Bakery Pastry**
- ☐ **Biscuits**
- ☐ **Bread** _____
- ☐ **Bread Crumbs**
- ☐ **Buns** _____
- ☐ **Crackers** _____
- ☐ **Croutons, Seasoned**
- ☐ **Graham Crackers**
- ☐ **Muffins** _____
- ☐ **Rolls**
- ☐ **Tortillas**
- □ _____

Snacks

- ☐ **Cookies** _____
- ☐ **Nuts** _____

Snacks (cont'd)

- ☐ Popcorn
- ☐ Potato Chips
- ☐ Pretzels
- ☐ Tortilla Chips
- ☐ Veggie Chips
- ☐ _____

Beverages

- ☐ 7-Up
- ☐ Beer
- ☐ Bourbon
- ☐ Club Soda
- ☐ Cola
- ☐ Gin
- ☐ Ginger Ale
- ☐ Mixers _____
- ☐ Mountain Dew
- ☐ Root Beer
- ☐ Rum
- ☐ Vodka
- ☐ Whiskey
- ☐ Wine _____
- ☐ _____

Pharmacy

- ☐ Alka-Seltzer
- ☐ Antacid
- ☐ Aspirin
- ☐ Band Aids
- ☐ Cold Medicine
- ☐ Laxatives
- ☐ Neosporin
- ☐ Pain Reliever _____
- ☐ Pepto Bismol
- ☐ Peroxide
- ☐ Pharmacy Drugs
- ☐ Rubbing Alcohol
- ☐ Vitamins
- ☐ _____

Household Staples

- ☐ All-Purpose Cleaner
- ☐ Bags _____
- ☐ Bleach
- ☐ Dish Detergent
- ☐ Dishwasher Detergent
- ☐ Fabric Softener
- ☐ Facial Tissues
- ☐ Foil
- ☐ Laundry Detergent
- ☐ Light Bulbs _____
- ☐ Napkins
- ☐ Paper Towels
- ☐ Plastic Bags
- ☐ Plastic Wrap
- ☐ Soap, Bath
- ☐ Soap, Facial
- ☐ Stain Remover
- ☐ Toilet Paper
- ☐ Wax Paper
- ☐ Window Cleaner
- ☐ _____

Miscellaneous

- ☐ Baby Supplies _____
- ☐ Combs/Brushes
- ☐ Conditioner
- ☐ Deodorant
- ☐ Drug Items
- ☐ Feminine Hygiene _____
- ☐ Dental Floss
- ☐ Personal Hygiene _____
- ☐ Pet Products _____
- ☐ Razors
- ☐ School Supplies _____
- ☐ Shampoo
- ☐ Shaving Cream
- ☐ Tooth Brushes
- ☐ Tooth Paste _____
- ☐ _____

You have an option on the previous 4 pages.

- You can either make multiple photo copies of the pages (back-to-back), so that you and your family can mark what you need each week (so that you don't forget), and throw them away when you are finished shopping;
- or make one master set and laminate the pages (back-to-back), and then mark on them with an erasable dry marker, what you need each week.

Chapter 6
Menu Planning & Shopping for
Singles, Couples & Families

Singles/Couples

Many single people find that cooking for one is a hard chore, and that it is easier to eat out. Eating out, however, is very expensive compared to eating at home.

If you are just setting up housekeeping, you could share meals with a co-worker, neighbor, and/or roommate. Not only does this provide companionship, but it also allows you the freedom of not having to cook every night of the week.

If you are a senior citizen, you might enjoy the activities of a local senior center. Senior centers are a wonderful way to meet others. At the senior center in my area, we have the following:

- Cafeteria
- Deli
- Exercise facilities with plasma TVs
- Indoor pool
- Garden area w/cookout
- Billiards/aerobics
- Crafts/quilting
- Outings
- Many more activities available year round

Singles may find that convenience foods, in some instances, are more practical and economical for them. For example, you can buy a box of Hamburger Helper for 50 cents a box when on sale and when using a double coupon. That's 50 cents a serving once you add meat and/or other add-ins. If you prefer other types of menu selections, you will want to use a food processor and either vacuum seal the food for use within 2-3 weeks (in the refrigerator) or freeze the food for a much later date. Or if you want to add a starch to your meal, you can get a box of Betty Crocker potato selections for 50 cents a box -- when on sale from the store at a dollar a box and with a double coupon (25 to 50 cents).

The perfect place to purchase food in the size packaging that you require, as a single person would be:

- Your local deli or meat market
- Your favorite seafood market
- Your favorite bakery
- The bulk food section of your favorite grocery store
- A farmer's market

Another way of getting variety in your meals would be to alternate having a meal at your home with another single or couple and having a meal at their home. Besides sharing meals, you can also share grocery shopping by dividing up food items that might be too large in quantity for just one person to consume. This method also promotes and develops friendships.

At one time I held a game night at my home once a month and my friends would each bring a dish to share with others. After eating, we would all play table games for a few hours. I still have fond memories of those Friday/Saturday evenings.

Another option is to join a cooking club in your local area.

Economical lunches for singles/couples might include:

- Grilled cheese sandwiches w/carrots and pickles for 50 cents a serving
- Grilled peanut butter sandwiches w/celery for 50 cents a serving
- Tuna salad, a piece of fruit and w/iced tea for $1.00 per serving
- Hamburger (1/4 pound w/bun), pretzels and iced tea for 90 cents per serving
- Pasta salad (pasta, bell pepper, tomatoes, onion, grated carrot & salad dressing) and iced tea for 75 cents a serving

Families:

The one thing you should begin striving toward right now is offering your family balanced meals. In today's society, these are not as common as they should be. We have come to expect a meal to include a large protein and small side dishes of vegetables and starches -- and sometimes we skip the vegetable! But this is not the healthiest option.

Each of your family's meals should include similar portions of the following:

- A protein
- A grain or starch
- A vegetable or fruit

Envision a plate as a circle. Vegetables should take up ½ of the plate; starches ¼ of the plate; and protein ¼ of the plate.

Another way to ensure a balanced meal is to offer many different colors. The more different colors your food has, the more healthful it is, as many essential nutrients are found in brightly colored food.

Many families find that their children have distinct preferences for their fruits and vegetables. It is fine to cater to those preferences at first, but you should also try to help them expand their repertoire. Experts say that it can take a person several exposures to a new food before he or she learns to like it. Serve new food to your children several times; after a while you may find that they enjoy it.

It can be difficult to get children to even try a new food they are convinced they will not like. This is where you might want to consider a little bribery. Tell your children that all they have to eat are three bites. If they eat those three bites, they can have a peanut butter sandwich or soup of their choice. If your children are anything like the children I know, that will be a powerful incentive! The next time you serve that food, move it up to four bites, and so on.

Also, remember that your children will be watching *you* to see how you treat a particular food! If you expect them to eat something they are resistant to, then you had better make sure you eat it, too.

You may also try preparing vegetables and fruits in such a way as to make them more enjoyable to children. For instance, one of my friend's children loves veggie chips. She thinly slices various vegetables (like carrots, zucchini, parsnips, sweet potatoes, and turnips), sprays them with olive oil spray and a little seasoning, places them in the oven on low heat for a few hours, and then serves them as a delicious side dish or snack. An added bonus is that veggie chips have a longer shelf life than fresh vegetables!

Planning meals can be a daunting task. One way to simplify it, at least at first, is to design "choice nights" for every night of the week. You can plan these with the help of the whole family. Find out what your family enjoys eating, and incorporate those favorite meals into choice nights based on what is on sale at the grocery store.

A few possible choices could include:

- Chicken
- Fish/Seafood
- Hamburger
- Pasta
- Breakfast-for-dinner
- Homemade pizza
- Tacos/Burritos
- Soup/Stew
- Salad
- Grilling a meal
- Vegetarian/Meatless
- Ethnic (this could include Asian, Greek, Tex-Mex, and so on)
- Leftovers

One thing I do not recommend is acting as a short-order cook -- making different meals for each member of the family. It does not help children learn to appreciate many types of food, and it places an unnecessary burden on whoever is cooking.

Children's Lunches

The same principles of menu planning and preparation may be successfully applied to school lunches.

Each child should have a thermal bag and one or two thermoses (one for a cold drink and one for a hot meal). Then each bag should have heavy duty plastic eating utensils (have the child bring these home so they can be washed and used again) and a napkin.

By doing a little brainstorming you can easily come up with a five-day (or more) rotation of meals that your children will like. Remember that selections will vary according to the age of the child and their likes, dislikes, and the time of year. With some planning, many parts of these meals can either be prepared on weekends or the night before. This will make getting the children out the door on school mornings much less stressful.

Day	Main Entrée	Fruit	Drink	Extra
Monday	Meatloaf sandwich	Small apple	Milk	Pretzels
Tuesday	Tuna sandwich	Raisins	Milk	Hardboiled egg
Wednesday	Lunch meat sandwich	Yogurt	Milk	Trail mix
Thursday	Spaghetti	Small apple	Milk	Small salad
Friday	Peanut butter sandwich	Pear	Milk	Celery

Chapter 7

Cooking with Children

Submitted by Mark Zacek

When I was 8 or 9 years old, my mother bought me the Betty Crocker Children's Cookbook. I still have that yellow-and-white cookbook with all those Sixties-era illustrations. I picked it up for the first time in decades a few weeks ago. I was amazed by the flood of joyful memories opening the book stirred in me. I remember every page of that book. I remember all of my successes and failures, as well as my occasional disappointment with the shortcomings of a recipe. I remember my flights of imagination away from the recipe on the page, and how my mom and dad encouraged and appreciated every one of my efforts. What I don't remember is either parent actually cooking with me. I think I was just turned loose in the kitchen. Somehow, this worked for me, as I have been cooking for as long as I can remember and still love it. But it is not the approach I have used with my own children.

I have bought children's cookbooks for my children. The cookbooks have never had the effect on them that my mother's gift had on me. Whether this was a shortcoming of these cookbooks or just my children's own responses to cooking, I am not certain. What does work is for me to ask them to help me cook. I find it very effective when enlisting my younger children to cook to ask them well in advance for their help. That builds anticipation and excitement. It also means they can help me decide on the recipe, write the grocery list, and shop with me. And most gratifying of all, it means that they value the time spent with me as much as I value the time I have with them.

I recognize that this approach may not work with many children. It has not worked for every one of my own children. Some children are receptive, and some are not. Do not force it on them, but draw them in wherever possible by doing something *fascinating* to a child (whipping cream, asking them to push the button for you to make bread crumbs with the food processor, slicing a hardboiled egg with an egg slicer). The child may turn out to be more interested than they had thought.

When you cook with your children, I have learned that it is essential to have all distractions minimized. Organize the time so there is no competition for your children's attention. No visiting friends, no homework, and no pesky little brother or sister to divert *your* attention. And most of all, NO TELEVISION. Be certain that you have plenty of your own time set aside because you must be totally patient and encouraging. Expect that cooking with children will slow you down. At least early on, they are not at all an extra pair of hands to lighten your load. Prepare to explain every step, why you are separating the eggs, why you cut off the bottoms of the asparagus spears, why you need baking powder in the cake.

Prepare yourself: your child will spill half the flour outside of the bowl and drop the carton of eggs on the floor. This is okay! It will happen, and it does not matter. You are building skills, confidence, and relationships, not competing for the Pillsbury Bake-Off or filming a Martha Stewart episode.

What should you cook with your children? A great start is to prepare a food that is special or particularly intriguing to them. Remember that something special to them may be as simple as a food that you have planned together for this week's menu. One possibility is to make together a familiar food that they have never seen prepared at home. Macaroni and cheese from scratch, for example. Other examples: a grilled hamburger, pancakes, a birthday cake, a green salad, or ice cream.

If you have only a few minutes together, teach them how to make hot chocolate from scratch, not from a packet. Show them how to make popcorn from popcorn kernels and a stapled paper bag (a few small metal staples are not a safety issue in the microwave). The Internet is the perfect resource for you if you have never attempted these things yourself. Of course, it is always essential to be vigilant with kitchen safety. A grease spatter from a frying egg, a steam burn from a carelessly opened microwave popcorn bag, or a cut from a knife must always be a concern.

In addition to cooking techniques, teach your children where their food comes from. The English chef and crusader for good nutrition Jaime Oliver revealed results of his test of otherwise well-educated American high school students that showed a truly shocking ignorance of food origins. Sausages come from cattails? Chocolate is harvested from lakes? Butter comes from corn? Astonishing! This is not a failure of our education system but rather an expression of how little we value where our food comes from. If a family relies on takeout, seldom eats meals together, and does not cook together, it is hardly surprising that this ignorance exists. If our children are not acquainted with the most basic facts of food sourcing, they cannot possibly have any understanding of nutrition or respect for those who labor to supply it.

Take your children to a farmers' market, or better yet, visit a biodynamic farm. From such a visit, they will also learn important lessons about soil, fertilizer, and replenishing the earth. Teenagers will enjoy tours of a winery, distillery, or brewery and acquire an appreciation of the plant-based nature of drinks they may (in the future!) enjoy. Visiting a dairy farm is an excellent way for a child to see firsthand the hard, long and often dirty chain of work required to produce the milk they drink every day. But the most important thing you can do is to cook with your children and talk to them about every ingredient that goes into the food as you cook together.

For "extra credit," compare your home ingredients to the ingredients on prepared foods you are buying. If you do not recognize the ingredients of purchased foods, you are buying the wrong foods! A general rule of thumb is that the fewer and more familiar the ingredients, the better and purer the product. And the sooner children learn that lesson, the better are their chances for a healthy life of good nutrition.

I think it is especially important to cook with children around the holidays. By doing so not only can you instruct your children and enjoy time with them, but you can also pass on family traditions and build special memories. One of my happiest memories is making plum puddings with my youngest daughter while Christmas carols played in the background and an evening snowfall covered the colored lights outside our kitchen windows. I do not know exactly how my daughter will remember these times, but I believe she will remember that this was an important part of Christmas and that baking with dad was fun. I hope it is also something she will want to do with her own children. You cannot ask for more than that.

Child Cooking Safety

Of course, there are many dangers for children in the kitchen, and it is important to do whatever you can to minimize these dangers. Burns, cuts, and falls are a few of the hazards for any cook, but even more so for children whose fine and gross motor skills are still developing.

The first thing to remember when you are in the kitchen with your children is to **give yourself a *lot* of time and be very patient**. You will need to teach them what to do, and this will add time and more steps to the cooking process. You will have to explain certain terms. You will also have to supervise them to make sure they don't grab a hot pot handle or bump into a hot pan.

Therefore, **any recipe that involves many quick steps are probably not suitable for teaching your children to cook**. Choose recipes that do not depend on quick actions, where it won't ruin the meal if it takes 20 minutes or longer between one step and another. Some simple cooking steps to start with might include icing cookies using a plastic bag; putting peanut butter on celery or apples; putting raisins on peanut butter; making peanut butter and jelly sandwiches; or making grilled cheese sandwiches using an electric skillet.

Be sure your children (and you!) **wash your hands** before you begin. This should be an automatic first step. Also be sure they wash their hands after handling any food with the potential to cross-contaminate, such as raw meat or raw eggs.

Have everyone **wear short sleeves.** Long sleeves are more likely to catch on pot handles or drag through fire.

Don't forget **aprons.** These protect clothing as well as skin! You could even purchase special aprons just for them.

Explain and demonstrate. Explain every step, and demonstrate when you can. These not only help children understand the proper ways to perform cooking tasks, but it also allows them to learn how to do things safely.

Be especially careful with knives and other cutting utensils. If your children don't yet have the motor control necessary to handle cutting, chopping, and so on, they may be able to use kitchen shears or vegetable/fruit peelers. But be sure to supervise and demonstrate even with these utensils. Encourage children to cut and peel away from themselves. You may want to begin a cutting demonstration by holding the food to be cut and having them place their hand over yours to help them feel the motion required. Then you can gradually move them towards making cuts on their own.

Keep pan handles turned in. Pan handles should never be jutting out from the stovetop. This prevents children grabbing hot handles or bumping into a handle and spilling hot food on themselves.

Use oven mitts. Towels should never be used to handle hot food containers, as they can drag through stovetop fire. Mitts are preferable to potholders because children can use them more securely.

Clean up spills. Spills can lead to slips and falls when they are on a floor. Even spills on a countertop can be harmful, as they can create slippery surfaces for tasks like cutting or stirring.

Keep an eye on the food. Anything can happen when food goes unattended; your children could get involved in a calamity, or a pot could bubble over and cause a fire.

Praise any successes. This isn't a matter of safety, but it is a matter of childhood enjoyment. Let your children know if they did a great job peeling vegetables, stirring a mixture, or using the blender. This will encourage your children to continue helping and go a long way towards making great memories!

Recipes for Children

Baby Wipes

1. Cut a single roll of heavy-duty paper towels (Viva is a good brand for this) in half with a sharp knife and get two miniature rolls.

2. Remove the cardboard center from the inside of one half and place the paper towels in an empty wipe box or a plastic container.

3. Mix together 1 1/2 cups water, 1 1/2 tablespoons baby oil, and 1 1/2 tablespoons baby shampoo. Mix it well.

4. Pour the mixture over the paper towels. Turn the towels over to make sure the mixture gets on both sides, close the wipe box, and shake it a bit.

5. Wait 10 minutes for the liquid to be completely absorbed before using.

Homemade Finger Paint
Yield: 2 1/2 cups

2 tablespoon sugar
1/3 cup cornstarch
2 cup cold water
1/4 cup clear dishwashing detergent

PLEASE NOTE: Because these paints contain a generous amount of dish detergent, they are not appropriate for toddlers or other children who put things in their mouths.

plastic spoons
food coloring
small plastic containers w/lids (empty yogurt cups would work well)

Combine the sugar and cornstarch in a small saucepan. Add the water and stir until all the lumps dissolve. Cook over very low heat, stirring constantly. Continue to cook and stir until the mixture becomes clear and thick like gelatin. Remove from the heat and cool to room temperature. Add the dishwashing detergent. Spoon a small quantity into each container and add a few drops of food coloring to create the desired color.

Homemade Play Dough

Yield: 2 1/4 cups

1 cup flour
1 cup water
1/4 cup salt
1 tablespoon vegetable oil
2 teaspoon cream of tartar
1 teaspoon or more food coloring

Combine all of the ingredients in a saucepan and mix well. Stir the ingredients over low to medium heat for approximately 5 minutes. When the mixture forms a ball, remove from the heat. Turn the ball of goop onto a cookie sheet and let it cool.

Once it is cool enough to handle, add food coloring and knead it with your hands for several minutes until the dough becomes smooth. Be sure to store in an airtight plastic container.

NOTE: Play dough is trouble if it gets ground into the carpet, so it's worth creating an easy cleanup play dough place. If you are using a nice table cover it with an oil cloth so that the food coloring will not stain it. Or use a very old folding table just for messy crafts.

Grilled Peanut Butter Sandwiches

Instead of grilled cheese, put peanut butter in between the bread. Yummy. Serve with tomato soup

Magic Milk Shakes

Serves: 4

1 1/2 to 2 cups iced water
1 1/2 cups nonfat dry milk powder
2/3 cup sugar
1/4 cup unsweetened cocoa
1 teaspoon vanilla
1 to 1 1/2 trays of ice cubes, as much as you can spare
2 tablespoons corn oil plus a 5-second squirt of non-stick spray for emulsification purposes

Place all of the ingredients into the blender, including the oil and the non-stick spray. Use less water for thicker milk shakes and more water for shakes that are easy on your blender motor. The blender should be about ¾ full. Place the lid on. Then process for a full 2 minutes. Pour into cups and serve.

Funnel Cakes

Serves: 6
Approximate 43 cents per serving.

2 beaten eggs
1 1/2 cup milk
2 cup sifted flour
1 teaspoon baking powder
1/2 teaspoon salt
2 cup cooking oil
Powdered sugar

Combine eggs and milk. Sift flour, baking powder, and salt together. Add to egg mixture and beat until smooth. If it is too thick, add a little milk. If too thin, add a little flour. The humidity in the air will cause the difference in the flour...for which you can make an adjustment for. Heat oil to 360 degrees. Pour 1/2 cup of the batter into a funnel and drizzle into the oil, forming a circle with drizzles in the center. Fry until golden brown. Flip and fry the other side. Drain on paper towels and dust with powdered sugar. You can also drip on chocolate syrup and apply sprinkles.

Banana Strawberry Pops

Serves: 10

1/2 cup fat-free milk
1/2 cup orange juice
2 tablespoon honey
1 pint fresh strawberries, hulled
1 medium ripe banana, cut into chunks

In a blender, combine the milk, juice, honey, strawberries and banana cover and process until blended. Fill each mold or cup with 1/4 cup strawberry mixture top with holders or insert sticks into cups. Freeze. Nutrition Facts: 1 pop equals 42 calories, trace fat, trace cholesterol, 6mg sodium, 10g carbohydrate, 1g fiber, 1g protein. Diabetic exchange: 1/2 fruit

Carmel Popcorn

Serves: 4

1 cup brown sugar
½ cup butter
½ teaspoon salt
¼ cup light corn syrup
½ teaspoon baking soda
3 to 4 quarts popped popcorn

Combine sugar, butter, salt, and corn syrup in a 1 ½ quart microwave dish. Bring to a boil in microwave on high. Stir then cook on high for 2 more minutes. Remove and stir in soda. Place popped popcorn in a brown paper grocery bag. Pour caramel over popcorn and roll down top of bag. Shake the bag to coat the popcorn. Place bag in microwave and cook on high for 1 ½ min. Shake bag, cook on high of 1 more minute. Pour into a pan to cool, or eat right out of the bag. This recipe is very comparable to Cracker Jack. Try it with peanuts.

Caramel Popcorn Balls

Serves: 12

1/2 cup butter
3 cups brown sugar
1 cup light corn syrup
14 ounces sweetened condensed milk
1 tablespoon vanilla extract
4 quarts to 6 quarts (16-24 cups) popped popcorn kernels (un-popped kernels removed)

In a heavy saucepan, combine butter, sugar, and corn syrup. Bring to a boil.
Pour in condensed milk. Return to a boil. Boil five minutes.
Remove from heat. Stir in vanilla extract.
Pour hot caramel over popcorn and stir with a wooden spoon or spatula.
Grease hands and form popcorn mixture into balls.
Let balls cool on greased cookie sheets or waxed paper.

Kool-Aid Jam

Yield: 3 ½ pints

2 cups mashed fruit
1 packages of MCP pectin
2 cups water
6 cups sugar
1 package unsweetened Kool-Aid

Mash the fruit and combine the fruit, water, Kool-Aid and MCP pectin in a large kettle. Never fill the kettle more than half full. Bring to a boil. Add sugar, and bring to a full boil. Stirring often, boil 3 to 5 minutes. While mixture is cooking, prepare jelly jars--they should be hot. Boil lids in boiling water to get the proper seal. When jam is thick, pour into hot jars and seal.

Chocolate Chip Pancakes

Yield: 11 pancakes

2 cups biscuit/baking mix
2 tablespoons instant chocolate drink mix
2 teaspoons baking powder
1 egg
1 cup milk
1/2 cup sour cream
1/4 cup miniature semisweet chocolate chips
Maple syrup and butter, optional

In a large bowl, combine the biscuit mix, drink mix and baking powder. Combine the egg, milk and sour cream and stir into dry ingredients just until moistened. Fold in chocolate chips.

Pour ¼ cup batter onto a greased hot griddle. Turn when bubbles form on top cook until second side is golden brown. Serve with maple syrup and butter if desired.
Cool remaining pancakes arrange in a single layer on baking sheets. Freeze overnight or until frozen. Transfer to a re-sealable plastic freezer bag.

 May be frozen for up to 2 months.

To use frozen pancakes: Place on a lightly greased baking sheet. Bake at 400 degrees for 4-6 minutes or until heated through. Serve with maple syrup and butter if desired.

No-Bake Cookies

Serves: 36

2 cups sugar
4 tablespoons cocoa
1 stick butter
1/2 cup milk
1 cup peanut butter
1 tablespoon vanilla
3 cups oatmeal
Waxed paper

 In a heavy saucepan bring to a boil, the sugar, cocoa, butter and milk. Let boil for 1 minute then add peanut butter, vanilla and oatmeal. On a sheet of waxed paper, drop mixture by a teaspoon, and leave until cooled and hardened.

Holiday Fudge

Serves: 12

4 cups sugar
1 12 ounce can evaporated milk
1 stick of butter or margarine
2 (7 ounce) chocolate bars
1 (10 ounce) bottle marshmallow crème
1 teaspoon vanilla

Butter a 9x13 glass pan. Break two giant Hershey bars into small pieces and place in a large bowl. Consider refrigerating half of the chocolate ahead of time, as this will help the fudge set quicker and make it creamier. Add marshmallow crème to the chocolate. Next, put evaporated milk in a heavy pot first and then add sugar and butter. Cook over medium heat stirring regularly and bring to softball stage (220 degrees Fahrenheit on your candy thermometer). Pour liquid over chocolate and marshmallow crème and then add vanilla. Stir until candy thickens and begins to lose its gloss. Add peanut butter, pecans, cashews, or walnuts at this point if you like.
Pour into 9x13 pan and let it set until firm. Serve and enjoy!

Fudgsicles

Serves: 8

Mix together:
3/4 cup sugar
1 tablespoon cornstarch
3 tablespoons cocoa
3 tablespoons flour
1/4 teaspoon salt
1 1/4 cup non instant dry milk powder

Beat into 4 cups boiling water and cook 1 minute. Add 1/2 teaspoon vanilla, pour into molds, and freeze.

Sloppy Joes

Serves: 8

1 pound ground beef chuck
1 can Sloppy Joe sauce
1 medium onion, finely chopped
3 tablespoons green bell pepper, chopped
1 tablespoon cooking oil

Sauté onion until translucent. Add bell pepper and ground chuck. When done add sauce, cover and simmer for 7 minutes. Serve on fresh grilled buns.

Corn Dogs

Serves: 12
Approximate 50 cents per serving

2 2/3 cup yellow cornmeal
1 1/3 cup all-purpose flour , plus more for hot dogs
3 tablespoon sugar
2 teaspoons baking powder
kosher salt
4 large eggs
1 1/2 cup whole milk
2 quarts vegetable oil, for frying
12 hot dogs

Whisk together cornmeal, flour, sugar, baking powder, 1 teaspoon salt, and 1 teaspoon pepper. Stir in eggs and milk. (You will have about 5 cups of batter). Fill a large heavy pot, Dutch oven, or a deep fryer with enough oil to submerge hot dogs heat until a deep-fry thermometer reaches 360 degrees. Meanwhile, pat hot dogs dry, and insert a 10 inch bamboo skewer through each lengthwise roll in flour to coat. Dip 1 hot dog into batter, turning, until completely coated let any excess batter drip off, and wipe away extra batter using your fingers so that the hot dog is coated evenly. Lower the hot dog into hot oil. Immediately repeat with 2 more hot dogs. Cook corn dogs, turning to cook evenly, until deep golden brown, 5 to 7 minutes. Transfer to a paper-towel-lined tray, turning to blot oil. Working in batches of 3, repeat with remaining hot dogs and batter.   Serving idea.....Nothing pairs better with a corn dog than yellow mustard.

Chapter 8

Calculating Recipe Costs

By calculating a recipe's cost, you will find out if preparing it from scratch is worth your time. It is easy but somewhat time consuming. List the ingredients of the recipe, then record the price of each next to it. Add the price of each ingredient, then divide it by the number of servings the recipe makes. You'll find the cost per serving. For example:

Ingredients	Quantity	Cost
Omelet, 3 eggs	3 @ $.10 each	.30
Bell pepper, onion, ham, 1 ½ tablespoon of each		.40
Cheddar cheese, 3 tablespoons		.25
Total		.95
2 servings		$ .47 each

Homemade Tortillas: to make 10- eight inch tortillas.

To figure my cost I need to know how much per cup flour is. It costs $1.29 for a 5-pound bag. From the chart above I found there are 3.5 cups of whole wheat flour per pound. $1.29 divided by 3.5 is $0.37 a cup.

I also need to figure the oil. Oil is $1.99 for 44 fluid ounces. There are 8 fluid ounces in a cup. So there are 5.5 cups in the bottle (44 divided by 8). There are 16 Tablespoons in a cup. So there are 88 Tablespoons in the bottle (5.5 times 16) so $1.99 divided by 88 Tablespoons of oil = $0.02 a Tablespoon.

Baking powder is another tricky one. There are 5.5 ounces in a cup of baking powder. I buy mine by the pound. There are 2.9 cups in a pound of baking powder (16 ounces in a pound divided by 5.5 ounces) and there are 16 Tablespoons or 48 teaspoons or 192 quarter teaspoons in a cup. So there are roughly 557 quarter teaspoons of baking powder in a pound (192 times 2.9). If baking powder costs $1.79 a pound, that is $0.003 a quarter teaspoon. (Not even worth figuring -- now we know!)

Now, for salt. Organic sea salt is $0.44 a pound. There are about 2 cups in a pound of salt. So 1 cup of salt costs $0.22. There are 16 Tablespoons or 48 teaspoons in a cup. $0.22 divided by 48 teaspoons = $0.004 a teaspoon for salt. (Not even worth figuring -- now we know!)

Ingredient	Amount	Cost/Unit	Total
			(Amount x Cost)
Whole Wheat Flour	2.5 cups	$0.37 / cup	$0.93
Oil	1 Tablespoon	$0.02 / Tablespoon	$0.02
Warm Water	1 cup	---	---
Baking Powder	.25 teaspoon	---	---
Salt	1 teaspoon	---	---
Total:			$0.95

Now I know a batch of homemade tortillas costs about $0.95. To buy them at the store is $1.67 -- and mine taste a whole lot better! It was a lot of work for me to figure out the costs of my ingredients, but after I do it once, I can record the costs in my notebook and never have to do those calculations again.

Of course, this can get a little trickier when you have measured ingredients. How do you figure out, for instance, the price of a cup of flour or a Tablespoon of basil?

That's where the following equivalency lists can help. It will show you how much measured ingredients will cost.

(Usually I do not figure in the costs of small amounts of seasoning like salt or pepper -- I do not find it worth my time to figure out a few pennies.)

NOTES:

_____

_____

_____

_____

Food Equivalencies

Baking Ingredients

1 cup baking powder	5 1/2 ounces
23 soda crackers	1 cup
15 graham crackers	1 cup
Flour	See note below
1 pound all-purpose flour	3 1/2 to 4 cups
1 pound cake flour	4 to 4 1/2 cups
1 pound whole wheat flour	3 1/2 cups
1 pound salt	2 cups
3 – 1/4 ounce packet	1/2 cup
1/4 oz packet unflavored gelatin	1 Tablespoon
1 pound brown sugar	2 1/2 cups
1 pound granulated sugar	2 cups
1 pound powdered sugar	3 1/2 cups
1 stick margarine or butter	1/2 cup
2 pounds margarine or butter	2 cups
1 ounce chocolate	1 square
6 ounce package chocolate chips	1 cup
16 ounces corn syrup	2 cups
12 ounces maple syrup	1 1/2 cups

When recipes in other books call for commercially canned or frozen foods, you may want to use your own home-preserved food. Use this chart to determine quantity needed.

Can Size	Weight	Size	Approx. Measure
	6 oz	Frozen juice, tomato paste	¾ cup
	8 oz		1 cup
	10 ½ oz	No. 1 or picnic	1 ¼ cup
	14 ½ oz	Evaporated milk	1 2/3 cup
	15 oz	Sweetened condensed milk	1 1/3 cup
	15 ½ oz	No. 300	1 ¾ cup
	1 lb.	No. 303	2 cups
	1 lb. 4 oz	No. 2	2 ½ cups
	46 oz	Juices and fruit drinks	5 ¾ cups
	6 lb. 9 oz	No. 10	3 quarts
Frozen Food	6 oz	Frozen juice concentrate	¾ cup
	10 oz	Box of vegetables	2 cups
	20 oz	Box of vegetables	4 cups

Ingredients/Food Guide and Equivalents

Food	Weight or Amount	Approximate Equivalent
Almonds, in shell	1 lb	1/3 cup ground almond meal
Almonds, shelled	1 lb	1 cup
Almonds, shelled, blanched	1 lb	3 cups whole, 4 cups silvered
Apples, each	1 medium	About ¾ to 1 cup chopped
Apples, each	1 large	About 1 cup chopped
Apples, fresh	1 lb	3 medium; 3 cups chopped or slice; 3 ½ cups shredded; 1 ¼ cups applesauce
Apples, dried	1 lb	4 1/3 cups finely chopped; 8 cups cooked
Apricots, fresh	1 lb	8-12 whole; 2 ½ cups sliced; 2 cups chopped
Apricots, dried	1 lb	2 ¾ cups; 5 ½ cups cooked
Artichokes	1 lb	2 Large
Artichokes, Jerusalem	1 lb	3 cups cut in 1" pieces
Asparagus, frozen cut	10 oz	2 cups
Asparagus spears, fresh	1 lb	16-20 spears; 2 2/3 cups cut in 1"-1 ½ " pieces
Asparagus spears, canned	14-16 oz	12-18 spears
Avocados	1 lb	2 Small; 2 ½ cups chopped; 1 cup mashed
Bananas, fresh	1 lb	3 medium; 2 cups sliced; 1 ½ cups mashed
Bananas, dried	1 lb	4 ½ cups sliced
Barley	1 cup	3 ½ cups cooked
Beans, canned	16 oz	2 cups
Beans, chickpeas, dried	1 lb	2 cups; 6 cups cooked
Beans, green, fresh	1 lb	3 ½ cups whole; 4-5 cups 1" pieces raw
Beans, green, frozen	9 oz	1 ½ cups
Beans, green, canned	16 oz	1 ¾ cups
Beans, kidney, dried	1 lb	2 ½ cups; 5 ½ cups cooked
Beans. lentils, dried	1 lb	2 ¼ cups; 5 cups cooked
Beans, lima, dried	1 lb	2 2/3 cups; 6 cups cooked
Beans, navy, dries	1 lb	2 1/3 cups ; 5 ½ cups cooked
Beets, fresh, without tops	1 lb	1 ¾ cups shredded; 2 cups chopped or sliced
Beets, canned	16 oz	2 cups
Blueberries, fresh	1 pt	2 cups
	1 qt	3 ½ cups
Blueberries, frozen	10 oz	1 ½ cups
Blueberries, canned	14 oz	1 ½ cups
Bread, dry	1 slice	1/3 cup dry bread crumbs
Bread, fresh	1 slice	½ cup soft bread crumbs
Broccoli, fresh	1 lb	1 large head, 2 cups florets + 2 cups stems
Broccoli, frozen	10 oz	1 ½ cups chopped
Broth, beef or chicken	1 cup	1 teaspoon instant bouillon or 1 envelope or cube bouillon dissolved in 1 cup boiling water
Brussels sprouts, fresh	1 lb	4 cups
Brussels sprouts, frozen	10 oz	18-24 sprouts
Bulgur	1 lb	2 ¾ cup; 3 ¾ cup cooked
	1 cup	3 cups cooked

Food	Weight or Amount	Approximate Equivalent
Cabbage, napa	1 head	6 cups shredded
Cabbage, red, green or savoy	1 lb	1 small head; 5 cups shredded; 3 cups cooked
Cantaloupe	1 lb	½ medium cantaloupe; 1 ½ cups cubes
Carrots, fresh, without tops	1 lb	4-6 medium; 3 cups shopped or sliced; 2 ¾ cups julienned; 2 ½ cups shredded or grated
Carrots, frozen	1 lb	2 ½ -3 cups sliced
Carrots, canned	16 oz	2 cups sliced
Cashews, shelled	6 oz 1 lb	1 cup 2 2/3 cups
Cauliflower, fresh	1 ½ lbs	1 head; 6 cups florets, 1 ½ cups chopped
Cauliflower, frozen	10 oz	2 cups chopped or sliced
Celeriac (Celery root)	1 lb	1 medium root; 2 cups chopped or shredded
Celery	1 medium rib 1 lb	½ cup chopped or sliced 3 cups chopped or sliced
Cheese, blue or feta	4 oz	1 cup crumbled
Cheese, Cheddar or mozzarella	1 lb	4 cups shredded or grated
Cheese, cottage	8 oz	1 cup
Cheese, cream	8 oz	1 cup
Cheese, parmesan	4 oz	1 1/3 oz grated
Cheese, ricotta	1 lb	2 cups
Cherries, fresh	1 lb	3 cups pitted
Cherries, frozen	10 oz	1 cup
Cherries, canned	1 lb	1 ½ cups
Chestnuts, in shell	1 lb	35-40 large; 2 ½ cups cooked and shelled; 1 cup puree
Chestnuts, shelled	1 lb	3 1/3 cups
Chicken breast halves, boneless, skinless	4 oz raw	1 piece; 2 cups cooked and chopped
Chocolate, Chips	6 oz	1 cup
Chocolate, squares	8 oz	8 squares (1 oz each)
Coconut, shredded	1 lb	5 2/3 cups
Coffee, ground	1 lb	5 cups; 80 Tablespoon; 40 brewed cups (6 oz each)
Corn, fresh	2 medium ears	1 cup kernels
Corn, frozen	10 oz	1 ¾ cup kernels
Corn, canned, cream style	16 oz	2 cups
Corn, canned, whole kernel	12 oz	1 ½ cups
Cornmeal	1 lb 1 cup	3 cups dry, 12 cups cooked 4 cups cooked
Cornstarch	1 lb	3 cups
Corn Syrup, light or dark	16 fl oz	2 cups
Crackers (See Graham crackers; Soda crackers)		
Cranberries, fresh	12 oz	3 cups
Cranberry sauce, canned	1 lb	1 2/3 cups
Cream, light or ½ & ½ or sour	½ pint	1 cup
Cream, heavy	6 ounces	2/3 cup
Cream, heavy	½ pint	1 cup; 2 cups whipped
Cucumber	1 lb	2 medium; 4 cups cubed; 3 cups sliced; 2 cups shredded

Food	Weight or Amount	Approximate Equivalent
Dates, unpitted	1 lb	2 cups; 2 ½ cups pitted and chopped
Egg, whole, extra large	1 doz	3 cups
Egg, whole, large	1 each	4 Tablespoons liquid
Eggs, whole, large	4 to 5	1 cup
Egg, whole, large	1 doz	2 1/3 cups
Egg, whole, medium	1 doz	2 cups
Egg, whites, extra large	1 doz	1 ¾ cups
Egg whites, large	1 doz	1 ½ cups
Egg whites, medium	1 doz	1 1/3 cup
Egg whites, small	1 doz	1 ¼ cups
Egg yolks, extra large	1 doz	1 cup
Egg yolks, large	1 doz	7/8 cup
Egg yolks, medium	1 doz	¾ cup
Egg yolks, small	1 doz	2/3 cup
Eggplant	1 lb	3 ½ cups chopped; 1 ½ cups cooked
Fennel bulb	1 lb	1 large bulb; 2 cups sliced
Figs, fresh	1 lb	12 medium
Figs, dried	1 lb	2 ½ cups chopped
Figs, canned	1 lb	12-16
Filberts (See Hazelnuts)		
Flour, all-purpose or bread or self-rising	1 lb	3 ¾ cups unsifted, 4 ¼ cups sifted
Flour, buckwheat	1 lb	3 ½ cups unsifted
Flour, cake or pastry	1 lb	4 cups sifted
Flour, gluten	1 lb	3 cups sifted
Flour, rice	1 lb	3 ½ cups sifted
Flour, rye	1 lb	3 ½ cups sifted
Flour, soy	1 lb	4 cups unsifted
Flour, whole wheat	1 lb	3 ½ cups unsifted, 3 2/3 sifted
Garlic	1 small clove	1 teaspoon minced
Gelatin, unflavored	¼ oz	1 envelope, 1 Tablespoon granulated; 3 ½ (4" x 9") sheets
Graham crackers	15	1 cup crumbs
Grapefruit, fresh	1 lb	1 medium; 1 ½ cups segments; 2/3 cup juice
Grapefruit, frozen	13 oz	1 ½ cups segments
Grapefruit, canned	16 oz	2 cups segments
Grapes, seeded or seedless	1 lb	75 grapes; 2 ½ - 3 cups
Greens, collards	1 lb	10 cups pieces; 2 cups cooked
Greens, Belgian endive	1 lb	5 ½ cups sliced into rounds
Greens, escarole	1 lb	12 cups torn leaves; 8 cups shredded
Greens, general, fresh	1 lb	2 cups cooked
Greens, general, frozen	10 oz	1 ½ - 2 cups
Grits	1lb	3 cups, 10 cups cooked
	1 cup	3 1/3 cups cooked
Hazelnuts, shelled, whole	1 lb	3 ½ cups
Herbs, fresh, chopped	1 Tablespoon fresh	1 teaspoon dried
Hominy	1 lb	2 ½ cups, 16 ¼ cups cooked
	1 cup	6 ½ cups cooked
Honey	1 lb	1 1/3 cups
Horseradish, bottled	1 Tablespoon	1 ½ teaspoon freshly grated

Food	Weight or Amount	Approximate Equivalent
Jicama	1 lb	3 cups chopped or shredded
Ketchup	16 oz	1 2/3 cup
Kiwifruit	1 medium	½ cup sliced or chopped
Leeks, white parts only	1 lb	2 leeks; 4 cups chopped; 2 cups cooked
Lemons	1 lb	4-6 medium; 1 cup juice
	1 medium	2-4 Tablespoon juice; 2-3 teaspoon zest
Lentils	1 lb	2 ¼ cups dry; 5 cups cooked
Lettuce, Bibb	1 medium head	4 cups leaves
Lettuce, iceberg	1 lb	1 medium head; 10 cups leaves; 8 cups shredded
Lettuce, leaf	1 medium head	8 cups leaves
Lettuce, romaine	1 medium head	8 cups leaves
Limes	1 lb	6-8 medium; ½ cup juice
	1 medium	1-2 Tablespoon juice; 1-2 teaspoon zest
Macaroni	1 cup dry	2 cups cooked
	1 lb	4 cups dry; 9 cups cooked
Mango	1 medium	1 ½ cups chopped; 1 cup pureed
Maple syrup	16 fl oz	2 cups
Marshmallows, large	1 lb	About 60 marshmallows
	1 cup	6-7 marshmallows
Marshmallows, miniature	10 ½ oz	400 marshmallows
	1 cup	85 marshmallows
Meat, ground	1 lb	2 cups raw
Melon	1 lb	1 cup cubed
Milk, powdered buttermilk	4 Tablespoons + 1 cup water	1 cup buttermilk
Milk, dry	1 lb	3 2/3 cups; 14 cups reconstituted
Milk, evaporated, whole or fat-free	14 ½ oz	1 2/3 cups;3 1/3 cups reconstituted
Milk, fat-free or whole, or buttermilk	1 qt	4 cups
Milk, sweetened condensed	15 oz	1 1/3 cups
	14 oz	1 ¼ cups
Millet	1 lb	2 1/8 cups; 5 ½ cups cooked
Mixed Vegetables, frozen	10 oz	2 cups cut
Mixed Vegetables, canned	16 oz	2 cups cut
Molasses	16 fl oz	2 cups
Mushrooms, fresh	1 lb	35 medium; 4 cups sliced; 2 cups sautéed
Mushrooms, dried	4 oz	1 lb fresh
Mushrooms, canned	4 oz	2/3 cup sliced or chopped
Nectarines	1 lb	3 medium; 2 ½ cups chopped
Noodles, Chinese, dry	¾ lb	5 cups cooked
Noodles, fine width	½ lb	5 ½ cups cooked
Noodles, Linguine	1 lb	5 cups cooked
Noodles, pappardelle	½ lb	3 ¼ cups cooked
Noodles, 1" pieces	1 lb	6-8 cups; 8 cups cooked
Nuts (See individual nuts)		
Oats, rolled	3 oz	1 cup dry; 1 ¾ cups cooked
	1 lb	5 cups dry; 9 cups cooked
Okra, fresh	1 lb	2 ¼ cups chopped
Okra, frozen	10 oz	1 ¼ cups chopped

Food	Weight or Amount	Approximate Equivalent
Onions, green (See Scallions)		
Onion, large	Each	3/4 to 1 cup
Onions, white, fresh	1 lb	4 medium; 3-4 cups chopped
Onions, white, frozen	12 oz	3 cups chopped
Oranges, fresh	1 lb 1 medium	3 medium, 1 cup segments; 1 cup juice; ¼ cup zest 1/3 cup segments; 1/3 cup juice; 1-2 Tablespoon zest
Oranges, Mandarin, canned	11 oz	1 ¼ cups fruit and juice
Orzo	4 oz	2/3 cup dry; 1 ½ cups cooked
Oysters	1 qt 1 dozen	50 shucked 1 cup meat after shucking
Papaya	1 lb	2 medium; 2 cups cubed; 1 cup pureed
Parsley, fresh	4 oz	1 bunch; 4 cups packed; 2 cups chopped
Parsnips	1 lb	4 medium; 2 cups chopped
Pasta (See Macaroni, Noodles: Orzo: Spaghetti)		
Peaches, fresh	1 lb	4 medium; 2 ¾ cups sliced; 2 ½ cups chopped; 1 cup puree
Peaches, frozen	10 oz	1 1/8 cups sliced with juice
Peaches, dried	1 lb	2 ¾ cups; 5 ½ cups cooked
Peaches, canned	1 lb	6 -10 halves; 2 cups sliced
Peanuts, in shell	1 ½ lb	1 lb shelled; 3 ½ -4 cups nuts
Pears, fresh	1 lb	3 medium; 2 cups sliced
Pears, dried	1 lb	2 ¾ cup; 5 ½ cups cooked
Peas, blacked-eyed, fresh	1 lb	2 1/3 cups
Peas, Black-eyed, frozen	10 oz	1 ½ cups cooked
Peas, dried, split	1 lb	1 cup shelled
Peas, green, frozen	10 oz	2 cups
Peas, green, canned	1 lb	2 cups
Peas, snow	3 oz 1 lb	1 cup 5-6 cups
Pecans	1 lb	4 cups halves; 3 ¾ cups chopped
Peppers, bell	1 lb	3 medium; 2 cups chopped
Peppers, Chile	1" segment	2 teaspoon finely chopped
Pimientos	1 jar (4 oz)	½ cup chopped
Pineapple	3 lbs	1 medium; 2 ½ cups chopped
Pistachios	1 ½ lb	1 lb shelled; 3 ½-4 cups
Plantains	1 lb	2 cups 1" pieces
Plums, fresh	1 lb	6 plums; 2 ½ cups pitted and sliced; 1 ½ cups puree
Plums, canned, whole	1 lb	Six to eight 2" plums; 3 cups sliced
Pomegranates	1 lb	3 medium; 1 ½ cups seeds; ¾ cup juice
Popcorn	½ cup kernels	4 cups popped
Potatoes, sweet	(See Sweet potatoes)	
Potatoes, white	1 lb	2-3 medium russet or 6-8 new; 3-3 ½ cups chopped, sliced or cubed; 1 ¾ - 2 cups cooked & mashed
Prunes, pitted	1 lb	2 ½ cups chopped; 4 cups cooked
Prunes, dried	1 lb	2 ½ cups; 4- 4 ½ cups cooked

Food	Weight or Amount	Approximate Equivalent
Pumpkin, fresh	1 lb	1 cup cooked and mashed
Pumpkin, canned	16 oz	2 cups mashed
Pumpkin, seeds, hulled	1 lb	3 ¼ cups
Radishes	½ lb	1 2/3 cups sliced
Raisins, seedless	1 lb	3-3 ¼ cups
Raspberries	½ pint	Scant 1 ½ cups
Rhubarb, fresh	1 lb	3 cups chopped; 2 cups cooked
Rhubarb, frozen	12 oz	1 ½ cups chopped and sliced
Rice, brown	1 cup	4 cups cooked
Rice, converted	1 cup	3 ½ cups cooked
Rice, quick-cooking	1 cup	2 cups cooked
Rice, white	1 cup	3 cups cooked
Rice, wild	1 cup	4 cups cooked
Rutabaga	1 lb	2 ½ cups cubed
Sausage, Italian link	1 lb	4 links
Scallions, fresh	1 bunch	9 with tops; 1 cup sliced; ¾ cup minced
Sesame seeds	1 lb	3 ¼ cups
Shortening, vegetable	1 lb	2 cups
Shallots	½ oz	1 medium; 1 Tablespoon finely chopped
Shrimp, in shell	1 lb	40-50 small 31-40 medium 26-30 large 21-25 extra large 16-20 jumbo
Soda crackers, saltines	28 crackers	1 cup fine crumbs
Spaghetti, 12" pieces	1 lb	About 7 cups cooked
Spinach, fresh	1 lb	10 cups torn pieces; about 1 cup cooked
Spinach, frozen	10 oz	1 ½ cups
Spinach, canned	15 oz	2 cups
Split peas (see Peas, dried, split)		
Sprouts, mung bean	½ lb	1 ½ cups
Squash, acorn	1 ½ lb	1 medium, 2 cups cooked and mashed
Squash, spaghetti	5 lb	1 medium, 6-6 ½ cups strands
Squash, summer, fresh	1 lb	3 medium, 3 ½ cups sliced, 3 cups shredded
Squash, summer, frozen	10 oz	1 ½ cups sliced or chopped
Squash, winter, fresh	1 lb	2 cups cooked; 1 ½ cups mashed
Squash, winter, frozen	12 oz	1 ½ cups
Strawberries, fresh	1 pint 1 quarts	1 ½ - 2 cups sliced or chopped 3-4 cups sliced or chopped
Strawberries, frozen, sliced	10 oz	1 cup
Strawberries, frozen, whole	1 lb	1 1/3 cups
Sugar, brown, light or dark	1 lb	2 ¼ cups packed
Sugar, confectioners'	1 lb	3 ½-4 cups unsifted; 4 ½-5 cups sifted
Sugar, granulated	1 lb	2-2 ¼ cups
Sugar, superfine	1 lb	2 1/3 cups
Sugar, turbinado	1 lb	3 1/8 cups
Sunflower seeds	1 lb	3 ¼ cup
Sweet potatoes, fresh	1 lb	3 medium; 3 cups shredded; 3 ½ cups chopped or sliced

Food	Weight or Amount	Approximate Equivalent
Tangerines	1 lb	4 medium; 2 cups sectioned
	1 medium	3-4 Tablespoon juice; 3-4 teaspoon zest
Tea leaves	1 lb	About 200 cups brewed
Tofu	1 lb	1 cake; 2 cups cubed; 1 ½ cups mashed
Tomatillos	1 lb	12 medium; 1 ¼ cups chopped
Tomatoes, fresh	1 lb	3-4 medium; 2 cups chopped
Tomatoes, canned	15 oz	1 ¾ cups drained pulp
Tuna, canned	6 oz	2/3 cup drained and flaked
Turnips	1 lb	3 medium; 2 ½ cups drained
Vegetables, mixed (see Mixed Vegetables)		
Wafer cookies, chocolate	18 wafers	1 cup crumbs
Wafer cookies, vanilla	22 wafers	1 cup fine crumbs
Walnuts	1 lb	3 ¾ cups halves; 3 ½ cups chopped
Watercress	¼ lb	1 bunch; 1 cup loosely packed
Wheat germ	1 lb	4 cups
Yeast, active dry	¼ oz	1pkg; 1 scant Tablespoon; 1.6 oz compressed fresh yeast
Yogurt	½ pint	1 cup

Flour

Flour can have different weights due to a variety of factors. Humidity, climate, temperature, and other things can affect flour's moisture level. Flour absorbs everything in its surroundings. To accurately measure flour, you really need a kitchen scale. A one cup measure may weigh anywhere from 6 ounces to 12 ounces.

This is important for baking, not for cooking. You do not need to measure flour that you use to coat food.

Basic Mathematical Conversions for Flour

3 teaspoons	1 tablespoon
4 tablespoons	1/4 cup
5 tablespoons + 1 teaspoon	1/3 cup
8 tablespoons	1/2 cup
16 tablespoons	1 cup
1 cup	8 ounces (1/2 pint)
4 cups	32 ounces (1 quart)
16 cups	128 ounces (1 gallon)

Notes:_____

_____

_____

_____

Baking Substitutions

1 teaspoon baking powder	1/3 teaspoon baking soda + 1/2 teaspoon cream of tartar or 1/4 teaspoon baking soda + 1/3 cup sour milk, buttermilk or yogurt
1 cup cake flour	1 cup minus 2 Tablespoon all-purpose flour
1 cup self-rising flour	1 cup all-purpose flour + 1 ½ teaspoon baking powder +1/2 teaspoon salt
1 Tablespoon cornstarch	2 Tablespoons flour
2 Tablespoons tapioca	3 Tablespoons flour
2 egg yolks	1 whole egg
1 cup whole fresh milk	1/2 c. evaporated milk + 1/2 c. water or 1/3 c. dry milk solids plus 1 c. water
4 T. Powdered milk + 1 cup water	1 cup buttermilk or mix 1 cup sweet milk w/1 T. Vinegar or 1 T. lemon juice or 1 3/4 teaspoons cream of tartar
1 cup sour milk	1/3 c. dry milk solids + 1 cup water or 1 cup buttermilk or yogurt or 1 1/3 buttermilk or yogurt or 1 1/3 tablespoon vinegar or lemon juice + enough milk to make one cup
1 cup sour cream (in baking)	7/8 c. buttermilk, sour milk or yogurt
1 cup sour cream (in casseroles, salad dressings, etc.)	7/8 c. buttermilk, sour milk or yogurt
1 cup sugar	3/4 c. honey, molasses or corn syrup or reduce liquid in recipe by 1/4 cup, add 1/4 teaspoon soda, and reduce oven temperature by 25 degrees.
1 cup brown sugar	Add 2 Tablespoons molasses to 1 cup (white) sugar, stir well and store in air-tight container.
1 cup light corn syrup	1 cup granulated sugar + ¼ cup water
1 cup dark corn syrup	1 cup light corn syrup or ¾ cup light corn syrup + ¼ cup molasses or 1 cup maple-flavored syrup
1 cup margarine, butter or shortening	3/4 cup bacon fat, chicken fat or 7/8 cup lard or oil (not suggested to use in baking)
1 square (1 ounce) unsweetened chocolate	3 Tablespoons cocoa
¼ cup apple cider vinegar	¼ cup white vinegar
1 Tablespoon balsamic vinegar	1 Tablespoon sherry or cider vinegar
1 cup beer	1 cup non-alcoholic beer, beef broth, or apple cider
1 cup red wine	1 cup non-alcoholic wine, beef broth, apple cider, tomato juice, or water
1 cup white wine	1 cup non-alcoholic wine, white grape juice, chicken broth, apple juice, or water
¼ cup dry bread crumbs	¼ cup finely crushed cracker crumbs or corn flakes
1 clove garlic, finely chopped	1/8 teaspoon garlic powder or ¼ teaspoon jarred minced garlic
1 Tablespoon ginger root, grated	1 Tablespoon candied ginger (rinsed & finely chopped) or 1 ½ dry ground ginger + ½ teaspoon lemon juice
1 Tablespoon fresh herbs, chopped	1 teaspoon the same herb, dried
1 Tablespoon yellow mustard	1 teaspoon dry mustard
1 Tablespoon lemon juice	1 Tablespoon bottled lemon juice, lime juice, or white vinegar

Healthy Substitutions

Replace This...	With This...
DAIRY	
1 cup whole milk	1 cup fat-free, 1%, or 2% milk
	1 cup buttermilk (for baking)
1 cup fat-free milk	1/3 cup nonfat dry milk mixed with ¾ cup water
1 can sweetened condensed milk (14 oz)	1 can fat-free sweetened condensed milk (14 oz)
1 can evaporated milk (12 oz)	1 can fat-free evaporated milk (12 oz)
1 cup heavy cream	1 cup 1 % milk + 1 Tablespoon cornstarch
	1 cup fat-free evaporated milk
1 cup whipped cream	1 cup frozen light non-dairy whipped topping, thawed
1 cup buttermilk	1 cup low-fat or fat-free plain yogurt
1 cup sour cream	1 cup fat-free plain yogurt
	1 cup fat-free sour cream
	1 cup fat-free evaporated milk + 1 Tablespoon lemon juice
1 cup shredded cheese (4 oz)	1 cup shredded reduced-fat or fat-free cheddar cheese
4 oz blue cheese, feta cheese, or goat cheese	2 oz appropriate cheese + 2 oz fat-free cream cheese
8 oz cream cheese	8 oz fat-free ricotta cheese
	8 oz dry-curd cottage cheese
	8 oz fat-free cream cheese (block-style or tub style)
	4 oz fat-free cream cheese + 4 oz reduced-fat cream cheese
	8 oz reduced-fat cream cheese (block-style or tub-style)
	8 oz mascarpone cheese
	4 oz mascarpone + 4 oz fat-free cream cheese
FAT	
½ cup oil	½ cup fat-free chicken broth (for salad dressings and marinades)
	¼ cup unsweetened applesauce + ¼ cup buttermilk (for baking)
	½ cup unsweetened applesauce or baby food prunes (for baking)
	1/3 cup vinegar + ¼ cup fat-free chicken broth + ¼ cup pineapple juice + 2 Tablespoon strong-flavored oil (to make 1 cup salad dressing or marinade)
½ cup margarine or butter (1 stick)	½ cup unsweetened applesauce (for baking)
1 cup butter	7/8 cup vegetable oil
	¼ cup unsweetened applesauce + ¼ cup buttermilk (for baking)
	½ cup baby food prunes (for baking)
	½ cup marshmallow crème (for frosting and fillings)
	½ light butter
2 Tablespoon oil	2 Tablespoon wine or fat-free broth (for sautéing)
Olive oil	Equal amount of any vegetable oil
1 cup chopped walnuts	½ cup chopped walnuts, toasted
1 cup chopped pecans	½ cup chopped pecans, toasted
1 cup slivered almonds	½ cup sliced almonds, toasted
	½ cup slivered almonds, toasted
PROTEIN	
6 oz pork sirloin, cooked	6 oz pork tenderloin, roasted
6 oz flank steak, cooked	6 oz round steak, roasted
6 oz chicken thigh, no skin, cooked	6 oz chicken breast, no skin, roasted
6 oz turkey meat, cooked	6 oz turkey breast, roasted

Replace This...	With This...
6 oz tuna in oil, drained	6 oz tuna in water, drained
1 lb ground beef	1 lb ground turkey breast 1 lb chopped pork tenderloin 1 lb chopped chicken breast 1 lb ground turkey 1 lb extra-lean ground beef (15 percent fat)
6 oz pork sausage, cooked	6 oz turkey sausage, cooked
MISCELLANEOUS	
1 cup frozen non-dairy whipped topping	1 cup light nondairy whipped topping
1 cup chocolate chips	½ cup chocolate chips ½ mini chocolate chips
1 cup flaked coconut	1 teaspoon coconut extract ½ cup flaked coconut
1 cup sliced olives	½ cup sliced olives
1 oz baking chocolate	3 Tablespoon unsweetened cocoa powder
Single pie crust	3 sheets phyllo dough (6 half-sheets)
1 can condensed cream of mushroom soup (10.7 oz)	1 can condensed reduced-free cream of mushroom soup (10.7oz)
1 cup sugar	¾ cup sugar
1 small package flavored gelatin mix (4 servings)	1 small package sugar-free gelatin mix (4 servings)
1 cup basic white sauce (1 cup whole milk + 2 Tablespoon flour + 1 Tablespoon butter)	1 cup basic white sauce (1 cup 1% milk + 1 Tablespoon cornstarch)

"Granny's Measurements"

Generally speaking, a "pinch" does indeed refer to the amount you can pinch between your thumb and forefinger. None of these so-called "Granny's Measurements" are meant to be precise, but the following chart will give you an approximate idea of amounts.

Measurement	Equivalent
A hint	Tiny amount (1/2 drop)
A drop	1/64 teaspoon (1/2 smidgen)
A smidgen	1/32 teaspoon (1/2 pinch)
A pinch	1/16 teaspoon (1/2 dash)
A dash	1/8 teaspoon (1/2 tad)
A tad	¼ teaspoon
¼ stick butter	2 Tablespoons
1 stick butter	½ cup
Juice of 1 lemon	3 Tablespoons
Juice of 1 orange	½ cup

Chapter 9

Food Storage &

Organization

Everyone stores their excess supply of food or pantry items according to space available. I am fortunate to have a walk-in pantry, a small pantry closet, lots of cupboards, and a large space in my garage.

Shown here is my walk-in pantry. I try to keep all like-minded items together and all labels facing out.

Be sure to keep an eye on the food in your pantry. Watch expiration dates, and always keep the items with the earliest dates in the front so they will be used first. If you have anything in your pantry that you do not use and/or like, give it away to make more space.

Particularly in the summer, pest infestation can be a real concern. This is where a vacuum sealer can be a valuable tool. Anything that comes packaged in a paper or cardboard container can normally be vulnerable to insects -- things such as oats, cereal, sugar, flour, etc. Remove these from their containers, place them in glass jars, vacuum seal them, and voila -- now you not only have food that will stay fresh longer, but you also have food that is

impervious to infestation. In order to keep my flour as fresh as possible, I freeze it in the bag it came in, slipped inside a plastic bag.

To the left are a couple of shelves in my garage. I have stockpiled enough so that I will not have to purchase any cleaning supplies for about 3 years.

Be sure to keep hazardous chemicals out of reach of children and pets. If you have locking cabinets, these are excellent places to keep cleaning products. If not, consider investing in a lock for a cabinet just for this purpose.

An alternative way to keep children and pets safe is to use non-toxic products for cleaning. (See Part II for homemade cleaning product recipes.)

Below are shelves in my laundry room over my washer and dryer.

Below are shelves that stock my storage items: jars, vacuum seal rolls, plastic wraps, and plastic bags.

We strongly encourage the use of a vacuum sealer for foods you store in the freezer and pantry. We will discuss vacuum sealers in more depth in Chapter 10.

As you can see in the photo on the previous page, I have a lot of plastic bags. I stocked up on these when they were on sale for 90 cents a box instead of their normal price of $2.49.

In your refrigerator, you can also use glass jars for storing some leftovers, like sauces; for other kinds of leftovers, or for portion control, you may want to use glass containers with plastic lids, plastic containers with lids, and plastic bags. Try not to microwave plastic containers, as toxins from the plastic can leak into your food.

Avoid buying disposable plastic containers. They are more expensive than plastic bags and do not last as long as other plastic containers.

Using the Freezer

These foods freeze well:

- Muffins and biscuits
- Pancakes and waffles
- Bread, bagels and English muffins
- Tortillas
- Raw and cooked bacon
- Raw and cooked sausage
- Ground chuck
- Hams
- Chickens or Cornish hens
- Shredded cheese

Bread-like items should not be kept more than 30 to 45 days in the freezer or they will pick up flavors from other foods and ice crystals will form inside the packages. You can also freeze most other kinds of raw meat, but do so carefully. You can stock up on meat when you find it on sale; however, when you get home from the store, you will need to do a little work before you put the meat into the freezer. It is a very bad idea to toss a bunch of meat into the freezer without dividing it up first, and then re-packaging it in vacuum-sealed bags.

Ground beef: Depending on how you plan to use it, you can prepare it for freezing in a number of ways. If it will be used for hamburgers, you can form patties in advance, wrap them in plastic, and then freeze them, or make patties, separate them by parchment or wax paper, then vacuum seal them. (Separating the patties helps keep them from sticking together.) Do you want to make meatballs? Shape the meatballs, place them on baking sheets covered with wax paper, and freeze; once they are frozen, you can place them all in a bag or container and return them to the freezer. Or you can make a meatloaf, place it into a loaf pan, and freeze it that way. If you will use the beef as is -- for instance, for tacos or hamburger stroganoff -- just divide the beef into meal-sized portions before freezing.

Beef or pork roasts: I cut these into slabs for pork chops, or into cubes or strips for stews or stir fries. I use a vacuum sealer and vacuum pack everything in meal-sized portions.

Chicken: If you buy large packages of individual pieces (legs and thighs tend to be cheapest), I would suggest that you vacuum seal enough for one meal. Sometimes I don't always know how many people will be eating, so I package the meat in different quantities. For example, I might package chicken in 3, 4, or 5 pieces portions. That way, if I need enough for 6 people I just pull out two packages of 3 pieces each or three packages if I have a big eater in the crowd.

Fresh fruit, cookie and biscuit dough, and dumplings can be quick-frozen if you know how to do it. The following directions apply to fruit, but minus the peeling and cutting, it can apply to other foods as well.

1. Place a sheet of wax paper on a baking sheet.
2. Cut the fruit away from the core or pit and peel (if needed). Cut fruit into pieces (again, if needed).
3. Place the baking sheet in the freezer for 10 to 15 minutes.
4. Transfer fruit to a plastic bag for vacuum sealing.

What if you forget and leave the food in the freezer for longer than 15 minutes? Just put the food into its bag to be vacuum-sealed when you remember. Be sure to label the bag with a permanent marker before you put it into the freezer, as labels do not stick to cold bags very well! If you freeze dough balls, remember to label with the baking time and temperature.

When you bake frozen dough balls, be sure you add 2 to 3 extra minutes to the baking time called for in the recipe. Alternatively, you could let the dough come to room temperature on the baking sheet before baking according to the recipe.

When freezing pancakes, waffles, or other baked goods, be sure you allow them to cool completely before placing into plastic vacuum sealing bags. This helps prevent the development of ice crystals inside the bag (and on the food), which will in turn prevent freezer burn.

For more information on Freezing and Food Safety please visit this web site developed by the United States Department of Agriculture:

http://www.fsis.usda.gov/factsheets/focus_on_freezing/index.asp#19

Inventory

If you keep a lot of foods in your freezer, you may want to keep an inventory of everything in the freezer and post it right on the door. This serves two purposes: **one,** you'll know at a glance exactly what you have and what you might want to restock; **two**, you will not forget about something and have to throw it away when it goes bad. Food *can* go bad in the freezer; just because it is frozen does not mean it will last forever.

Whenever you remove something from the freezer, cross it off your inventory list; when you add something, add it to the list. Every so often – say, every 3 to 4 months – take a good look at your inventory and rewrite your list.

I laminated my inventory list which I attach to the freezer with a magnet. If you laminate your list, use markers that can be easily erased.

Thawing

When you are ready to eat the foods from your freezer, if they are ready-to-eat – that is, they do not require reheating – you have a few options for thawing. **First,** you could pop them in the refrigerator the night before. This is the safest way. **Second**, you could thaw in the microwave. Many microwaves have "defrost" settings. **Third**, if you are pulling out pancakes or waffles, you can pop them right into the toaster. If they are frozen, you may need two toasting cycles to heat them all the way through. You may want to lower the toaster setting before you do this to prevent burning.

Proper Food Storage in the Refrigerator

The following are a few basic refrigeration principles to keep in mind when you stock your refrigerator. Certain spots are better for certain foods than for others.

- The top shelf and door of the refrigerator tends to be a few to several degrees warmer than the rest of the refrigerator. Therefore you should not place foods here that can spoil when they become warm, such as milk, eggs, or mayonnaise. Anything with a high vinegar or sugar content, such as fruit juices, icing, pickles, salad dressings, or other condiments can be placed here. So can butter and margarine.

- Raw meat should be kept in the back of the lowest shelf of the refrigerator -- that is where the temperature is coldest. Be sure to minimize the possibility of cross-contamination due to leaking or dripping juices.

- Never place produce near the back of your refrigerator. It can freeze and even ruin some frost-sensitive fruits and vegetables. Crisper drawers are better places for produce.

- Keep track of when you put food into the refrigerator, especially leftovers, and try to use the oldest items first. This reduces the proliferation of "science experiments" in the refrigerator. (Of course, always keep an eye and nose out for signs of spoilage before consuming.)

- Cutting up vegetables, then storing them in bags or containers with a damp (not wet) paper towel, will help prevent them from drying out and keeps them fresh longer.

- Storing lettuce, greens, and fresh herbs with a paper towel in a plastic bag or container will help keep them fresh longer. Check the towel every few days and replace with a fresh one when it gets too damp.

- Eggs will stay fresher in their own cartons. I try to use store-bought eggs within 6 weeks of purchase, and eggs I get directly from the farm, within 10 weeks.

Food Storage Limits at 70 degrees

Item	Storage	Notes
Baking powder	18 months	Keep dry & tightly closed
Baking soda	2 years	Keep dry & tightly closed
Cereals, unopened	6 to 12 months	Refold package liner tightly after opening
Chocolate, semisweet	2 years	Keep cool & dry
Chocolate, unsweetened	18 months	Keep cool & dry
Cocoa mixes	8 months	Cover tightly
Chocolate syrup	2 years	Refrigerate after opening
Coffee, canned	2 years	Refrigerate after opening
Coffee, instant	1 to 2 years	Keep cool & dry
Cornmeal	18 months	Keep dry & tightly closed
Cornstarch	6 to 8 months	Keep dry & tightly closed
Flour	6 to 8 months	Keep cool, airtight
Honey	12 months	Cover tightly. Refrigerate after opening
Molasses	12 months	Keep tightly closed
Marshmallows	2 to 3 months	Keep cool, airtight
Mayonnaise	2 to 3 months	Refrigerate after opening
Milk, condensed	12 months	Once opened, keep airtight
Milk, nonfat dry	6 months	
Pasta	2 years	Once opened, keep airtight
Salad dressing	10 to 12 months	Refrigerate after opening
Salad oils	6 months	Refrigerate after opening
Shortening	8 months	No refrigeration required
Brown sugar	4 months	Keep cool, airtight
Confectioners' sugar	18 months	Keep cool, airtight
Granulated sugar	2 years	Keep dry & tightly closed
Vinegar	1 year	
Biscuit/brownie/muffin mix	9 months	Keep cool & dry
Cake mix	9 months	Keep cool & dry
Cake mix, angel food	1 year	Keep cool & dry
Casserole mix	9 to 12 months	Keep cool & dry
Cookies, packaged	2 months	Keep dry & tightly closed
Crackers	8 months	Keep dry & tightly closed
Frosting, canned	3 months	Refrigerate leftovers
Frosting, mix	8 months	
Hot roll mix	18 months	Keep cool, airtight
Pancake mix	6 to 9 months	Keep cool, airtight
Pie crust mix	8 months	Keep cool & dry
Potatoes, instant	6 to 12 months	Keep cool & dry
Pudding mix	12 months	Keep cool & dry
Sauce & gravy mixes	6 to 12 months	Keep cool & dry
Soup mixes	12 months	Keep cool & dry
Canned food	12 months	Keep cool
Dried fruit	6 months	Keep cool, airtight
Canned fruit juices	9 months	Keep cool, airtight
Dried vegetables	12 months	Keep cool, airtight
Ketchup, chili sauce	12 months	
Mustard, prepared yellow	2 years	May be refrigerated
Spices & herbs	6 months	Keep cool & dry
Vanilla extract, opened	2 years	Keep tightly closed
Other extracts, opened	1 year	Keep tightly closed

Chapter 10

Growing, Raising & Preserving Food

Gardening

Contributed by Mark Zacek

Do you remember in the go-go Nineties how the catch phrase for conspicuous consumption was "living large"? We live in very different times now. "Living small" is a more appropriate response to today's economic realities. Many people's vision of living small is self-sufficiency. But what does self-sufficiency really mean? You may have a romantic vision of "returning to the land," thinking of self-sufficiency in pioneer terms. Like Ma and Pa of Little House in the Big Woods. Now that was real self-sufficiency. Or was it? After all, Pa sold furs to buy calico for Ma and gun powder for himself. If Pa was not able to grow, hunt, or make *everything* his family needed to be truly self-sufficient, what chance do we have? In fact, true self-sufficiency is impossible and even undesirable. After all, if we were truly self-sufficient, we on our ½-acre suburban properties would be out foraging for firewood every day.

I suspect that for most of us, self-sufficiency simply means, what can we grow or provide for ourselves that we normally would be buying? Vegetables? Fruits? Eggs? Wool? Meat? Fertilizer? Compost? Those who live on a farm need no instruction from me on how to provide for their families from the fruits of the land. And those who are truly committed to a more stringent definition of self-sufficiency (alternative fuels to power the house and car, for example) will require resources beyond the scope of this book and can readily find them on the Internet or in a library. But many of us can be far more self-sufficient than we realize on our yards of half acre or less. While this will not result in complete independence from consumerism, it can be healthful, emotionally enriching, and a meaningful statement to our community and our families.

Some of the advantages of a home garden are obvious. There are few things more satisfying than walking out the back door, plucking a red-blushed peach from the tree, and biting into the succulent fruit with the sun-warmed juices dripping down your chin. I always have a childish delight in showing my children the glories of nature by simply pulling up a potato or carrot that has taken the place of that piece of potato or tiny seed that we planted together a couple of months before. I have the fondest memories of my grandfather and I planting and harvesting vegetables together in his beautiful Montana garden. (Wonderful as my garden carrots are today, they can never taste as good as the carrots of my memory in my grandfather's garden. Maybe my children will feel the same about the carrots we have planted together). I never lose my wonder that the table scraps my hens are happy to devour turn into the eggs, sometimes still warm from the chicken, that I scramble or poach every morning.

Freshness, flavor, healthfulness, and togetherness; a home garden can provide all this. The flavor of just-ripened hand-picked fruits and vegetables of varieties grown for flavor rather than appearance and pack ability is a great advantage of the home garden. The flavor that comes from heritage tomato varieties, for example, has only recently been reclaimed after having nearly been lost in recent decades. The shapes or color of these varieties are thought not to look enticing on store shelves. And these fruit are also too delicate to survive modern transit. A home gardener of course will trade the flavor of any of the approximately 600 varieties of heirloom tomatoes for the supermarket product. The only transportation that concerns the gardener is getting the fruit from the garden to the kitchen without eating it on the way.

A home garden is likely to be inherently organic. Few gardeners spray with chemicals for bugs, preferring to surrender a portion of their crop to them, pick them off by hand, or spritz them with a soap solution. To nourish the soil, home gardeners often have their own compost piles composed of scraps from the kitchen and garden that are then recycled back to the earth in a perfect life cycle. The healthfulness of the fruits of the home garden cannot be exceeded by any other source.

The psychological health benefits of the garden can be just as important as the nutritional benefits. The feeling of warm, rich, friable soil between the fingers is balm to a gardener's soul. The informal instructions of a parent to a child in the garden are hours that will reap their own harvest in years to come. The patience and enthusiasm that parents cultivate in themselves will be key to growing a love of gardening in their children.

A well-tended vegetable garden and/or a neatly pruned grove of fruit trees are beautiful additions to your yard and sources of justifiable pride to the gardener. A fruit and vegetable garden can show the same care of arrangement as a well-designed flower garden. Kales, lettuces, and many other vegetables can be regarded as ornamental as well as fruitful. Herbs have been used for centuries in intricate geometries for knot gardens. Rosemary, thyme, lemon balm, and marjoram earn their place in the kitchen as well as in an artfully arranged herb planting. If you are planting a garden for beauty as well as productivity, consider banishing the rectangle or square from your garden shape. Multiple gardens of contrasting shapes and levels lend visual interest to your landscape. Small plots can be linked by fruit trees or flowers beds into one overarching design. Think vertically with multiple levels of raised beds and small arbors and staked vegetables, which increase the productivity of small beds as well as adding tremendously to the visual appeal.

You may be thinking that this all sounds lovely, but is it really making any difference for self-sufficiency or thrift? A beautiful garden is soul-nourishing as well as body-nourishing, and that brings its own justification. The beauty created by thoughtful design is likely to be little more expensive than a casual, rectangular garden. The internet is loaded with information for creating beautiful, low-cost vegetable gardens. However, low cost is relative. Are you truly going to save money by growing your own vegetables rather than buying them? Is it thrifty? If you really are striving for a significant measure of self-sufficiency, the garden must be of substantial size and will require an investment (preparing the space, building the soil, providing structure for raised beds, purchasing garden equipment). Considerable self-sufficiency does not necessarily mean thriftiness. When your garden is at its peak, the fruits and vegetables in the stores will also be most plentiful and therefore at their lowest prices of the year. A chicken coop, chicken run, and flock are not inexpensive to operate responsibly.

In my experience, and I think that this is a commonly held truth, you build a garden for reasons that are more philosophical (e.g. self-sufficiency, nourishment of the soul, instilling values within the family) and nutritional than for thrift. Of course, once you have made that initial investment in building the structure of the garden and equipping it, subsequent gardening years will be considerably less expensive. And then, after that initial investment and a few years of soil building, you just may have it all: freshness, flavor, healthfulness, togetherness, *and* thriftiness.

Having said this, it is perfectly acceptable to start small when it comes to gardening, particularly if you have never had much of a green thumb. You could start with a container herb garden, for instance, or you could devote a patch of ground to planting your favorite fruit or vegetable. For the best rate of success, start with those fruits and vegetables that are easiest to grow. Starting such plants from seeds is the most economical option.

With some dedication and perseverance, you will see the fruits of your labor. Then you will not only save money on the food you grow, but you will enjoy the satisfying emotional reward of knowing that you were able to grow something delicious all by yourself. Involve your children, and you will find them reaping the very same rewards.

Preserving Garden Produce

We all know the benefits that the home garden has on our family's nutrition, our property's aesthetics, and even our own mental health. But we also know that a productive vegetable and fruit garden is a lot of work, and not just because it should be kept tidy and attractive. When a substantial garden has produce ready for harvesting, you may have only a few days to process the armloads of produce. This requires a lot of preparation and setting aside of time to work in the kitchen as well as the garden. Root vegetables, certain squashes and varieties of apples may keep for several weeks or months and do not require your concentrated effort. However, peas, peaches, peppers, pears, beans, berries, cucumbers, melons, tomatoes, summer squash and zucchini (among many others) all require processing in the kitchen if they are to be preserved beyond a few days from harvesting.

The savvy gardener will have planted multiple varieties of some of these fruits and vegetables and staggered their planting to sequence the ripening. This is wise because it allows an extended period in which the produce can be eaten fresh from the garden. But there will come that time when you find that you have two bowlfuls of tomatoes beyond those needed for tonight's *insalata caprese*. Then you know it is time to plan the roasting, saucing, jamming, freezing, pickling, and canning.

Roasting: Slow roasting tomatoes with olive oil, garlic, and herbs produces an incredibly delicious side dish, pasta sauce, or condiment and makes the kitchen smell wonderful in the process. When roasted, covered with olive oil and stored in the refrigerator, the tomatoes can be kept for two weeks. That is not a long time compared to the other preserving methods, but that is beside the point because something this delicious simply will not be hanging around in your refrigerator for long. The truly amazing thing about roasting surplus tomatoes is that the same alchemy works for semi-tasteless supermarket tomatoes, so you can enjoy oven-roasted tomatoes from grape and plum tomatoes in February when you most need to be jolted by that memory of summer.

Saucing: This is one of the most satisfying and efficient methods for using a variety of vegetable garden produce. You can modify your sauce recipes (typically, tomato-based) according to what is currently most prevalent in the garden. Perhaps celery and carrots this week, and zucchini and peppers next week. Canning the sauces will provide a fresh-tasting, wonderfully nutritious pasta sauce or soup base that will nourish and warm your family throughout the long winter months.

Fruit sauces are wonderful for the cold-weather months as well. Everyone knows apple sauce, but peaches and pears make delicious sauces too. Keep cooking them down, add spices, and you have an apple butter or peach butter. Try using your crock pot for cooking these sauces down. The fruit butters will be like spreading summer sunshine on your English muffin at breakfast or your scone at teatime, if you are in an English frame of mind!

Jamming: When you think of preserving the fruits of your garden, you are most likely to think of making jam. To those who have made it, that may conjure images of a sweltering kitchen of hot water baths waiting for the hot jam-filled preserve jars. You have the satisfaction of knowing that it will all be worth it in the end, but it is usually not a lot of fun on a hot summer day. There is an option: freezer jam. Most freezer jam recipes do not require cooking the fruit. Therefore, your jam retains that bright, just-picked flavor. Another advantage is that you do not need to sterilize jars. You simply pour the fruit-sugar-pectin-water mixture into clean freezer-safe jars and pop them into the freezer. Your kitchen does not heat up and you still have jam that will keep for a year or so. Cherries, blueberries, raspberries, gooseberries, currants, pears, peaches, rhubarb, and, of course, strawberries can all be preserved this way. If you don't have fruit trees on your property, you might consider going to "pick-your-own" farms.

There is one caveat with freezer jam. Because the fruit undergoes very little processing and because the fruit/sugar/water/pectin ratios for successful jelling do not allow room for recipe improvisation, the quality of the jam is almost entirely dependent on the quality and ripeness of the fruit. Under-ripe fruit may cause the jam to over-gel and be less flavorful. Overripe fruit may cause the jam to be runny and may introduce off-notes to the jam. Fortunately, when the fruit is from your own garden, the ripeness at harvest is easy to control.

You can make jam from your vegetables too. Peppers, onions, and tomatoes (yes, I know; tomatoes are a *fruit,* but it is usually is used as a vegetable) make delicious jams that you will enjoy as condiments for your autumn and winter table. I purchased some onion jelly at our local farmers market and love using it on goat cheese crostini.

Freezing: Freezing is a preserving technique for which there are a lot of pitfalls. Most fruits and vegetables cannot be frozen whole or cut up without causing texture and taste problems. Water expands when it freezes. This breaks the cell walls, which explains why frozen fruits and vegetables typically are mushy when they thaw. A rule of thumb is that fruits and vegetables typically eaten raw, such as blueberries, tomatoes, and lettuce, have the most textural damage when thawed. Those high in starch, such as lima beans, peas, and corn, are less damaged. To control the damage to texture from freezing, freeze as quickly as possible by having your freezer on its coldest setting. Rapid freezing reduces the size of the ice crystals and does less damage to cell walls than slow freezing. Thawed fruit can also be eaten partially frozen to reduce the watery texture.

According to the University of Minnesota Extension Service, blanching vegetables is essential for producing quality frozen vegetables. Blanching (boiling or steaming vegetables briefly) inactivates enzymes in vegetables. These enzymes cause the loss of color, flavor, and nutrients in frozen fruits and vegetables. In fruits, enzymes are responsible for the development of brown spots and loss of vitamin C. Fruits are not blanched before freezing. Ascorbic acid (vitamin C), when added to the fruit prior to freezing, interrupts the chemical reactions caused by the enzymes. A soak in vinegar or coating the fruit with lemon juice or sugar may be helpful but is less effective than ascorbic acid.

Contact with air causes oxidation, which results in rancid flavors (that freezer-burn taste). Wrap or double wrap produce tightly with a material than does not allow air to transfer to the product. By rapid freezing, deactivating the enzymes, and preventing oxidation, you will avoid the all-too-common disappointment of tasteless, mushy thawed garden produce.

Pickling: Pickling preserves food by fermenting it in brine (a solution of salt in water) and storing it in an acid solution (usually vinegar). The acid in the solution is sufficient to kill most bacteria. Thus, unlike the canning process, pickling does not require the food to be sterile before it is sealed. Pickling typically uses herbs and spices (mustard seed, cinnamon, garlic, cloves) that are themselves anti-microbial as well. Foods commonly pickled include tomatoes, peppers, eggs, watermelon rinds, peaches, beets, beans, mushrooms, shrimp, and, of course, cucumbers.

Canning: Jams, pickles, and sauces are great ways to extend the lives of fresh produce, but they must themselves be preserved. Their high water content makes them highly perishable. Unless canned (or frozen, in the case of freezer jam), they will spoil due to the growth of molds, bacteria, and yeasts and the activity of food enzymes. Canned products have shelf lives of 1-5 years because the canning process defeats these spoiling mechanisms. The canning process includes:

- Careful selection and washing of the food to be canned
- Hot packing the food
- Adding acids (lemon juice or vinegar) to some foods
- Using appropriate jars and self-sealing lids
- Processing the filled in a boiling-water or pressure canner to create a sealed, sterile environment.
- Key to successful canning is the selection of high quality produce. Micro-organisms live on the surfaces of fresh food and on the inside of bruised and damaged food. Start with the best produce to assure the best quality product. Always remember that not following canning guidelines can result in the proliferation of toxic **bacteria. If the sealing lid of a stored jar has lost its seal or appears "swollen,"** unquestionably, it must immediately be disposed of as the proliferation of dangerous microbes could result in death if consumed.

If after all this saucing, jamming, freezing, pickling, and canning you still have surplus produce, remember that you can always compost the rest for an even richer harvest next year or give it to a food pantry!

Special note: The Internet is an invaluable asset when studying how to preserve garden product. Consult university extension service websites for instructions, recipes, and, especially, safety instructions, which are so important for the canning process. Another great resource for produce-processing equipment and anything else a homeowner and gardener could possibly want is Lehman's Hardware of Kidron, Ohio. Fortunately, Lehman's has a strong online presence and ships its wares all over the world. And of course, the "Bible of Canning ", the Ball Blue Book of Preserving. *This sells for around $6.00 on Amazon.com plus shipping.*

Some Tips:
When it comes to canning, keep in mind these three important tips:

- **Mind the brine**: Do not change the amounts of vinegar, salt or sugar in a canning recipe. They are the preservatives and must be kept at a specific ratio. Changing spices is fine.
- **Keep it hot.** Sterilize the jars and keep them hot. Be sure the jars are covered by more than an inch of boiling water during processing.
- **Check the seal.** After processing, press on the lid. If you can press it up and down, the seal is not complete. Put the canned product in the refrigerator and use within three weeks.

Other Reading Resources & Web Sites:

- Putting Food By, by Janet Greene, Ruth Hertzberg, and Beatrice Vaughan.
- Complete Book of Home Preserving by Judi Kingry and Lauren Devine
- Preserving Summer's Bounty by McClure, Susan and the staff of Rodale Food Center
- Put'em Up! by Vinton, Sherri Brooks
- The Joy of Pickling by Linda Ziedrich
- Ball Blue Book 100th Anniversary Edition, www.freshpreserving.com
- USDA Complete Guide to Home Canning, www.extension.purdue.edu/store
- So Easy to Preserve, www.soeasytopreserve.com
- National Center for Home Food Preservation, www.uga.edu/nchfp/index.html
- Pick your Own, www.pickyourown.org
- Simply Canning, www.simplycanning.com
- Using and Caring for a Pressure Canner, www.Cals.uidaho.edu/edComm/pdf/PNW/PNW0421.pdf

Suppliers:

1. Canning Pantry
   800.285.9044
   www.canningpantry.com

2. Pomona's Universal Pectin
   www.pomonapectin.com

3. Lehman's
   877.438.5346
   www.Lehmans.com

4. All American Canner
   www.allamericancanner.com

5. Ball
   www.freshpreserving.com

6. Canning Supply
   www.canningsupply.com

7. Freundcontainers.com
   www.freundcontainers.com

8. Pressure Cooker Outlet
   www.pressurecooker-outlet.com

Educational Classes

Many evening adult educational classes teach classes on home canning, as well as County Extension Services (funded by the local universities) and Facebook. In the Columbus, Ohio an area class is the Rooster Cannery in Sunbury, Ohio which regularly holds classes for around $45.00. Their phone number is 614.499.2958.

You might also check with:

- The Canning Boot Camp, located at 1941 Hart Road, Lebanon, Ohio. Their web site is http://jamandjellylady.com
- Indy Hall located at 20 N. 3rd Street, 2nd floor, Philadelphia, PA. Their email address is foodinjars@gmail.com
- www.canningacrossamerica.com

Backyard Chickens

When Mark Zacek was a lad growing up in Montana, he occasionally had to fetch eggs from the chicken coop on the neighboring ranch. The stench and the cranky hens were enough to put him off chicken coops forever. So when his wife asked him to build a chicken coop and chicken run for her prospective flock of hens, he was less than thrilled. Now, one year after the construction of the coop and establishing the flock, he can at last appreciate his wife's vision. Chickens are cool.

He pre-ordered six hen chicks and picked them up in early May as 3-day-olds from their local farm supply. At that tender age, any assurances of their sex is a dicey proposition. They got lucky. Not a rooster in the bunch. They raised the chicks indoors in a large cardboard box with a heating lamp and the proper bedding and feed. That served as their "brooder." Their cheep-cheep-cheep provided a constant but friendly background noise to their day. Their care was simple, just a daily replenishment of their water, shavings, grit, and feed.

From the beginning, the differences were evident according to breed. Their two Plymouth Rocks were mostly black; the two Buff Orpingtons were indeed a soft buff; and the Rhode Island Reds were a rich, velvety red; so much more interesting and beautiful than the white chickens raised commercially. It is usually a bad idea to give "farm" animals names, but they went ahead anyway and named them: Lucky, Clara, Lemon Drop, Lulu, and Rosebud, and Henry. They were worried with the growth of Henry's comb that it was a Henry, not a Henrietta. When Henry started laying for them, they had their proof that the chicken was a "she," but they never did get around to renaming her Henrietta.

In the late spring, Mark constructed a chicken coop and chicken run of his own design, although based on established standards. The coop and run are things of beauty (or at least he like to pretend that they are!) with their clever features and the wonder of the neighborhood. He constructed an elevated sloped perch with three roosting bars. The droppings fall from the perch, which is enclosed by wire to keep the chickens from using the space. The perch is placed against a wall of the coop so a cutout door gives them access to rake out the space beneath the perch as needed. A brooding box with two compartments, lined with paper shreddings, is more than adequate for six chickens. The door that gives the chickens access to the run, raises and lowers with a simple pulley. The action cord and pulley is so slick that it gives Mark satisfaction each morning as he lets them out to the run.

However, the single feature that is most amazing to him is not even an aspect of construction design; it is the "odor-reduction" system. It was so simple. His family read that a 4-inch bed of wood shavings will prevent the highly objectionable chicken coop odor when raked lightly every day to keep the bed dry. Mark was dubious, but it turned out to be true. They just recently changed the wood shavings for the first time after 12 (!) months. The chicken coop has never in that time developed that horrible coop smell. Instead, it simply has an earthy smell that is not at all objectionable. Amazing! (When Mark built the coop, he tacked linoleum scraps on to the wooden floor to provide a more cleanable, durable surface. This also helps when raking as the rake glides over the linoleum rather than scraping over the wood.) The shavings also provide good insulation for the floor.

About four weeks after bringing the chicks' home, the coop and run were completed and the chicks were ready to move in. They took to it immediately. They cluck happily every morning as the family tosses table scraps and kitchen waste (watermelon rinds, overripe fruits and vegetables) into the run. They give them fresh water in the coop and in the run every day, twice a day when the weather is very hot. On the hottest days, they hose down the mulch in their run even though their outdoor area is shielded by shade trees. They have a feeder in the coop that they replenish weekly. They point a fan toward them on hot summer nights and provide a heating lamp in the winter. And that is about it for care, although he will admit that ensuring that their water stays drinkable (i.e. not frozen) in the depths of the winter is no pleasure. They might consider investing in a water heater for the winter.

An essential aspect of chicken care is security. In western Massachusetts, they have weasels, fishers, coyotes, hawks, and of course dogs that pose a threat to any unprotected chicken flock. Of all this family's chicken-owning acquaintances, they are the only ones who have not lost chickens to predators. Mark designed their coop and chicken run to be safe and completely enclosed; thus he never has to be concerned for their security. The picket fence he built around the run has pressure-treated boards buried partway into the ground. Masonry tiles are placed around the exterior and interior perimeters to further remove any threat from digging animals. Chicken wire is stapled on the inside of the fence. The run is covered with green netting strips that they can peel back to gain access to all areas of the run yet provide the cover the hens need from birds of prey and leaping animals.

One beast that their chickens do not need to fear is their cockapoo, Chloe. Chloe is very territorial and totally prevents squirrels and wild rabbits from even thinking of setting foot on her property. But they introduced their flock to Chloe as friends. Chloe has a large vocabulary (they think she is a canine genius). Understanding the hens to be "friends" makes a difference to her. Chloe can calmly be in the chicken run and the chickens just cluck around her. However, Chloe does love to eat roasted chicken and salivates at the word "chicken." So they are always careful when discussing the hens within Chloe's earshot to refer to them as "the girls" rather than "the chickens" just to be on the safe side.

It was November when the chicks were six months old and started laying. They knew from their friends' experience that the hens' egg production would be way down in the winter, so it was a pleasant surprise for them to regularly collect one egg per chicken even in February. With very rough control of heat in the coop via a heating lamp and light to provide approximately 12 hours of daylight, Lucky, Lulu, and the rest of the brood were content to keep producing an egg a day each. To maintain this laying rate, they also make sure that the coop and run are kept clean and that the hens are well nourished. This, along with generous space, ensures a stressless, largely unvarying environment that keeps at bay the problems that can afflict a flock, such as dangerous pecking at each other or eating the eggs.

What they had not realized when buying into this whole chicken thing was that the hens' laying rate really drops off after 3 or 4 years. As a well-cared for chicken can live up to 15 years and sometimes even longer, they could be accumulating a lot of unproductive hens in a few years. Butchering them was not an option for them, though it would be for many other families. Mark is thinking about sending them "to camp" at a farmer friend's house and pretending not to know what their fate will be. They will then have to replace the flock at a single time because introducing young hens to an established flock activates the "pecking order," upsetting their currently contented flock and upsetting their family. When they do replace the flock, they will be certain to disinfect the henhouse. This is a critical point to observe even though they have a healthy flock.

In having a flock of their own, they have also learned about eggs. All of their chickens produce lovely brown eggs. Their brooding boxes are lined with clean shredded paper. When their family gathers the eggs, they are always clean and dry. They have learned not to wash their eggs before refrigerating them. Washing removes the "bloom" (a microscopically thin protective membrane) from the shell. The bloom protects the egg by blocking the pores to prevent the transfer of germs and air to the interior and possibly contaminating and aging the egg. They have learned that eggs do not have to be refrigerated, although many "city folks" will not understand this. In many French kitchens, eggs sit in a bowl on the counter for days and days. And guess what? The French are right! Eggs can be kept at room temperature for two weeks or so.

One last word about their chickens: they are just plain fun to be around. Mark told me that he was more surprised than anyone about this. Commenting on how beautiful and entertaining the birds were, he found that they were also inquisitive and suspicious, yet always seem pleased to see him. He even commented to me how comforting it was to hear their cluck-cluck-cluck from the far end of the yard. They never squawk or crow. Even their neighbors seem to enjoy their background chatter.

But of course, ultimately, it is all about the eggs. Their beautiful brown eggs never cease to feel like a gift for the family when they gather them at midday. They know that their bright, golden yolks will stand proudly and firmly above the white in a way that supermarket eggs just never do. It is intensely gratifying to know that he is feeding his family a staple in their diet that is completely within his control, knowing that their eggs are fresh from their coop, knowing the hens' diet; he knows that the food is delicious and nutritious, and that he has provided something simple but extraordinary and important for his family.

Since I live in Ohio and cannot enjoy eggs from Mark's Massachusetts chickens, I have two places that I get mine from. One is nearby; the chickens are caged, but fed a nutritious diet. The other is a two hour drive (one way) where the farmer's 35 chickens follow her all over the yard. The taste of her chicken's eggs are so much better that when I have the time (usually on the weekend), I make the long trip and get about 14 dozen eggs at one time. I keep 8 dozen for me (I use one dozen a week when I am not doing a lot of baking), and give 6 dozen to friends. Unlike Mark, I keep all my eggs refrigerated.

As for the cost, I probably only pay 25 to 50 cents more per dozen (not counting gasoline) but feel that even with the long drive, the taste of the eggs makes it well worth it. This is one luxury I do not want to do without!

Chapter 11

Farmer's Markets & CSA's

If you have never visited a farmer's market, summer and early autumn are the perfect times. I set my alarm clock extra early on Saturday mornings so that I can get there before the rush. I empty most of my purse the night before so that it will not be heavy the following day. And I never forget my canvas tote.

I love shopping at one of the small town markets. I love the sights, smells, the friendly people, the aisles piled high with herbs, flowers, fruits, vegetables, dairy, and other delectable offerings. I can't wait to get the ever-berries, which are strawberries that are only available from July till the first frost in the autumn in our area. Then it is on to corn, green beans, homemade dog biscuits, a bunch of flowers and herbs, and maybe even an Amish pie or dinner rolls.

Shopping at a Farmer's Market offers many benefits. First and foremost is the quality of selection. You can also find organic meat, eggs, plants, handmade soaps, and of course, the freshest fruits and vegetables available, when you purchase in season. There is also the ethical benefit that many appreciate of supporting the local economy.

As delightful as it can be to shop at Farmer's Markets, you will need a strategy if you are to make the most of the experience.

Here are some tips:

1. Dress comfortably.
2. To get the best selection, arrive early. You will find the choicest selections picked over if you arrive at the same time as you might arrive at the grocery store. Also, the food will be fresher, as it will not have spent as much time in the warm summer air.
3. Bring a cooler. I also take ice in my coolers when I go shopping at the farmer's markets in order to keep my purchases cold and the vegetables as fresh as possible.
4. Take your time and enjoy browsing.
5. Introduce yourself and get to know your vendors. Some offer Community Supported Agriculture (CSA) options and can tell you how to get their product when the market is closed. They might even invite you to the farm!
6. Most vendors are happy to discuss their products and how they raised them, so you can ask them about:

- Growing practices, including soil care and chemical use.
- When an item was picked, how to tell if it is ripe and how to properly store it.
- Ways to use the food in cooking. Some farmers may have recipes to even share.
- Estimated time of arrival of a regional favorite, such as sweet cherries, and how its quality looks this year.

7. Before you purchase anything, do some investigating. Normally the selection of a Farmer's Market changes every week, as it all depends on what is in season and what has been harvested. <u>Your job is to discover which market has the best product.</u> See a lot of people buying red leaf lettuce at one market and bell peppers at another? That is a sign that they are onto something. Follow them.

8. <u>Ask questions early and often.</u> The people who run Farmer's Markets have a passion for great food, and they will be more than happy to let you know the growing conditions for the food as well as how to cook it. Talk to your fellow shoppers, too. You may run into some local chefs who can share new and interesting recipes with you.

9. <u>Shop only at markets where you can choose your own product.</u> Vegetables are better the heavier they are for their size, and they should be firm with no soft spots. These are things you cannot tell without touching the produce. You also should be free to take a sniff. If you are at a location where touching and sniffing is discouraged, shop elsewhere.

10. <u>Try the free samples being offered;</u> perhaps you might find something new that you will like. It is part of the fun to experiment with a fruit or vegetable you have never tasted.

11. <u>Bring cash</u>, preferably small bills. Most Farmer's Markets run with cash, and few will take your credit card or be able to give you change for a $100 bill, as most stand will not have this available. It is also a good idea to bring your own packaging—boxes, baskets, and/or bags.

12. Most Farmer's Markets in small areas are open only on weekends, but markets in larger metropolitan areas may have a permanent facility that is open year-round. Or different areas of the city might have market's open on different days of the week.

Shopping at Farmer's Markets can be a tremendously rewarding experience that you can share with your children, too. Some Farmer's Markets allow you to pick your own produce, and such places are fantastic for children. The investment children often have with fruits and vegetables they have picked (or helped to pick) they can be similar to that of produce they have helped to harvest in home gardens. They are often more excited about cooking -- and tasting! -- their harvests.

CSAs

Community Supported Agriculture (CSA) began 30 years in Japan when a group of women recognized that more and more of their food was being imported. They organized a group that bought directly from a farmer, inaugurating the system that came to be known as CSA.

Most CSAs begin with a farmer and sometimes a core group of members, who draw up a budget that includes all farm production costs, including salaries and overhead, for one year's operation. The total cost is divided by the number of families the farm will provide for, and that determines the cost of one share of the harvest. Each week, shareholders go to the farm or to a pickup site to collect their produce, with one share's worth enough to feed a family of four for a week. Most CSAs offer half shares, as well, and make arrangements for installment payments. The benefits and the risks of the harvest are then shared by the farmer and the members.

This is a nice way to get a variety of produce throughout the season. Do be aware, though, that the subscription may result in choices you may not necessarily have selected on your own. The upside of this is that you will have the opportunity to try new produce -- and possibly find new favorites! This subscription is very expensive and not beneficial for singles or couples unless you share with a friend or neighbor.

Chapter 12

Appliances That Make
Cooking a Breeze

Immersion Blender Stick

When I think of the benefits of using the Immersion Blender Stick, three things immediately come to mind: it's easy and fun to work with, it helps make nutritious foods, and it's easy to clean. It makes anything from mouthwatering smoothies on ice to steamy creamy vegetable soups effortlessly. Sorry, your excuses for not eating healthy just got chopped. It's great for baby food, too, by the way. The Immersion Blender Stick will become your number one can't – live-without kitchen tool in any time. Just stick it into any pan, pot, glass, or bowl and it will turn your food into puree at the push of a button. Once you're done, simple let the Immersion Blender Stick run in a bowl of hot water for a bit and it cleans itself. Preparing healthy meals and snacks doesn't get any easier than this.

Vacuum Sealing

I would be lost in my kitchen without my vacuum sealer, which I have used for over 30 years. If you have had to throw away food because of spoilage, this is a great tool to reduce "lost money." The website for the FoodSaver is www.foodsaver.com

The FoodSaver will save food that you purchase up to 5 times longer and will stop wasteful throwing away of spoiled food, which translates into money.

With this machine you can cook ahead for a week or month and either freeze the meals or leave them in the refrigerator. I find that using canning jars is more economical then the containers they sell. And if you are careful when opening vacuum-sealed disc lids (I pry them gently with a butter knife to break the seal), you can reuse the jars many times. I prefer the wide-mouth jars, which come in many different sizes from half-pint to 2 quart.

This chart shows the amount of time that you can freeze food using the advantages of a FoodSaver compared this using foil, plastic bags or plastic containers.

Food	Conventional Storage	Food Saver
Freezer		
Beef & Poultry	6 months	2 to 3 years
Fish	6 months	2 years
Soups & Stews	3 to 6 months	1 to 2 years
Coffee Beans	6 to 9 months	2 to 3 years
Vegetables	8 months	2 to 3 years
Bread	1 to 4 months	1 to 3 years
Refrigerator		
Cheese	1 to 2 weeks	4 to 8 months
Lettuce	3 to 6 days	2 weeks
Berries	1 to 6 days	1 to 2 weeks
Wine	1 to 3 weeks	2 to 4 months
Pantry		
Flour & Sugar	6 months	1 to 2 years
Rice & Pasta	6 months	1 to 2 years
Nuts	6 months	2 years
Cookies	1 to 2 weeks	3 to 6 weeks
Oils	5 to 6 months	12 to 18 months

Crock-Pots / Slow Cookers

Another kitchen appliance that I cannot live without is my slow cooker (Crock-Pot). When I talk with individuals who do not cook much, or would like to improve their cooking abilities, I always suggest that they purchase a slow cooker. With just around 20 minutes of prep work in the morning or the night before, you can have a wonderful fragrant meal greeting you when you come home from work in the evening.

The slow cooker has many advantages over oven or stove-top cooking. One major advantage is that it does not heat up the kitchen as much, which is of particular benefit during the summertime.

Slow cooking has changed over the past 20 years. Similar to microwaving in the past, people use slow cooking for just about everything nowadays - even baking!

Believe it or not, the slow cooker offers great flexibility, both in the types of food you can cook and the recipes you can make. You can cook breakfast, lunch, or dinner with dessert. Chinese, Greek, French, Italian, or Mexican cuisines: all can be prepared in the slow cooker.

When you prepare your menu for the week, try using your slow cooker on the days that you do not have the time prepare a meal for the family, or you are running short on time with extra activities or work you need to accomplish at home. You might even find that you need more than one slow cooker because of the menu you have planned. But be careful that you do not blow a fuse, or you will not have dinner at all -- and then you will have to throw out all the food you put in the slow cooker!

Ingredients for the Slow Cooker

Baking Foods: Condensation will naturally form on the inside of the lid when cooking and can drip onto your baked goods. To avoid this, layer 3 to 5 paper towels under the lid to catch the drips as your food bakes.

Beans: Dried beans should always be soaked before adding to a slow cooker recipe. Sugar, salt and acidic ingredients, such as vinegar, have a hardening effect on beans and will prevent them from becoming tender. So it is best not to cook beans with these flavorings, but to cook them separately and add them to the slow cooker thereafter. Lentils and split peas do not need to be soaked.

Condensed Soups: Condensed soups can be cooked in slow cookers for extended periods of time with minimal curdling concerns.

Couscous: For better results, cook couscous separately on the stove rather than in the slow cooker.

Cutting Vegetables and Other Ingredients: Try to cut vegetables and other ingredients to the same size so that they cook evenly. When cooking with larger cuts of meat, place vegetables in the slow cooker first, then top with meat. This ensures that the vegetables are tender when the meat is done.

Dairy: Milk-based products may break down (curdle) when cooked in a slow cooker. When practical, add those ingredients toward the end of the cooking time.

Fat: When preparing meat or poultry for the slow cooker, trim off excess fat. Fat retains heat, so large amounts of fat could raise the temperature of the cooking liquid and cause the meat to overcook.

Frozen Meat: Frozen meat should be completely thawed before placing in a slow cooker.

Liquid: When adapting a stove-top recipe to use in a slow cooker, <u>use only half of the liquid called for unless using long grain rice in the recipe.</u>

Meats: It is usually not necessary to brown meats before placing them in a slow cooker. However, browning may improve color of the meat and produce a richer flavor. Inexpensive cuts of lean meat that require long, slow cooking to break down fibers are just the type of meat that do well in a slow cooker. Even the toughest cuts come out fork-tender and flavorful. I have made pot roasts, stews, and soups in a slow cooker that when in use make me very hungry when I enter my home after a day at work.

Oats: Quick-cooking and old-fashioned oats are often interchangeable in recipes. However, old-fashioned oats retain their shape and hold up better.

Orzo: To prevent orzo or other small pastas from becoming mushy, add them to a slow cooker during the last hour of cooking.

Pasta: Avoid adding dry pasta to a slow cooker since it becomes sticky. It is better to cook it according to package directions and stir it into the slow cooker just before serving.

Rice: Converted rice is ideal for all-day cooking in a slow cooker. If using instant rice, add it during the last 30 minutes of cooking.

Roasts: When cooking a roast larger than 3 pounds in a slow cooker, cut it in half before placing it in the slow cooker. This ensures thorough cooking.

Seafood: Seafood tends to break down when cooked in a slow cooker. If used, add seafood toward the end of the cooking time.

Vegetables: Vegetables, especially potatoes and root vegetables (such as carrots), tend to cook more slowly than meat. Place these vegetables on the bottom and around the sides of the slow cooker and put meat on top of the vegetables. Add tender vegetables, like peas and zucchini, or those you'd prefer to be crisp-tender, during the last 15 to 60 minutes.

Tips for Using Your Slow Cooker

Cooking with Ground Meat: For food safety, cook and drain all ground meats first.

Filling: To cook food properly and safely, manufacturers and the USDA recommend that the <u>slow cooker be filled at least half full, but never more than two-thirds full.</u>

Leftovers: Slow cookers should not be used to reheat leftovers. Use a microwave, stovetop, or conventional oven to reheat foods to 165 degrees.

Lid: Each time you remove the lid from your slow cooker you may need to increase the cooking time by 20-30 minutes.

Old vs. New Slow Cookers: Some newer slow cookers seem to heat up more quickly than older ones. If you have an older model and a recipe directs to cook on low, you may want to set it on the highest setting for the first hour of cooking to ensure food safety.

Power Outage: After a power outage of less than two hours, you can finish cooking your food on the stove or in the microwave. If it has been more than two hours, or you are unsure how long the power has been out, discard the food.

Preheating/Refrigeration: Many slow cooker recipes cook all day. It may be easier to place all ingredients in the crock the night before, then cover and refrigerate overnight. In the morning, place the crock in the slow cooker and select the temperature. *Do not preheat your slow cooker.*

Reducing Fat: Because slow cookers retain moisture, you do not need to begin with as much fat. Often you do not need to add any fat at all. Any flavorful liquid, such as a broth, condensed soup, or salsa can stand in for fat and become a delicious sauce or gravy.

Settings: Most slow cookers have two or more settings. Food will cook faster on the high setting. However, the low setting is ideal for all-day cooking and/or for less tender cuts of meat. If your slow cooker has a "warm" setting, use it to keep your food warm until you are ready to eat it.

Slow Cooker Size: Use this chart to determine the ideal slow cooker size for your family:

Household Size	Slow Cooker Size
1 person	1-1/2 qt
2 people	2- to 3-1/2 qt
3 or 4 people	3-1/2 to 4-1/2 qt
4 or 5 people	4-1/2 to 5 qt
6 or more people	5-7 qt

Hints for Cleaning Slow Cookers

✓ For easy clean-up, spray the crock with non-stick cooking spray before adding food.

✓ Removable stoneware inserts make cleanup a breeze. Be sure to cool the insert before rinsing or cleaning with water to avoid cracking. Do not immerse the metal base unit in water. Clean it with a damp sponge.

✓ Wash the insert in the dishwasher or in warm soapy water. Avoid using abrasive cleansers since they may scratch the stoneware.

✓ To remove mineral stains on a crockery insert, fill with hot water and 1 cup white vinegar; cover. Turn heat control to high for 2 hours, then empty. Allow to cool, then wash with hot sudsy water and a cloth or sponge. Rinse well and dry with a towel.

✓ To remove water marks from a highly glazed crockery insert, rub the surface with vegetable oil and allow it to stand for 2 hours before washing with hot sudsy water

✓ Today with slow cookers coming in so many different sizes, if a recipe suggests a certain size, you will want to make sure to use that size, so that you get better results with the recipe.

Slow Cooker Capacity

Slow-Cooker Capacity	Serving Size	Suggested Foods to Cook
1 quart	1-2	Appetizers, Dips
2 quart	2-3	2 serving meals, Desserts
3 ½ quart	4	Family Meals, Desserts
4 quart	5-6	Family Meals
5 quart	6-8	Large Family Meals, Soups
6 quart	8-10	Roasts, Hams, Whole Chickens

Food Processors

There are many different styles of food processors, and costs will range from $49 to $399. It depends on how much you will use it and what you expect to get from it. I personally use mine to make fresh bread crumbs, pesto sauce, slicing vegetables, and grating cheese.

They also come in different sizes, so your purchase will depend on how much food you generally prepare. Some will even make snow cones or shaved ice/granitas, which are beloved by children and adults alike during the hot summer months!

Here are some of my favorite ways to use a food processor:

Puréeing Soups and Sauces – A food processor makes quick work of pureeing vegetables for soups and sauces.

Making Salsas, Pesto, Dips, and Spreads – Fine chopping and grinding for such recipes is a breeze with a food processor.

Chopping or Grinding Nuts – A food processor will help immensely for any recipes calling for chopped or ground nuts.

Making Nut Butter – Keep those nuts in the food processor a little longer and you'll have homemade nut butter!

Making Homemade Mayonnaise – If you make your own mayonnaise, you will find using a food processor far easier and quicker than hand-whisking.

Making Bread Crumbs and Cookie Crumbs – You could buy bread crumbs or prepared cheesecake crusts at the store, or you could use a food processor to whip up very fine bread crumbs to use for coating and topping or to grind cookies into crumbs.

Shredding Cheese and Vegetables – *So* much easier and quicker than shredding by hand!

Slicing Vegetables – Many recipes call for sliced vegetables. Use a food processor and make quick work of it.

Bread Machines

You can buy bread machines that make 1-lb loaves up to about 2 1/2-lb loaves. They are great for baking bread, homemade pizzas, dinner rolls, coffeecakes, and quick breads.

Newer models have timers so you can start the bread before you go to work and have it warm and ready for dinner that night. Just be sure that nothing you put in the bread machine will spoil during that time. (Be wary of recipes that require fresh milk or eggs, for example.)

For baking bread, you will need yeast. Rather than buying the small quarter-ounce packages, buy it by the 1-lb container. This should last over a year and is more economical, and should be stored in a Mason jar (in your freezer) to prevent spoilage.

By making bread yourself, you can create loaves of bread for about 50 cents a loaf – far cheaper than the prepackaged loaves of bread you would find at any store!

Yogurt Makers

Yogurt makers are wonderful convenience for busy families. There is no need to watch a yogurt maker -- it does all the work of creating yogurt for you.

You may ask yourself, "why should I make yogurt when you can buy it easily at the grocery store?" The biggest reason is that it can save you a lot of money. All you need to make your own yogurt is water, powdered milk, and starter -- the latter is a small amount of yogurt that contains the live cultures required to make more yogurt. One box of powdered milk will last you a long time. So in addition to being more economical, making your own yogurt also means you do not need to make a trip to the grocery store every time you want more.

Yogurt is also a very nutritious food. Alone it is packed with calcium, protein, B vitamins, and "good" bacteria that actually improve your digestive and immune systems. In fact, many doctors suggest eating yogurt with active cultures whenever you are taking antibiotics, as it helps prevent the gastrointestinal upset that may accompany a round of antibiotics. And if you mix fruit into it, you will improve the nutritional profile even more!

Yogurt can also be used in place of buttermilk in baking recipes, so if you make your own yogurt you can save money on that expense, too (buttermilk tends to be very expensive).

Finally, homemade yogurt can be used to make even more dairy products that you would normally buy at the store. From yogurt you can make cream cheese, sour cream, cottage cheese, and some forms of pressed cheese. Think of that -- all kinds of dairy products you do not have to buy. Yet more monetary savings!

You can make yogurt without a yogurt maker, but it requires more effort to maintain the proper temperatures required. You can always begin your yogurt-making efforts through other means, and then when you have the chance, you can purchase a yogurt maker. Generally they are not very expensive; they can run anywhere from $20 to $45.

You will find some great recipes for making your own yogurt, plus other kinds of dairy products, under "Powdered Milk."

Making Your Own Yogurt
by Mark Zacek

Many people are surprised to learn that making yogurt at home is possible. Making yogurt in your own kitchen is not only possible, but it is a very simple and inexpensive process. If your family eats a lot of yogurt, making your own will save you a lot of money. Once you have established your yogurt culture, the cost per ounce of your yogurt will be the same as the cost as the cost per ounce of the milk you make it with plus the cost of any flavorings or additives, such as honey, vanilla, granola, jam, or fruit. Your own 6 oz serving of plain yogurt will cost you about 15 cents. Contrast that with the standard $1.00 for a 6 oz container of commercial yogurt. You can make almost 7 servings of yogurt for the cost of a single store-bought serving.

At least as important as the cost-effectiveness of homemade yogurt is that it is delicious. It may be the most delicious yogurt you have ever tasted. A plain commercial yogurt tends to be sharp and acidic. To make it palatable, a surprising amount of sugar is added. There is frequently as much sugar in commercial flavored yogurts as there is in pudding, which of course defeats the "health food" expectation of yogurt. The lowest fat yogurts frequently have the most sugar. You can control your homemade plain yogurt to be less sharp than the commercial equivalent. That means that you may not have to add any sweetening beyond fruit or granola. You have the satisfaction of controlling exactly what goes into your yogurt.

The plain yogurt you make in your kitchen requires only two ingredients: milk and starter. The starter is simply a small amount of plain yogurt (1 tablespoon per 1 quart of milk). The starter is either from a commercial container of plain yogurt or retained unflavored from your last yogurt batch. (You can also buy ridiculously expensive envelopes of dry yogurt starter.) The milk can be skim, low fat, or whole milk, pasteurized or raw.

There are many online articles about making yogurt in a crockpot or in the oven. There is no excuse then for not making your own yogurt as you can make it with equipment already in your kitchen. However, a reasonable alternative for its sheer convenience is a commercial yogurt maker. A basic yogurt maker can be purchased for under $35. The advantages of a yogurt maker are that it requires no attention after you have added the milk/starter mix and that you make the yogurt in individual containers to which you can add flavorings and which become your serving jars.

You will note quite a lot of variation in the home yogurt-making techniques documented on the Internet. The variety of techniques simply shows that it is hard to screw it up. It is a forgiving process. The outline of the process is to heat 1 quart of milk to around 185 degrees and hold for 20-30 minutes. (How long you hold it is one way to control the thickness of the yogurt.) You then let the milk cool to about 110 degrees and stir in a starter. The yogurt is held warm for 7-10 hours. The length of "cook" time dictates the resulting tang of the yogurt as the bacteria are producing lactic acid while they reproduce. It is then thoroughly chilled in the coldest part of the refrigerator to stop the reaction. The yogurt will keep in your refrigerator for 2-3 weeks.

Once your family experiences your creamy, sweet homemade yogurt, there will be no returning to the store-bought variety. Your product will be fresher, more nutritious, and far less expensive. And most of all, delicious.

Freezers

Many food items taste better frozen than canned. This year I froze 8 dozen ears of corn, still on the cob. It is a lot easier to remove the kernels when I need them, than all at once. And I personally like freezer jam better than canned jam.

I also purchase 6 hams a year, at 99 cents a pound, that lasts me all year; then there was an 18 pound turkey for $5.00; 40 pounds of butter at $2.00 a pound; chicken thighs at 89 cents a pound; FREE loaves of bread (buy 1 get 2 free); and my favorite bacon at 50% off. Since I made the investment of purchasing a freezer, I wanted to make sure that it paid for itself.

A full freezer is not just a sign of a thrifty home cook; it is also energy efficient. When an empty or near-empty freezer is opened, cold air rushes out and is replaced by warm air. Excess energy is wasted by continually lowering the temperature. Since a full freezer holds less air, your freezer does not have to work as hard to re-cool it. If yours is empty, you may want to reconsider your cooking habits. You can also pour water into empty water bottles and place them in the freezer to take up space. Just be sure to leave a 1" head room so that the bottle does not bust open. You can also then pack these bottles packed in a picnic basket to keep food cold.

Chapter 13

Food Pantries

If you are receiving Federal, State, or other assistance, you need to be able to stretch your food dollars to last until the end of the month. If you are willing to change some old habits, you can do this, have better food and more of it.

If you have a problem and do run out of food, be familiar with the different food pantries in your area that will supply you with emergency food that should last for a few days. You need to sign up ahead for some of them, as they may allow you to obtain this assistance only once a month.

If you are in a dire situation, and your family does not have enough to eat, please do not hesitate to seek assistance from your local Job and Family Services (County or State office), your church, local food pantries, etc. Do not let pride get in the way of getting enough food for your family. These organizations are here to help you. There is no reason for anyone to go hungry. There is no shame in not having enough to eat in this economy and there are many organizations that will help you.

When you go to a food pantry for the first time, you may need to provide them with identification for each family member you are claiming assistance for. That would mean driver's licenses for the adults and birth certificates for the children. They will also want to verify that you reside in their county, so you will need proof for that also (utility bill, phone bill, doctor's statement, etc.). Most food pantries will provide you with enough food for 3 to 5 days depending what location you are in, and how hard your area has been hit. You can also go to more than one food pantry in your area. I live in an area with 9 food pantries, and you are allowed to go to each one, once per month. However, every area is different, so be sure to check first.

A typical allotment of food might consist of milk, eggs, one pound of meat, cereal, pasta, spaghetti sauce, canned fruit and vegetables, day old/er bread, peanut butter, and maybe some cheese. During the farmer's growing season, you might also be able to get local produce. There is very little, if any, food for pets.

There are also many area churches that provide very tasty weekly/monthly dinners for people in need. This could also be a way of meeting other people who are experiencing the same difficulties that you and your family are.

When money is tight, it is tempting to eat cheap and filling foods such as macaroni and cheese or stuffed baked potatoes. Though they provide many calories per dollar, these foods are high in fat and starch. Such foods are not nutritious, and if eaten often, they can lead to health complications such as high cholesterol, high blood pressure, obesity, diabetes, and auto-immune disorders.

If you are having trouble locating help, such as agencies, churches, food pantries, free medical/dental assistance, employment, certain government agencies, help with foreclosure on your home, housing, or childcare, in the State of Ohio all you need to do is dial 211 on your local phone system. You will then be put in touch with someone that can provide you with assistance.

And now let me tell you a true story:

Hundreds of cars were turning into the drive at the church in Sunbury, with the huge welcoming doors.   But what I found inside was even bigger hearts filled with all the volunteers that make everyone feel welcomed. The décor makes you feel like you were visiting a lodge. It is filled with lots of wooden tables and chairs, and comfortable furniture. Then there were the smells drifting from the kitchen enticing you to a meal that you know you are going to enjoy.

As I sat in the crowded room, looking around at the people, young and old alike, I wondered what had brought them all together. Seniors, young married couples with children, and families. It made me stop and think that many families are just payday away from asking for help or assistance. The game of "people watching" almost seemed like an intrusion, until you realized that everyone was here for the same purpose: Needing free food and/or free medical help. Help that they required for themselves or their family. The members of the congregation made everyone feel welcomed, and greeted them with open arms as they would any friend or family member, while they waited for their number to be called.

They started arriving 2 hours before the sign-in time, and then waited patiently for the lines to start moving so they could receive the help they so desperately needed. Many seemed to be used to these services, but then there were the new ones that had never been there before. They looked like my neighbors next door, family members, or friends. You would never have guessed that they were in need. But I found there really is not a "look."

While they were waiting, the church members will serve over 200 meals that evening, and numerous glasses of lemonade or coffee.

There was a comfortable calmness about the place once you got over the feeling of being embarrassed to be here, wondering if you would see someone you knew or if they would see you. You would think that it would quiet here. But it was not. There were conversations going on everywhere: groups gathered around the wooden tables eating what may be their only meal for the day, adults keeping the children entertained or watching the children play in front of the fireplace, and still others watching and listening to those around them, waiting for their turn to go and receive their share of food for the evening. This was all there was between existence as we know it for some, or maybe going to bed hungry, not knowing where your next meal would come from.

The church started a new procedure this evening. When your number is called, someone takes you in the other room, where there are tables full of food for you to select from. You may have 2 cans of vegetables, 1 can of soup, 1 loaf of bread, 5 pounds of potatoes, toilet paper, one pound of ground turkey or ground beef, ½ gallon of milk and eggs, or more depending on the size of your family. If you were lucky there was also some pet food for you to take home for the "forgotten ones". This is not talked about very much, the pets that people cannot afford to keep or feed anymore. It makes you stop and wonder how a child would feel if they suddenly did not see their beloved Rover around anymore. Or the senior whose only companion was their cat, dog or bird, who must wonder where they would get food for their friend that keeps them company all day. Do you buy food for yourself or your cherished pets?

This special church in Sunbury started this program five years ago with just five families. On this evening they would give away enough food for almost 400 people. That is 125 families and still growing. And in two weeks, they will do it all over again.

This is just one place in Delaware County. In Ohio this is the county with the highest employment rates, the nicest homes, a great school system, and yet there are at least eight more places that provide such services every month. And what about counties that are not as fortunate? There are so many families that are in need. Not just the ones that have always taken advantage of the welfare system, but **those that just need a helping hand, not a handout.**

A poor economy affects so many today. It used to be that it would never touch you personally. But now everyone knows of someone, or heard or read about families it has left its mark on. Life will never be as we once knew it, but maybe that is for the better. Gives us more time to appreciate what we have: not just material things, but the people around us, our friends and family, neighbors, and if we are fortunate enough to be employed, co-workers, as well as those we just see on the street while passing by. It may impress upon us the importance of sharing what we have with others. Not taking so much for granted, and helping others when we can.

It is hard to believe, but there are thousands of places like this one, all over the United States, they help anyone who comes through its' doors. Places that will help provide that helping hand that is so desperately needed.

Chapter 14

Make Your Own

Convenience Foods & Recipes

Powdered Milk

Powdered milk has an astonishing number of uses. Of course it is not just for drinking; it can also be used to make a surprising number of delicious dairy products. And since powdered milk has a much longer shelf life than fresh milk, you can stock your pantry with it and supplement your family's diet with it very economically.

The following recipes are all for non-instant powdered milk. You'll be amazed at all the wonderful things you can create!

Milk measurement	Amount of water needed	Amt of powdered milk needed
1/4 cup	1/4 cup	2 teaspoons
1/2 cup	1/2 cup	4 teaspoons
1 cup	7/8 cup	3 tablespoons
2 cups	2 cups	1/3 cup
3 cups	3 cups	1/2 cup
1 quart (4 cups)	3 1/2 cups	2/3 cup
2 quarts	8 cups	1 1/3 cups
1 gallon	3 3/4 quarts	2 2/3 cups

Basic Powdered Milk Yogurt

Serves: 4
Keeps for 2 weeks in refrigerator

2 cups warm (100 degree) water
1 cup non-instant milk powder
2 tablespoons unflavored yogurt

Pour warm water into blender and turn on at low speed. Add milk powder slowly. Blend until smooth. Add yogurt and blend a few more seconds. Pour into jars or glasses. Set with one of the following methods:

Method 1 - Place jars neck-deep in warm water. Cover pan with lid. Set on yogurt maker and keep temperature at 100-120 degrees. Will take 4-8 hours to set up. Chill immediately.

Method 2 - Turn on a heating pad to the medium setting. Place a folded towel over the heating pad. Set jars on towel. Cover with another towel. Let set 4-8 hours. When set, chill immediately.

You can allow yogurt to set overnight or while you're at work. Save some yogurt to use as a starter for your next batch.

You should not use a yogurt starter for more than one batch of homemade yogurt. You may want to purchase a container of yogurt and then use that container only for starters. In other words, use the yogurt a little at a time for starter until you have used it up. You can also use a container's full of homemade yogurt in the same way, using a little at a time as starter until it is finished.

Homemade Yogurt

Yield: 4 cups

5 cups milk (I use ½ powdered milk and ½ 2%)
¼ cup plain yogurt with active cultures

In a heavy bottomed 4 quart saucepan, heat the milk, stirring frequently over medium heat to 185 degrees. Remove and heat, and let cool to 110 degrees.

Place yogurt in a medium bowl. Using a whisk, gradually stir in cooled milk, about ½ cup at a time, stirring until smooth between additions. Cover the bowl with plastic wrap, poking two or three holes for ventilation. Transfer to a warm place (about 90 degrees) and let sit until milk begins to thicken around the edges and the yogurt is set, about 5 hours. Or put mixture into a yogurt maker following their directions.

Place bowl in refrigerator until completely chilled. Reserve at least ¼ cup of this yogurt to begin your next batch. Refrigerate for up to 2 weeks in an airtight container.

Yogurt Cream Cheese or Sour Cream

2 cups homemade yogurt
2 paper towels
colander
large bowl

Place a paper towel in the bottom of a colander. Put homemade yogurt on the paper towel. Cover with another paper towel. Set colander inside a larger bowl to catch liquid. Place the whole thing in the refrigerator overnight. The result is cream cheese.

For sour cream, drain for less time.

Crème Fraiche

Serves: 8
Yield: 2 cups

1 cup heavy cream (not ultra-pasteurized)
1 cup dairy sour cream

Whisk both together in a bowl. Loosely cover with plastic wrap and let stand in the kitchen or other reasonably warm spot overnight, until thickened. Cover and refrigerate for at least 4 hours, after which the crème fraiche will be quite thick. The tart flavor will continue to develop as it sits in the refrigerator. Good for at least two weeks in refrigerator. Makes 2 cups.

Use as a thickener for soups or sauces, as a dessert topping, or in boiled recipes as it will not curdle. Stir a few spoonfuls into butter-warmed vegetables for a simple sauce. Whisk some into salad dressing for extra flavor and texture.

Veggie Dip

Yield: 18   2oz servings

Thoroughly blend:
2 cups unflavored homemade yogurt
2 cups homemade cottage cheese

Sprinkle in:
1/4 cup toasted sesame seeds
1/4 cup wheat germ
1/2 teaspoon celery salt
1/4 teaspoon garlic powder

Blend well, salt to taste. Chill and serve with crackers or veggies.
VERY GOOD!!!

Suggestion:

I would suggest that you always read recipes thoroughly first and pull all of the ingredients. There is nothing worst that getting half way through a recipe and find that you are missing one or more ingredients.

Sweetened Condensed Milk

Yield: 1 can

Place 1/2 cup hot water in blender.
Turn on and slowly add 3/4 cup sugar and 3/4 cup powdered milk. Blend until smooth.

Greatest-Ever Yogurt Dressing

Serves: 12

1 cup plain yogurt
3 tablespoons vegetable oil
1 tablespoon tarragon white wine vinegar
2 teaspoons chopped parsley
2 tablespoons grated onion
1/8 teaspoon ground oregano
1/2 teaspoon salt
1/4 teaspoon garlic powder
1/8 teaspoon white pepper

Place ingredients in a blender container. Cover and blend on high for 2 minutes or until smooth and creamy. Chill
for about 2 hours before serving to allow flavors to mingle.

Bleu Cheese Dressing

Yield: 14 2oz servings

1 cup sour cream or plain yogurt
1 teaspoon dry mustard
1 tablespoon black pepper
1 tablespoon vinegar
1/2 cup milk
1/2 teaspoon salt
1/2 teaspoon garlic powder
1 teaspoon Worcestershire sauce
1 1/3 cup mayonnaise
4 ounces bleu cheese

Blend all ingredients (except bleu cheese) well. Add cheese in very small pieces and stir well. For maximum flavor,
chill for 24 hours before using.

Ranch Salad Dressing

Yield: 8 2 oz servings
Version 1:
3 minced garlic cloves
1/4 cup mayonnaise
1/2 cup buttermilk
1 teaspoon dried parsley flakes
1 teaspoon onion powder
1/2 teaspoon salt
1/2 teaspoon pepper

Combine all ingredients and blend well until smooth. Chill for at least 30 minutes. For the best taste, chill overnight before serving.

Yield: 16 two ounce servings
Version 2:
Blend together:
2 cups mayo
2 cups homemade yogurt
1/2 teaspoon garlic powder
1/2 teaspoon pepper
1-1/2 teaspoon onion powder
1-1/2 teaspoon salt
2 teaspoons parsley flakes

Prepare in the same manner as Version 1.

Simple Vinaigrette

In a small jar, combine salt ground black pepper and vinegar. Cover and shake until the salt has dissolved. Add the coil and shake again until all of the ingredients are combined. The oil and vinegar will eventually separate, so shake the mixture just before using. A good ratio of ingredients is 3 parts oil to 1 part vinegar, with salt and pepper to taste.

Emulsified Vinaigrette

Add a small amount of prepared or powdered mustard to your vinaigrette. This will help to keep the oil and vinegar from separating.

Raspberry Jam Vinaigrette

3 tablespoons seedless all-fruit raspberry jam
1/3 cup red wine vinegar or cider vinegar
¼ teaspoon salt
¼ teaspoon black pepper
1 cup vegetable oil

Put the jam in a 2 cup glass measuring cup and microwave, uncovered, on high power until the jam just melts, about 15 seconds. Or melt it in a small pan over low heat. Remove the container from the microwave and add the vinegar, salt, and black pepper. Whisk until well combined. Slowly add the oil in a thin stream, whisking constantly until it is thoroughly blended. Serve at once or cover and refrigerate until ready to serve.

Flavored Butters

Stir desired recipe ingredients into ½ cup butter (1 stick), softened; cover and chill for 8 hours.

Herb butter: 2 tablespoons chopped fresh dill and 1 tablespoon chopped fresh parsley. Serve on assorted steamed vegetables, fish or chicken.

Citrus butter: 1 tablespoon grated lemon rind and 1 tablespoon grated orange rind. Serve on any seafood, chicken or pasta.

Honey butter: 2 tablespoons honey and 1 teaspoon grated lemon rind. Serve on sweet potatoes, waffles, winter squash, or ham.

Bourbon butter: 2 tablespoons bourbon. Serve on pork chops or ham, toasted pound cake, waffles, or sweet potato biscuits.

Pesto butter: 2 tablespoons pesto. Serve on chicken breasts, baked potatoes, assorted steamed vegetables or pasta.

Croutons

Yield: approximately 60
6 tablespoons unsalted butter
1 baguette cut into cubes

Preheat oven to 350 degrees.
Lightly brush baking sheet w/butter.
Place bread slices on sheet. Brush top w/remaining butter.
Toast in oven until crisp and golden, 15 to 20 minutes.
Transfer croutons to a wire rack.
Keeps 1 to 2 days.

Yield: 8 large croutons
8 slices (1/2 thick), crusty, Italian bread
2 tablespoons extra-virgin olive oil

Heat grill to medium heat. Lightly brush each side of bread with oil, and place on grill. Cook on each side until lightly charred, about 4 minutes total.
Remove from grill; drizzle croutons with a little more oil if desired. Serve warm or at room temperature.

Yield: 90 croutons
6 to 8 slices of day-old white sandwich bread
4 tablespoons unsalted butter
Coarse salt & pepper to taste

Cut bread into 1/2 inch cubes, yielding about 4 cups.
Heat a large nonstick pan over medium heat. Melt 1 1/2 tablespoons butter until bubbling. Add half the bread cubes; cook, tossing occasionally, until crisp and golden, about 2 minutes. Add 1/2 tablespoon butter to pan, swirl to melt, and cook croutons 5 minutes longer. Set aside on a plate. Repeat process with remaining butter and bread cubes. Season croutons with salt & pepper & serve.

Glossary:

1. Sandwich bread. Sprinkle these cubes into soups, or toss them into salads. Flavor with butter, olive oil, garlic or fresh herbs including flat leafed parsley, chive, thyme or dill.

2. Baguette topped with a spread; these rounds become tasty hors d'oeuvers. Flavor with butter, olive oil, garlic, fresh herbs, or Gruyere or other cheese.

3. Pita bread. Pair wedges with Mediterranean salads or dips such as hummus. Flavor with sesame oil, olive oil, sesame seeds, cumin, coriander, garlic or fresh herbs, including thyme, oregano, or parsley.

4. Brioche. Sweet croutons made with this delicate bread add will and crunch to ice cream, yogurt, or poached fruit. Flavor with butter, cinnamon, sugar or melted caramel sauce.

5. Rustic breads. Sourdough, miche, levain, and other dense breads work best for these hand-pulled croutons. Use them to enhance soups or salads. Flavor with olive oil, garlic, fresh rosemary or thyme, or grated parmesan.

6. Italian bread. Float one of these hearty slices in a savory soup, or top with a spread to make an appetizer. Flavor with olive oil, garlic, fresh herbs, including oregano, basil or flat-leaf parsley, or parmesan, asiago or other cheese.

All-Purpose Baking Mix

6 cups all-purpose flour
3 tablespoons baking powder
2 teaspoons salt
3/4 cup shortening

In a large bowl combine the flour, baking powder and salt. Cut in the shortening with a pastry knife or fork until the mixture is well blended. Use in recipes that call for Bisquick or all-purpose mix.

Fire-Roasted Salsa

Serves: 6

1 (14 1/2-ounce) can fire roasted diced tomato, drained
1/2 cup sliced onion
1/2 cup diced green bell peppers
1 tablespoon dried cilantro
1 tablespoon dried parsley
1 tablespoon or more, lime juice
1 teaspoon sugar
1/4 teaspoon salt
1/8 teaspoon pepper

In a food processor, combine the tomatoes, onion, bell peppers, lime juice, sugar and salt. Cover and process until desired consistency. Stir in parsley and cilantro. Let sit for 20 minutes before serving.

NUTRITION FACTS: 2 tablespoons equals 13 calories, trace fat, 0 cholesterol, 141mg sodium, 3g carbohydrate, trace fiber, trace protein. Diabetic Exchange: Free Food

Homemade BBQ Sauce

Serves: 12

1 ¼ cups ketchup
1/3 cup molasses
2 tablespoons cider vinegar
½ teaspoon hot sauce
1/8 teaspoon liquid smoke.

Whisk together all ingredients until well blended. Refrigerate.

Steak Sauce

Serves: 20

1 cup ketchup
1 minced garlic clove
1/3 cup chopped onion
1/4 cup lemon juice
1/4 cup water
1/4 cup Worcestershire sauce
1/4 cup rice vinegar
2 tablespoons soy sauce
2 tablespoons packed dark brown sugar
1 tablespoon prepared mustard

Combine all ingredients in a saucepan and bring to a boil. Reduce to a simmer and cook for 30 minutes. Refrigerate.

Ketchup

Yield: 8 ounces

1   8 ounce can of tomato sauce
¼ cup of sugar
Dash of cinnamon
1 tablespoon of vinegar

Pour the tomato sauce into a small saucepan and boil away some of the water until it begins to thicken. Then add the sugar, cinnamon, and vinegar. Simmer again for 3 to 4 minutes. Refrigerate when cool.

Mayonnaise

Serves: 20
Yield: 2 ¼ cups

2 large egg yolks
1 whole large egg
1 tablespoon Dijon style mustard
Pinch of salt
Pepper, to taste
2 tablespoons of fresh lemon juice
2 cups vegetable oil

Combine the egg yolks, whole egg, mustard, salt, pepper, and 2 tablespoons of the lemon juice in a food processor. (Process for 1 minute or whisk until blended and bright yellow.)

With the motor running, add the oil through the feed tube in a slow, steady stream. (Or gradually whisk in half the oil, a few drops at a time, and then the remaining oil in a steady stream. You will need to whisk continuously for about 10 minutes.) When the mayonnaise is thoroughly blended, turn off the food processor and scrape down the sides of the bowl. Taste the mayonnaise and correct the seasoning and lemon juice if necessary.

Scrape the mayonnaise into a container, cover, and refrigerate. It will keep for 5 days.

NOTE: Since this recipe uses raw eggs, make sure they are very fresh, ideally organic. Never serve raw eggs to pregnant women, infants, or anyone with a weakened immune system.

Best Homemade Mustard Ever

Serves: 60

1/4 cup dry mustard powder
2 teaspoons light brown sugar
1 teaspoon kosher salt
1/2 teaspoon turmeric
1/4 teaspoon paprika
1/4 teaspoon garlic powder
1/2 cup sweet pickle juice
1/4 cup water
1/2 cup cider vinegar
1/4 cup mustard seed

In a small, microwave-safe bowl whisk together the dry mustard, brown sugar, salt, turmeric, paprika and garlic powder. In a separate container, combine the pickle juice, water and cider vinegar and have standing by. Place the mustard seed into a spice grinder and grind for a minimum of 1 minute, stopping to pulse occasionally. Once ground, immediately add the mustard to the bowl with the dry ingredients and add the liquid mixture. Whisk to combine. Place the bowl into the microwave and heat on high for 1 minute. Remove from the microwave and puree with a stick/immersion blender for 1 minute. Pour into a glass jar or container and allow to cool uncovered. Once cool, cover and store in the refrigerator for up to 1 month.

Overnight Apple Butter

Serves: 16 (1/4 cup)
Yield: 4 cups

1 cup packed brown sugar
1/2 cup honey
1 tablespoon ground cinnamon
1/4 teaspoon ground cloves
1/8 teaspoon ground mace
10 (about 2 1/2 pounds) apples, peeled, cored, and cut into large chunks

Combine all ingredients in a 5 quart electric slow cooker. Cover and cook on LOW for 10 hours or until apples are very tender.

Place a large fine-mesh sieve over a bowl; spoon one-third of the apple mixture into sieve. Press mixture through sieve using the back of a spoon or ladle. Discard pulp. Repeat procedure with remaining apple mixture. Return apple mixture to cooker. Cook, uncovered, on HIGH for 1 1/2 hours or until mixture is thick, stirring occasionally. Spoon into a bowl, cover and chill up to 1 week.

Serve over toast or English muffins as a healthy alternative to butter; or serve it as a condiment with pork chops or chicken. This apple butter also makes a terrific gift. Just divide it into jars and label each one with a tag telling recipients to keep it in the refrigerator.

A mixture of apple varieties, rather than just one type, will produce apple butter with a rich, complex flavor. Balancing a tart apple, such as a Granny Smith with a sweeter variety, will make an ideal combination. Whatever combination you choose, look for firm, vibrantly colored apples that smell fresh and don't have bruises.

Chicken Stock

Yield: 12 cups of stock

Place the chicken parts in a 4 1/2 quart soup pot. Add enough cold tap water over the chicken to cover it (about 10 1/2 cups).

Next, add 1 peeled onion cut in half; 2 medium size carrots cut in half (no need to peel them); and a rib or two of celery cut in half. If you have any saved vegetable trimmings you can add these now as well. Cover the pot. Bring the water to a boil over high heat, then lower the heat and simmer, covered, for 1 1/2 to 2 hours. Check the stock from time to time, adding more water, if necessary, and spooning off any foam that collects on top.

When the stock has cooked, transfer the chicken pieces to a bowl to cool. (The meat can be removed from the bones for later use.) Discard the vegetables. Cool the stock a little and ladle it through a strainer.

After the stock has been refrigerated for several hours, skim off any fat from the surface.

Freeze or refrigerate in 1 or 2 cup batches in an airtight, hard plastic containers. Covered and refrigerated, the stock will keep for up to 2 days; covered and frozen, for up to 2 months. Thaw frozen stock overnight in the refrigerator, or defrost it in the microwave.

Condensed Cream Soup Substitute

Yield: Replaces 1 can of soup

Condensed Cream Soup Substitute - version 1
1 tablespoon butter
3 tablespoon flour
½ cup broth (beef, chicken, or vegetable)
½ cup milk (you can use reconstituted dry milk)
And any Mushrooms, celery, asparagus, chicken -- anything that might normally be found in a cream soup, cooked and chopped.
 Salt and pepper to taste.

Melt butter in a saucepan over medium-low heat. Stir in flour gradually until smooth, then remove from heat. Add broth and milk gradually, stirring as you add to maintain the mixture's smoothness. Stir in vegetables or chicken. Return pan to heat and bring sauce to a gentle boil. Stir constantly until mixture thickens. Add salt and pepper to taste.

Yield: Replaces 1 can of soup

Condensed Cream Soup Substitute - version 2
2 cups nonfat dry milk powder
¾ cup cornstarch
¼ cup reduced-sodium chicken bouillon granules or chicken base
1 teaspoon onion powder
½ teaspoon dried thyme
½ teaspoon dried basil
¼ teaspoon pepper

Combine all ingredients and store in an airtight container until ready to use. In a small saucepan, whisk together 1/3 cup of the mixture with 1 ¼ cups water until smooth. Bring to a boil over medium heat. Cook and stir for 2 minutes or until thickened. You can add any of the mix-ins mentioned in version 1: mushrooms, celery, chicken, or asparagus. Nutritional information when prepared as written (without the mix-ins): 152 calories, trace of fat, 5 mg cholesterol, 557 mg sodium, 26 g carbohydrate, trace fiber, 10 g protein.

Yield: Provides enough mix for 7 cans of soup

Condensed Cream Soup Substitute - version 3
2 cups instant nonfat dry milk powder
½ cup plus 2 tablespoon cornstarch
½ cup mashed potato flakes
¼ cup chicken bouillon granules
2 tablespoon dried celery flakes
1 teaspoon onion powder
½ teaspoon dried marjoram
¼ teaspoon garlic powder
1/8 teaspoon white pepper
Combine all ingredients in a food processor or blender; process until vegetable flakes are finely chopped. Store mix in an airtight container until ready to use. On the stovetop, in a 1-qt sauce pan combine 1/3 cup soup mix and 1 ¼ cups water. Bring to a boil, stirring constantly. Cool or chill as needed. You can also prepare in the microwave. Simply combine the ingredients in a microwave-safe bowl and microwave on high for 1 ½ to 2 minutes.

Maple Flavored Syrup

Yield: 12   2 ounce servings
Approximate cost to make 60 cents.

2 cups sugar
1/2 cup water
1/2 cup corn syrup
1 teaspoon maple extract
1 teaspoon butter flavoring

Bring water, sugar and corn syrup to a slow boil over low heat stirring constantly.
Remove from heat before it comes to a rolling boil in order to keep crystals from
forming. Add flavorings as it is cooking. Store in refrigerator. Great over pancakes &
corn fritters.

Brown Sugar Syrup

Makes: 2 cups

1 cup packed light brown sugar
1 cup sugar
¼ cup light corn syrup
2 cups water
3 tablespoon unsalted butter

In a medium saucepan, bring the sugars, corn syrup and water to a boil. Reduce the
heat and simmer vigorously until thickened to a syrupy consistency, 10 to 15 minutes.
Stir in the butter. Let cook slightly (it will thicken more as it cools) and serve. Optional:
add ¼ cup chopped toasted walnuts for a different taste. Add them in with the butter.

Juice Syrup

Serves: 6

1   6-fluid ounce can favorite juice concentrate, thawed
1   6-fluid ounce can water
1   tablespoon cornstarch

Mix cornstarch and water until cornstarch is completely dissolved. Whisk mixture into cold juice concentrate. Heat
over medium heat until boiling, stirring constantly. (Try Cherry, Raspberry, Peach, Pine-Orange-Banana, Pine-
Passion-Banana; is your mind rolling with the possibilities?)

Chocolate Syrup

Serves: 16

1 cup unsweetened cocoa
2 cups sugar
1/4 teaspoon salt
1 cup cold water
1 tablespoon vanilla extract

Combine cocoa and sugar and blend until all lumps of cocoa are gone. Add salt and water and mix well. Cook over
medium heat, bringing it to a boil. Remove from heat once it boils. When cool, add vanilla.

Spaghetti Herb Mix

Yield: 8 ¼ cup mixes

1/2 cup garlic powder
1/2 cup onion powder
1/2 cup dried oregano
3 tablespoons dried basil
3 tablespoons dried thyme
3 tablespoons salt
2 tablespoons sugar

Mix well and store in an airtight container.

To use, blend 16 ounces of diced tomatoes with 1/4 cup of the mix.

Taco Spice Mix

Yield: Enough for 12 mixes

1/4 cup red pepper flakes or chili powder
1/4 cup ground cumin
1/4 cup dried oregano
2 tablespoons cayenne pepper
1/4 cup garlic powder
1/4 cup onion powder
3 tablespoons salt

Mix well together. To use add 2 tablespoons to one pound of ground meat. Mix well and then cook.
For dips add 2 tablespoons to 1 cup sour cream or yogurt.

Pumpkin Pie Spice

Yield: 5 tablespoons

3 tablespoons ground cinnamon
1 tablespoon ground ginger
1 teaspoon ground cloves
½ teaspoon ground nutmeg
¼ teaspoon ground cardamom

Apple Pie Spice

Yield: 5 tablespoons

2 tablespoons ground cinnamon
2 teaspoons ground allspice
1 teaspoon ground nutmeg
1 teaspoon ground ginger
¼ teaspoon ground cardamom

In a small bowl, combine all ingredients; stir to blend well. Store in a small airtight container. Makes great gifts for friends anytime of the year. Use as directed in recipes.

Beverages

Hot Apple Cider

Serves: 6

6 cups apple cider
1/2 teaspoon whole cloves
1/4 teaspoon ground nutmeg
3 sticks cinnamon

Heat all ingredients to boiling in 3-quart saucepan over medium-high heat; reduce heat. Simmer uncovered 10 minutes. Strain cider mixture to remove cloves and cinnamon if desired. Serve hot.

Hot Buttered Rum Spiced Cider: Make as directed. For each serving, place 1 tablespoon butter (do not use margarine or vegetable oil spreads), 1 tablespoon packed brown sugar and 2 tablespoons rum in mug. Fill with hot cider.

Rich Vanilla Coffee Mix

Serves: 10

1/3 cup instant coffee
1 cup instant dry milk powder
1/2 cup powdered coffee creamer
1/3 cup sugar
1/4 cup store-bought instant vanilla pudding mix

Measure all of the ingredients into a clean, dry bowl. Use a fork to combine everything evenly. If you are ambitious, you can powder everything in a blender. Transfer the mixture to a re-sealable container, or a pretty jar. This makes a good gift, especially in the winter time.

To Prepare: Place 1/4 cup of dry Rich Vanilla Cafe mix into a coffee cup. Add hot water to fill up the cup (about 3/4 cup hot water). Stir and serve.

Instant Cappuccino Mix

Makes about 2 ¼ cups of mix, makes 28 1-cup servings

1 cup powdered chocolate milk mix
¾ powdered non-dairy creamer
½ cup instant coffee
½ teaspoon ground cinnamon
½ teaspoon ground nutmeg

In a medium bowl, combine all ingredients. Store in an airtight container. **To serve;** place 1 heaping tablespoon and mix in a cup or mug. Add 1 cup boiling water and stir. Adjust mix amount for personal preference.

Hot Cocoa

Yield: 4 cups

1/3 cup sugar
3 tablespoons unsweetened chocolate extract
dash salt
1/2 cup hot water
3 cups milk
1/4 cup miniature marshmallows, if desired

Version 1:
In medium saucepan, combine sugar, cocoa, salt and water mix well. Bring to a boil. Reduce heat to low simmer 2 minutes, stirring occasionally.

Add milk cook until thoroughly heated. DO NOT BOIL.

Just before serving, beat until frothy with wire whisk. Top each serving with marsh-mallows.

Nutrition Information Per Serving: Serving Size: 1 Cup * Calories: 180 * Calories from Fat: 35 * % Daily Value: Total Fat: 4 g 6% * Saturated Fat: 3 g 15% * Cholesterol: 15 mg 5% * Sodium: 125 mg 5% * Total Carbohydrate: 30 g 10% * Dietary Fiber: 1 g 4% * Sugars: 27 g * Protein: 7 g * Vitamin A: 8% * Vitamin C: 2% * Calcium: 25% * Iron: 4% * Dietary Exchanges: 1 Fruit, 1 Low-Fat Milk or 2 Carbohydrate

Version 2:
4 cups instant nonfat dry milk powder
1-1/2 to 2 cups sugar
1 cup powdered non-dairy creamer (coffee lightener like Creamora)
2/3 cup unsweetened cocoa
1 package of instant store-bought chocolate OR vanilla pudding mix (optional, but very good)

Measure all ingredients into a bowl. Use a whisk to stir everything together. If the cocoa clumps, smash the little balls with a fork. When everything is evenly distributed, transfer the Hot Cocoa Mix to a clean coffee can, or a sealed canister. Use 2 cups of sugar if you are making this for kids. The extra sweetness makes it especially kid-friendly. For grown-ups you could add 1/4 cup of instant coffee for a nice mocha flavor.

To Prepare: Spoon 1/3 cup of the hot cocoa mix into a cup or mug. Add boiling water to the top, stir and serve.

This tastes really, really good. It is great for cold weather when you have been out sledding or picking apples. If you go camping, bring along a big bag. It tastes best when sipped from inside a sleeping bag on a cool October morning, in the middle of the woods.

Ice Capped Coffee

Serves: 1

1 cup of whole or 2% milk
1 heaping teaspoon of instant coffee
1 teaspoon of vanilla
6 ice cubes
4 teaspoons of sugar

Mix all in blender until ice is crushed. Pour in glass and drink with a straw.

Or

2 oz boiling water
2 tablespoons instant coffee (regular or decaf)
2 heaping tablespoons sugar (or a sugar substitute)
4-6 ice cubes
1/3 cup 15% cream (or chocolate milk...or white milk)

Mix the first 3 ingredients together to make a syrup and put into the blender. Add ice cubes and blend until slushy. The add cream and blend until frothy.

Frozen Mocha Coffee

Serves: 1

1/4 cup strong brewed coffee, chilled
1/4 cup Chocolate Sundae Syrups Ice Cream Topping
1 tablespoon vanilla flavored syrup
1/4 cup cold milk
1 1/2 cups ice cubes
Whipped cream
Chocolate decorator sprinkles, for garnish

Place coffee, chocolate sundae syrup, vanilla syrup and cold milk in blender container. Cover. Blend on medium speed until combined. Add ice cubes. Process until thick and slushy.

Pour into tall glasses. Top with whipped cream. Garnish with sprinkles.

Iced Mocha Latte

Serves: 5

½ cup cold water
2 tablespoons instant coffee
1 (14oz) can Sweetened Condensed Milk, chilled
2 tablespoons chocolate syrup ice cream topping
Ice cubes

Combine water, coffee crystals, sweetened condensed milk and chocolate syrup in a blender container and blend until crystals are dissolved (2 minutes?).Pour over ice in tall glasses. Serve immediately with a straw.

Creamy Instant Iced Coffee

Serves: 5

1 (12 ounce) can evaporated milk, chilled
2 tablespoons instant coffee
1/3 cup sugar or to taste
Ice cubes
Whipped cream

Combine evaporated milk, coffee crystals and sugar in a blender container until coffee crystals and sugar is dissolved. Pour over ice in tall glasses. Top with whipped cream. Serve immediately.

Mocha Espresso Coffee Mix

Serves: 24

1/2 cup instant coffee
1/2 cup sugar
2 cups instant dry milk powder
1/2 cup powdered coffee creamer
1/4 cup unsweetened cocoa
1/4 teaspoon cinnamon (optional)
1/4 cup instant vanilla or chocolate flavored pudding mix (optional)

Measure all of the ingredients into a clean, dry bowl. Use a fork to combine everything evenly. If you are ambitious, you can powder everything in a blender. Transfer the mixture to a re-sealable container, or a pretty jar.

To Prepare: Place 2 tablespoons of Mocha Espresso powder in a small coffee cup. Add hot water to fill the cup (about 1/2 cup hot water.) If you are using a large coffee cup, increase the amount of Mocha Espresso powder you add. For instance, use 3 tablespoons to an average size coffee cup, (adding about 3/4 cup hot water). Stir well and serve.

Bavarian Mint Coffee Mix

Serves: 12

1/3 cup instant coffee
1 cup instant dry milk powder
1/2 cup powdered coffee creamer
1/2 cup sugar
1/4 cup unsweetened cocoa
1/4 cup store-bought instant chocolate pudding mix
6 to 8 red & white candy mints, crushed

Measure all of the ingredients (even the crushed candies) into a blender container. Put the lid on. Process the mixture for about a minute, or until it is all powdery smooth, and the texture is even. The finished result will have an impressively professional consistency. It might even inspire you to blend all of your coffee mixes from now on. Store the mixture in a container with a good lid. Makes 2-3/4 cups.

To Prepare: Combine 3/4 cup of boiling water and 3 tablespoons of the mix. Stir to dissolve and serve.

Cafe Vienna Coffee Mix

Yield: 26 servings

1/2 cup instant coffee
2/3 cup sugar
1/2 cup instant non-fat dry milk powder
1/4 cup powdered coffee creamer
1 teaspoon cinnamon
1/4 cup store bought instant butterscotch or vanilla flavored pudding mix (optional)

Measure all of the ingredients into a clean, dry bowl. Use a fork to combine everything evenly. If you are ambitious, you can powder everything in a blender. Transfer the mixture to a re-sealable container or a pretty jar.

To Prepare: Place 2 tablespoons of dry Cafe Vienna into a coffee cup. Add hot water to fill up the cup (about 3/4 cup hot water). Stir and serve.

Instant Cafe Au Lait

Serves: 1

1 1/2 teaspoons instant coffee
1 1/2 teaspoons powdered creamer
1 1/2 teaspoons sugar
2 tablespoons dry milk

Measure all of the ingredients into a coffee cup. Add hot water and stir to dissolve. Savor the flavor of savings.

1-1/2 teaspoons is the same as 1/2 a tablespoon or 1 very heaping teaspoon. Every time you drink this instead of buying coffee from the local coffee shop, you save $2 to $3. If you are out of either powdered creamer or dry milk, then double up on the one you do have. This would be ¼ cup of dry milk powder or 1 tablespoon of powdered creamer.

Cafe Latte Mix

Serves: 11

1/2 cup instant coffee
1/3 cup sugar
1 cup instant non-fat dry milk powder
1/2 cup powdered coffee creamer
2 teaspoons vanilla

This recipe has to be powdered in a blender. The vanilla makes it clumpy, and the heaviness of the sugar makes it sink to the bottom while the coffee creamer rises to the top. Blending the mixture solves these problems. Measure all ingredients into a blender. Put the lid on. Process the mixture for about a minute, or until it is powdery smooth, and the texture is even. This is actually a lot less work than it sounds like, and the texture is so impressively professional, that you may want to blend all of your coffee mixes from now on. Store in a container with a tight-fitting lid. Makes 1- 2/3 cups.

To Prepare: Combine 3/4 cup of boiling water and 2 to 3 tablespoons of the mix. Stir to dissolve and serve.

Ginger Tea Mix

Serves: 26

1 1/2 cup plain instant tea
1 teaspoon ground ginger
1/2 cup sugar
1 cup instant powdered milk
1/4 cup powdered coffee creamer

In a re-sealable container, combine all of the ingredients and stir with a fork or a whisk to distribute everything evenly. Then store on the pantry shelf.

To Prepare: Combine 2 tablespoons Ginger Tea Mix with 3/4 cup boiling water. Stir the ingredients in a tea cup to dissolve. Serve with lemon cookies at tea time.

Note: The English prefer milk in their tea, while most Americans prefer lemon. I have an English grandmother who taught me to appreciate both methods of service. This recipe is very English in origin, so it contains milk instead of the lemon most of us are more accustomed to. It is an odd little recipe, and the first time I made it I thought it would be fine for my personal consumption, but probably not worthy of sharing.

Then friends and family members got a taste of it, and begged for the recipe. It tastes a little strange at first, certainly exotic, and then it grows on you, eventually becoming an addiction of almost shameful proportions. I recommend you make half the recipe the first time to give it a try, and then see if it casts its spell upon you, demanding you prepare it in ever-growing quantity. This would make an excellent gift for the holidays.

Chai Tea Mix or Spiced Milk Tea

Serves: 10

1/2 cup instant tea
1/2 cup nonfat dry milk
1/4 cup powdered coffee creamer
1/2 cup white or (better) brown sugar
1 tablespoon instant vanilla pudding mix
1/2 teaspoon cinnamon
1/2 teaspoon ginger
1/4 teaspoon nutmeg
1/4 teaspoon ground cloves
1/4 teaspoon ground cardamom
1/8 teaspoon black pepper

In a re-sealable container combine all of the ingredients and stir with a fork or a whisk to distribute evenly. Store on the pantry shelf.

To Prepare: Combine 3 tablespoons Chai Tea Mix with 1 cup boiling water. Stir well to dissolve. Sip and savor.

Note: Cardamom is the ingredient that gives this recipe an authentic Indian flavor. To tell the truth, it can be expensive and hard to find. If desired you can omit it completely or replace it with an equal amount of allspice. It will not be authentic Chai at that point, but it will be authentic Spiced Milk Tea, which is pretty much what Chai means. Some people add ground fennel or lemon peel to their Chai. I prefer this recipe made with brown sugar, but white sugar is cheaper and makes a prettier mix. Feel free to experiment with the flavors as you see fit.

Homemade Spice Tea

Serves: 40

2 to 3 cups of sugar (depending on your sweet tooth)
2 packets orange Kool-Aid mix
1 or 2 packets lemon Kool-Aid mix (depending on your sour tooth)
1/2 cup instant tea
1 or 2 teaspoons cinnamon
1/4 teaspoon ground cloves

Measure the sugar into a large bowl. Open the Kool-Aid packets and add them to the sugar. Stir well with a wire whisk or a clean dry fork. Add the instant tea, cinnamon and cloves. Stir again to mix well. This makes about 4 cups of mix. Store it in a well-sealed container.

To Prepare: Combine a tablespoon of Spiced Tea Mix with hot water in a cup or mug. Stir to dissolve. Serve hot.

Dry Your Own Mint for Tea

Some techniques commonly used to dry mint are:

BUNDLE AND HANG :
Bundle and hang them from stems in a dark, very dry place. If possible put paper bags around the bundles.

Use a fan on low to circulate the air. The leaves are dry enough if they crush when you press a few of them together in your fingers. Strip the dry leaves off of the stems gently. Lay all of the leaves out on a flat surface to make sure that you have dried every leaf within the bundle.

Store the dry leaves in an airtight glass jar in a cool, dry and dark area. You can use a spoonful of crumbled leaves for each cup of tea. Always use a dry, wooden spoon to remove the leaves from the jar when you need them.

DRY THE LEAVES IN AN OVEN:
Use your oven to quickly dry mint leaves. Put the washed and dried leaves on a cookie sheet and set in an oven at 180 degrees for 2 or more hours. The leaves will dry without a loss of any oils or fragrance.
Remove the leaves from the oven and strip them from the branches.
Store the dry leaves in an airtight glass jar in a cool, dry and dark area. You can use a spoonful of crumbled leaves for each cup of tea.

WHEN TO PICK:
The best time to pick the mint is right before it flowers in the early to mid-morning. This is when the most essential oils are present sending all of its plant goodness into the reproductive process and producing all that aroma, flavor and other magic!

Homemade Eggnog

Serves: 9

2 large eggs
1 1/2 cups sugar
1/2 teaspoon salt
2 quarts milk
2 tablespoons vanilla extract
2 cups heavy whipping cream
Ground nutmeg

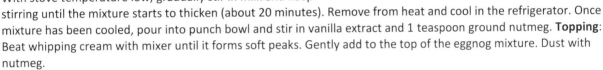

Beat eggs then place eggs, sugar and salt into a large saucepan.
With stove temperature low, gradually stir in milk and keep
stirring until the mixture starts to thicken (about 20 minutes). Remove from heat and cool in the refrigerator. Once mixture has been cooled, pour into punch bowl and stir in vanilla extract and 1 teaspoon ground nutmeg. **Topping**: Beat whipping cream with mixer until it forms soft peaks. Gently add to the top of the eggnog mixture. Dust with nutmeg.

Party Punch

Serves: 15

1 (6-ounce) can frozen lemonade concentrate, thawed
1 (6-ounce) can frozen orange juice concentrate, thawed
2 cups white Catawba grape juice, chilled
1 (1-liter) bottle (4 1/2 cups) lemon-lime soda
Chilled ice ring or ice mold, if desired

Just before serving, in punch bowl, combine lemonade and orange juice concentrates and blend well. Add grape juice and carbonated beverage stir gently. Place ice ring in bowl.

Nutritional Information Per Serving: 1/2 Cup * Calories: 100 * Calories from Fat: 0 * % Daily Value: Total Fat: 0 g 0% * Saturated Fat: 0 g 0% * Cholesterol: 0 mg 0% * Sodium: 10 mg 0% * Total Carbohydrate: 25 g 8% * Dietary Fiber: 0 g 0% * Sugars: 23 g * Protein: 1 g * Vitamin A: 0% * Vitamin C: 35% * Calcium: 0% * Iron: 0% * Dietary Exchanges: 1 1/2 Fruit or 1 1/2 Carbohydrate

Tomato Juice from Tomato Paste

1 can tomato paste
4 cans of tap water

Use any size can of tomato paste. Usually they come in 12-oz or 6-oz sizes. Open the can and scrape the thick concentrated tomato paste into a large jar or juice pitcher. Fill the can with water 4 times, and pour the water in with the tomato paste. Stir well. It will be unsalted, which I believe makes it taste fresher, but you may add salt to taste if you like. Some folks like to add a little Hot Sauce or Worcestershire Sauce for flavor. Personally, I like it well chilled and straight from the fridge. It has a tangy refreshing flavor that reminds me of summertime tomato harvesting. Use it anywhere you would regular canned tomato juice. This substitute which costs less than a third of its commercial counterpart, and actually tastes ten times better. Being thrifty in this instance pays off in flavor, health and savings.

Fruit Sangria

Serves: 10

2 cups dry red wine, chilled
2 cups orange juice
2 tablespoons lime juice
1/4 cup sugar
1 cup club soda, chilled

In large non-metal container or bowl, combine wine, orange juice, lime juice and sugar stir until sugar is dissolved. Just before serving, slowly add club soda, stirring gently to blend. Serve over ice.

Nutritional Information Per Serving: 1/2 Cup * Calories: 70 * Calories from Fat: 0 * % Daily Value: Total Fat: 0 g 0% * Saturated Fat: 0 g 0% * Cholesterol: 0 mg 0% * Sodium: 10 mg 0% * Total Carbohydrate: 11 g 4% * Dietary Fiber: 0 g 0% * Sugars: 11 g * Protein: 0 g * Vitamin A: 0% * Vitamin C: 35% * Calcium: 0% * Iron: 0% * Dietary Exchanges: 1 Fruit or 1 Carbohydrate

Kiwi Lemonade

Serves: 4

6 kiwis, pureed and strained if necessary to remove seeds
1 cup sugar
¾ cup lemon juice

Blend ingredients thoroughly. Mix with sparkling water or a lemon-lime soda to a taste that appeals to you.

Lemonade

Serves: 10

2 cups of lemon juice
2 cups of sugar
Tap water to make 1 gallon (about 3-1/2 quarts)
Gallon sized pitcher

In a large gallon-sized pitcher combine the lemon juice and sugar. Stir and stir to dissolve the sugar. If necessary, add a little hot tap water to help the process along. A cup or two of hot tap water will be plenty. When the sugar is dissolved add cold tap water to fill the pitcher. Serve over tall glasses of ice. If you prefer a stronger flavor, you may slice a fresh lemon into the pitcher. I usually use bottled lemon juice because it is the cheapest and most available to me. Adding the fresh lemon slices makes the bottled lemon juice taste much fresher. You can also cut this recipe in half.

Best Homemade Lemonade

Serves: 14   1 cup servings

1½ cups sugar
1½ cups fresh lemon juice (about 8 large lemons)
1 tablespoon fresh grated lemon peel (optional) water and ice cubes

Prepare syrup: in a one quart jar, stir sugar, lemon juice, lemon peel, and 1½ cups hot tap water until sugar dissolves. Cover and refrigerate. For each serving, pour ¼ cup syrup over ice cubes in a 12 ounce glass stir in about ¾ cup cold water. Slice a lemon very thinly and add these pieces to the pitcher of lemonade as well as each glass.

Tips:
To make sparkling lemonade, prepare the syrup as above, then substitute club soda for the water.
Prepare 2 hours before serving.

Mocha Coffee Mix

Makes about 3 ½ cups of mix, or 13 one cup servings

1 cup nonfat dry milk powder
1 ¼ cups granulated sugar
2/3 cup powdered non-dairy creamer
½ cup unsweetened cocoa
½ cup instant coffee
1 teaspoon ground cinnamon

Combine all ingredients in a food processor; pulse until ground and blended. **To serve**, place a rounded ¼ cup mixture in a cup or mug. Add ¾ cup boiling water and stir until mix is dissolved.

Homemade Chai Tea

Makes about 10 cups of individual servings or 2 cups of mix

¾ cup and 2 tablespoons brown sugar
1 teaspoon vanilla
1/3 cup non-fat dry milk powder
1/3 cup powdered non-dairy creamer
¾ teaspoon ground ginger
¾ teaspoon ground cinnamon
¼ teaspoon ground cloves
¼ teaspoon ground cardamom
Pinch of black pepper

In a food processor, pulse sugar and vanilla until vanilla is incorporated. Add milk powder and non-dairy creamer. Pulse to combine. Add ginger, cinnamon, cloves, cardamom and pepper; process until mixture is the consistency of fine powder. **To serve**: Mix 2 heaping tablespoons of mixture into 1-cup hot water.

Convenience Foods & Some of My Favorites

Polenta

Serves: 8

This recipe makes 2 loaf pans of Polenta.
2 cups corn meal
3 cups water
4 cups chicken broth
4 Tablespoons butter or margarine
1/4 cup grated parmesan cheese (optional)

Whisk the cornmeal and water together in a medium sauce pan. Gradually add the chicken broth, stirring constantly for 25 to 30 minutes. The mixture will become thick and pull away from the sides. Stir in butter and parmesan cheese, or add mushrooms, herbs or peppers.

Creamy Parmesan Sauce:
2 Tablespoons flour
1 Tablespoon olive oil or butter
1 Teaspoon Dijon mustard
1 1/4 cup milk
3 Tablespoons grated parmesan cheese

In a medium sauce pan, combine flour and oil. Stir to make a roux (a mixture of flour and fat) cooking for 3 minutes. Add milk a little at a time, whisking constantly, until the sauce is thick and comes to a boil. Whisk in the mustard. Pour over polenta. This is also good with steamed vegetables. Steam your vegetables first, then pour the sauce over the vegetables and spoon over polenta.

Crème Brulee French Toast

Serves 6 or more

1 stick unsalted butter
1 cup firmly packed brown sugar
2 tablespoon light corn syrup
6 large eggs
1½ cups half-and-half
2 tablespoon vanilla
¼ teaspoon salt
1 loaf Challah or other old dense bread

In a small saucepan, heat together first 3 ingredients until smooth. Pour into a 9 x 14 baking dish. Cut Challah into 1-inch thick pieces from middle. Remove crust and chunk. Place pieces on top of above mixture, squeezing pieces tightly into pan. Whisk together eggs, half-and-half, and salt. Pour over bread and press down to make sure all bread absorbs mixture. Cover with plastic wrap, pressing down so the top cannot get any air, and refrigerate overnight. Bring to room temperature before baking. Bake uncovered in a preheated oven at 350 degrees for 35 to 40 minutes or until edges are brown.

Cherry Cheese Blintzes

Serves: 4

4 cups all-purpose flour
4 cups milk
8 eggs
2 teaspoons vanilla
Dash of salt
1 pound ricotta cheese or 2 eight ounce cream
cheese, softened
1 to 1/3 cup sugar
1 1/2 tablespoon vanilla extract
Dash of cinnamon
Sliced almonds (optional)
Raisins (optional)
Cherry pie filling & whip cream

For blintzes: In blender, add flour, milk, eggs, the 1/2 teaspoon vanilla and a dash salt. Cover; blend till smooth. Let stand 30 minutes.

For filling: In a large bowl, mix cheese, sugar and 1 teaspoon vanilla, dash of salt and if you like, cinnamon. Beat until nearly smooth. Heat a lightly greased 8 inch nonstick skillet over medium heat until a few drops of water sizzle. Remove skillet from heat. For each blintz, spoon slightly less than 1/4 cup batter into hot skillet. Quickly lift and tilt to spread into a thin, even circle. Return to heat; cook 1 to 1 1/2 minutes or until top is set and edges are lightly browned. Invert over parchment paper to remove blintz. Repeat with remaining batter, greasing skillet occasionally to make 8 to 10 blintzes. **To serve**, spoon 1/4 cup cheese filling across each blintz just below center. If you like, add nuts. Fold blintz bottom over filling. Fold in sides, roll up. Serve with fruit and nuts. Optional includes adding raisins, whip cream, etc.

Buttermilk Waffles

Serves 6-8

2 cups all-purpose flour
¼ cup light brown sugar, firmly packed
1 teaspoon baking soda
1 ½ teaspoon baking powder
½ teaspoon ground cinnamon
½ teaspoon salt
3 large eggs, separated, room temperature
2 cups non-fat buttermilk, room temperature
8 tablespoons unsalted butter (1 stick), melted
1 each vanilla bean, split and scraped, or 1 teaspoon good quality vanilla extract

Heat waffle iron to high. Heat oven to 200°. In a large bowl, sift together flour, sugar, baking soda, baking powder, cinnamon, and salt. In a medium bowl, whisk together egg yolks, buttermilk, butter, and vanilla bean scrapings. Pour into dry mixture combine. In a medium bowl, beat the egg whites until stiff but not dry. Fold whites into the batter. Ladle about 1/2 cup batter into each section of the waffle iron spread batter almost to the edges. Bake until no steam emerges, 5 to 7 minutes. Transfer cooked waffles to a baking sheet and transfer to oven to keep warm while baking the remaining batter.

Cinnamon Rolls

Serves: 16

Dough:
1 tablespoon dry yeast
1 cup warm milk
1/3 cup granulated sugar
1/2 cup soft butter
1 teaspoon salt
2 eggs
4 cups flour

Filling:
1/4 cup soft butter
1 cup brown sugar
3 tablespoons cinnamon

Icing:
1/2 cup soft butter
1 1/2 cup powdered sugar
1 ounce cream cheese
2 tablespoons whipping cream
1 teaspoon vanilla extract
Pinch of salt

DOUGH INSTRUCTIONS:
Dissolve yeast in warm milk. Add the rest of the ingredients and mix well. Knead into a ball or put in a bread machine on the dough setting. Let rise until double in size. When ready, roll out to about 1/4 inch thick. Spread with filling.

FILLING INSTRUCTIONS:
Spread butter evenly on dough. Sprinkle sugar and cinnamon evenly over buttered dough. Roll up dough. Slice roll into 1 inch slices. Place on a greased pan. Let rise until double in size. Bake 10 minutes at 400 degrees.

ICING INSTUCTIONS:
Combine all ingredients and beat until fluffy. When rolls are hot spread lots of icing on them.

Rum French Toast

Serves: 4

3 eggs
¾ cup milk, half-and-half, or cream
3 tablespoon dark rum
1 tablespoon sugar
¼ teaspoon nutmeg
Pinch of salt
6 slices dense bread
4 tablespoon butter
2 tablespoons oil

Garnish: fresh fruit, butter/maple syrup

Stir together eggs, milk, rum, sugar, nutmeg, and salt in a shallow bowl. Dip both sides of each slice of bread in the batter. Place the slices on waxed paper. Heat 2 tablespoons butter and 1 tablespoon oil in a skillet large enough to hold 3 slices at a time. Fry bread over medium heat until lightly browned, turning once. Keep cooked slices warm while frying remaining slices in the oil and butter. **To serve,** slice bread in half (at an angle) and arrange on plates. Garnish with fruit and serve with butter and warm maple syrup.

Other suggestions: Use raisin toast as a base.
Sprinkle with chopped nuts.
Put rum raisin ice cream on top and serve as a dessert.

Sweet Red Pepper Strata

Serves: 6

6 thick slices of sourdough bread (or one whole 16 oz loaf), crusts removed
Softened butter for spreading
1 pound sausage, cooked & drained
½ med red pepper, cut in spirals (circles)
¼ cup chopped onion
2 cups shredded cheddar cheese
1 can cream of asparagus soup
2 cups milk
½ teaspoon Dijon mustard
4 eggs
½ teaspoon ground pepper

Spread one side of bread with butter and cube it. Place this in a greased 9 x 13 pan or a large quiche dish, butter side down. Add sausage, red pepper, onion and cheese in this order. Mix soup, milk, eggs, mustard and pepper, and pour over casserole. Refrigerate overnight. Let set for 30 minutes at room temperature, then bake for 1 hour at 325 degrees. Let set 5-10 minutes before cutting.

Bananas Foster French Toast

Serves: 4

4 eggs
1/4 teaspoon ground cinnamon
1/2 cup 2 percent milk
6 tablespoons firmly packed dark brown sugar, divided
Kosher salt to taste
4 slices day old bread 1" thick
6 tablespoons (3/4 stick) unsalted butter
4 bananas cut on bias into 1/2" slices
1/4 cup dark rum
1/2 teaspoon vanilla extract
3 tablespoons water

In a bowl whisk egg, cinnamon, milk, 1 Tablespoon brown sugar and a pinch of salt. Pour half of egg mixture into deep pie dish. Soak 1 bread slice, turning once after 1-2 minutes (lightly browned). Repeat with remaining bread and egg mixture. Pour any remaining mixture over bread until absorbed. In an 11" skillet over medium heat, melt 1 1/2 tablespoons of butter. Add 2 bread slices; cook, turning once, until golden, 2-3 minutes per side. Transfer to wire cooling rack set over baking sheet keep warm in 200 degree oven. Repeat with 1 1/2 tablespoons butter and remaining bread. In another skillet over medium high heat, melt 3 tablespoons butter. Add bananas cook, stirring occasionally, until lightly browned, 2-3 minutes. Carefully pour in rum, then add 5 tablespoons of brown sugar, vanilla, water and a pinch of salt. Simmer until bananas are soft, 2-3 minutes. Serve French toast with bananas.

Blueberry French Toast

12 slices day old white bread with crusts removed
2   8 ounce packages of cream cheese
1 cup fresh or frozen blueberries
12 eggs
2 cups milk
1/3 cup maple syrup or honey

Cut bread into 1" cubes and place half of them in a greased 9 x 13 baking pan or dish. Cut cream cheese into 1" cubes and place over bread. Top with blueberries and remaining bread. In a large bowl, beat eggs, add milk and syrup, and mix well. Pour over bread mixture. Cover and chill for 8 hours or overnight. Remove from refrigerator 30 minutes before baking. Cover and bake at 350 degrees for 30 minutes. Uncover and continue baking another 25-30 minutes or more, until golden brown and the center is set.

SAUCE:
1 cup sugar
2 tablespoon cornstarch
1 cup water
1 cup fresh or frozen blueberries
1 tab;es[ppm butter
In a saucepan combine sugar and cornstarch, add water. Bring to a boil over medium heat, and boil for 3 minutes, stirring constantly. Stir in blueberries, reduce heat, and simmer for 8-10 minutes or until berries have burst. Stir in butter until melted. Serve over French toast.

Corn Fritters

Serves: 4

1 1/2 pound fresh corn (or 2 large or 3 to 4 medium ears), husks and silk removed.
or
the equivalent in canned corn, 15 or 16 ounce can.
1 large egg, beaten lightly
3 tablespoons unbleached all-purpose flour
3 tablespoons fine-ground cornmeal
2 tablespoons heavy cream
1 small minced shallot
1/2 teaspoon salt
Pinch of cayenne pepper
1/2 cup corn or vegetable oil
Maple syrup to go over fritters

If you are using fresh corn, remove the kernels and place them in a bowl; or if using fresh kernels, empty a can and put it into the bowl. Stir in egg, flour, cornmeal, cream, shallot, salt and cayenne pepper. Heat oil in a large heavy-bottom, nonstick skillet over medium-high heat until shimmering. Drop 6 heaping tablespoons of batter in skillet. Fry until golden brown, about 1 minute per side. Transfer fritters to a paper towel-lined plate. If needed add more oil to skillet and heat until shimmering. Then fry remaining batter. Serve fritters immediately, with maple syrup if desired.

Old Tavern Corn Fritters

Serves: 8

1 cup all-purpose flour
1 1/2 teaspoon baking powder
2 eggs
1/3 cup milk
1 (15 1/4-ounce) can whole kernel corn , drained
1 tablespoon melted butter
Oil for deep-fat drying
Confectioners' sugar
Maple syrup, warmed

In a bowl, combine flour and baking powder set aside. In another bowl, beat the eggs and milk stir in corn and butter. Stir into dry ingredients just until blended. In a deep-fat fryer or electric skillet, heat oil to 375 degrees. Drop batter by heaping teaspoons into hot oil fry for 2 to 3 minutes or until golden brown. Drain on paper towels. Dust with confectioners' sugar. Serve with syrup.

Frosty Morning Oatmeal

Serves: 5

1/2 cup old-fashioned oats
1 cup water
1/4 cup dried cherries
Dash cinnamon
1/8 teaspoon salt
Brown sugar, walnuts, milk, as desired

Place oats, water, dried cherries, cinnamon, and salt in microwavable 2-cup bowl. Cook for 3 minutes, stir. Top with brown sugar, walnuts, and milk.

Homemade Granola Bars

Serves: 12

2 cups old-fashioned oatmeal
1 cup sliced almonds
1 cup shredded coconut, loosely packed
1/2 cup toasted wheat germ
.3 tablespoons unsalted butter
2/3 cup honey
1/4 cup light brown sugar, lightly packed
1 1/2 teaspoons pure vanilla extract
1/4 teaspoon kosher salt
1/2 cup chopped pitted dates
1/2 cup chopped dried apricots
1/2 cup dried cranberries

Preheat the oven to 350 degrees. Butter an 8 by 12-inch baking dish and line it with parchment paper.

Toss the oatmeal, almonds, and coconut together on a sheet pan and bake for 10 to 12 minutes, stirring occasionally, until lightly browned. Transfer the mixture to a large mixing bowl and stir in the wheat germ.

Reduce the oven temperature to 300 degrees.

Place the butter, honey, brown sugar, vanilla, and salt in a small saucepan and bring to a boil over medium heat. Cook and stir for a minute, then pour over the toasted oatmeal mixture. Add the dates, apricots, and cranberries and stir well.

Pour the mixture into the prepared pan. Wet your fingers and lightly press the mixture evenly into the pan. Bake for 25 to 30 minutes, until light golden brown. Cool for at least 2 to 3 hours before cutting into squares. Serve at room temperature.

Granola

Serves: 6

3 cups rolled oats
1 cup slivered almonds
1 cup cashews
3/4 cup shredded sweet coconut
1/4 cup plus 2 tablespoons dark brown sugar
1/4 cup plus 2 tablespoons maple syrup
1/4 cup vegetable oil
3/4 teaspoon salt
1 cup raisins

Preheat oven to 250 degrees. In a large bowl, combine the oats, nuts, coconut, and brown sugar. In a separate bowl, combine maple syrup, oil, and salt. Combine both mixtures and pour onto 2 sheet pans. Cook for 1 hour and 15 minutes, stirring every 15 minutes to achieve an even color. Remove from oven and transfer into a large bowl. Add raisins and mix until evenly distributed.

Granola To-Go Bars

Serves: 36

3 1/2 cups quick cooking oats
1 cup chopped almonds
1 egg beaten
2/3 cup butter, melted
1/2 cup honey
1 teaspoon vanilla
1/2 cup sunflower kernels
1/2 cup flaked coconut
1/2 cup chopped dried pineapple
1/2 cup dried cranberries
1/2 cup packed brown sugar
1/2 teaspoon ground cinnamon

Combine oats and almonds in a 15" x 10" x 1" baking pan coated with cooking spray. Bake at 350 degrees for 15 minutes or until toasted, stirring occasionally. In a large bowl, combine the egg, butter, honey and vanilla. Stir in the sunflower kernels, coconut, apples, cranberries, brown sugar and cinnamon. Stir in oat mixture. Press into a 15" x 10" x 1" baking pan coated with cooking spray. Bake at 350 degrees for 13-18 minutes or until set and edges are lightly browned. Cool on a wire rack. Cut into bars. Store in an air tight container.

Best Buttermilk Pancakes

Makes 9 6" pancakes

2 cups all-purpose flour
2 teaspoon baking powder
1 teaspoon baking soda
½ teaspoon salt
3 tablespoons sugar
2 large eggs, lightly beaten
3 cups buttermilk
4 tablespoons unsalted butter, melted, plus ½
teaspoon for griddle
1 cup fresh blueberries (optional)

Heat griddle to 375 degrees. Whisk flour, baking
powder, baking soda, salt, and sugar in a bowl. Add
eggs, buttermilk, and 4 tablespoons butter whisk
to combine. Batter should have small to medium
lumps.

Heat oven to 175 degrees. Test griddle by
sprinkling a few drops of water on it. If water
bounces and spatters off griddle, it is hot enough. Using a pastry brush, brush remaining ½ teaspoon of butter (you could also use reserved bacon grease) onto griddle. Wipe off excess.

Using a 4-oz ladle (which holds about ½ cup), pour batter in pools two inches apart. If using berries, scatter over *batter pools*. When the pancakes bubble on top and are slightly dry around the edges (which takes about 2½ minutes), flip. Cook until golden on bottom, about 1 minute. Repeat with remaining batter. Keep finished pancakes on a heat-proof plate in the oven.

Foolproof Popovers

Serves: 8

3 tablespoons melted butter , divided
2 eggs
1 cup milk, warmed in a microwave for 30 seconds (should be lukewarm)
1 cup all-purpose flour
1 teaspoon kosher salt

Preheat the oven to 400 degrees.

Using a pastry brush, or a paper towel, coat 8 muffin cups with 1 tablespoon of the melted butter and put the tin in the oven for 5 minutes. Meanwhile, mix the eggs in a blender until light yellow. Add the warmed milk and blend. Add the flour, salt and remaining melted butter, and blend until smooth. Pour the batter into the warmed muffin tin and return it to the oven to bake until golden, about 35 minutes. Remove from the oven and serve warm.

Favorite Oatmeal Pancakes

Serves: 12

1 1/4 cups all-purpose flour
1/2 cup oats (quick or old fashioned, uncooked)
2 teaspoons baking powder
1/4 teaspoon salt (optional)
1 1/4 cups fat-free milk
1 egg, lightly beaten
1 tablespoon vegetable oil

Optional Stir-ins (choose one)
 1 cup fresh or frozen blueberries (do not thaw)
 1 medium-size ripe banana, mashed, and 1/8 teaspoon ground nutmeg
 3/4 cup finely chopped apple, 1/4 cup chopped nuts and 1/2 teaspoon ground cinnamon
 1/2 cup semisweet chocolate chips

In large bowl, combine flour, oats, baking powder and salt; mix well. In medium bowl, combine milk, egg and oil; blend well. Add to dry ingredients all at once; stir just until dry ingredients are moistened. (Do not over-mix) Add one of the stir-in options, if desired; mix gently. Heat skillet over medium-high heat (or preheat electric skillet or griddle to 375degrees). Lightly grease skillet. For each pancake, pour 1/4 cup batter into hot skillet. Turn when tops are covered with bubbles and edges look cooked. Turn only once.

Pumpkin Pancakes w/Cinnamon Brown Butter

Serves: 7

1/2 cup butter, cubed
1/4 cup maple syrup
1/2 teaspoon ground cinnamon
1/4 teaspoon ground nutmeg
1/2 cup chopped pecan, toasted
1 1/2 all-purpose flour
2 tablespoons packed brown sugar
2 tablespoons baking powder
1 teaspoon salt
2 eggs
1 1/3 2% milk
3/4 cup canned pumpkin
1/2 cup ricotta cheese

In a small heavy saucepan, cook butter over medium heat for 8 to 10 minutes or until golden brown, stirring occasionally. Add the maple syrup, cinnamon and nutmeg. Remove from the heat; stir in the pecans.
In a small bowl, combine the flour, brown sugar, baking powder and salt. In another bowl, whisk the eggs, milk, pumpkin and cheese. Stir into dry ingredients just until moistened.
Drop batter by 1/4 cupful onto a greased hot griddle; turn when bubbles form on top. Cook until the second side is golden brown. Serve with maple syrup and toasted pecans and brown butter.

Pumpkin Bread

2/3 solid shortening
2 2/3 cups sugar
4 beaten eggs
2/3 cup canned pumpkin
2/3 cup water
3 1/3 cups flour
1/2 teaspoon baking powder
2 teaspoons baking soda
1 1/2 teaspoon salt
1 teaspoon cinnamon
1/2 teaspoon cloves
OPTIONAL:
2/3 cup pecan or other nuts or 2/3 cup dark raisins

Preheat oven to 350 degrees. Grease and flour two loaf pans. Cream shortening and sugar. Add eggs, pumpkin, and water. Sift together flour, baking powder, soda, salt, cinnamon, and cloves. Add nuts and raisins if desired. Mix together. Do not overbeat. Bake for an hour or until a toothpick inserted in the center comes out clean. .

Light, Crisp Waffles

Yield: 4 or 5   8" waffles

¾ cup all-purpose flour
¼ cup cornstarch
½ teaspoon salt
½ teaspoon baking powder
¼ teaspoon baking soda
¾ cup buttermilk
¼ cup milk
6 tablespoons vegetable oil
1 large egg, separated
1 tablespoons sugar
½ teaspoon vanilla

Heat the oven to 200 degrees and heat up the waffle iron. Mix the flour, cornstarch, salt, baking powder, and baking soda in a medium bowl. Measure the buttermilk, milk, and vegetable oil in a glass measuring cup; mix in the egg yolk and set aside. In another bowl, beat the egg white almost to soft peaks. Sprinkle in the sugar and continue to beat until the peaks are firm and glossy. Beat in the vanilla.

Pour the buttermilk mixture into the dry ingredients and whisk until just mixed. Drop the whipped egg white onto the batter in dollops and fold in with a spatula until just incorporated. Pour the batter onto the hot waffle iron (mine takes about 2/3 cup) and cook until the waffle is crisp and nutty brown. Set the waffle directly on the oven rack to keep it warm and crisp. Repeat with the remaining batter, holding the waffles in the oven (don't stack them). When all the waffles are cooked, serve immediately. Serve with melted butter and warm maple or brown sugar syrup.

Waffle- Making Tips

- Despite nonstick surfaces, you'll still need to grease most waffle irons the first few times you use them. Use a cooking spray.
- Use wooden utensils to preserve the integrity of non-stick surfaces.
- Start with about ½ cup of batter for the smallest irons and 2/3 cup for bigger ones; increase as necessary to fill out waffles.
- Don't open the waffle iron prematurely.
- The first waffle is usually a throwaway; adjust the amount of batter and the color control settings until you get the results you like.

Cream Scones

Makes: 1 dozen

2 cups all-purpose flour
1 tablespoons baking powder
¼ teaspoon salt
¼ cup sugar
1/3 cup butter, cut up
1 cup whipping cream

Combine first 4 ingredients. Cut in butter with a pastry blender or two forks until crumbly. Add whipping cream, stirring until just moistened. Turn out onto a lightly floured surface; knead 5 or 6 times. Roll to ½ inch thickness; cut with a 2 inch round cutter and place in lightly greased muffin pans or 2 inches apart on greased baking sheets. Bake at 375 degrees for 15 minutes or until golden brown. Serve with preserves and whipped cream.

Apple-Walnut Sausage Stuffing

Serves: 16

5 thinly sliced celery ribs
2 medium chopped onions
3 teaspoons rubbed sage
2 teaspoons dried thyme
1 cup cubed butter
3/4 cup grated parmesan cheese
1 tablespoon dried parsley
1 teaspoon salt
1/2 teaspoon pepper
1 pound bulk sausage
16 cups cubed day-old bread
5 medium tart apples, peeled and thinly sliced
1 (14 1/2-ounce) can chicken broth
1/2 cup chopped walnuts, optional

In a large skillet, sauté the celery, onions, sage, and thyme in butter until vegetables are tender. Transfer to a very large bowl cool slightly. Stir in the parmesan cheese, parsley, salt and pepper set aside.

In the same skillet, cook sausage over medium heat until no longer pink, then drain. Add to celery mixture. Add the bread cubes, apples, broth and walnuts toss to coat.

Transfer to a greased 3 quart baking dish (dish will be full). Cover and bake at 350 degrees for 25 minutes. Uncover and bake 10-15 minutes longer or until heated through and light browned.

Hashbrown Casserole

Serves: 14

13 ounce cream of chicken soup
9 to 10 ounce grated Colby cheese
1 medium onion, chopped
¾ cup melted margarine
½ teaspoon ground black pepper
2 teaspoons salt
3 pounds frozen shredded potatoes (1 bag)

Preheat convection oven to 350 degrees. Combine soup, cheese, onion, margarine, pepper, and salt. Add potatoes and mix until just blended. Pour mixture into casserole dish and bake, uncovered, for 30 minutes. Using a spatula, loosen the casserole from the sides of the pan. Cut into 12 equal portions and serve.

Variation: Mix in ham and/or bacon.

Quiche Lorraine

Serves: 6

5 ounces pie crust mix or preformed piecrust
1 tablespoon butter or margarine, softened
8 ounces sliced bacon diced, cooked, and cooled
1 medium onion chopped, sautéed, and cooled
4 eggs
2 cups heavy or whipping cream
¾ teaspoon salt
1 cup Swiss cheese, shredded

Prepare pie crust mix as label directs for a one crust pie. Use this to line a 9-inch pie plate. Spread the pie crust with butter or margarine. Refrigerate while preparing filling. Preheat oven to 425 degrees.

In a skillet over medium-low heat, cook bacon until browned and crisp. With slotted spoon, remove bacon to paper towels to drain.

Sauté onions either in a microwave or skillet.

In a medium-sized bowl, using a wire whisk or fork, mix eggs, cream, and salt until well blended.

Sprinkle bacon, onion, and cheese on pie crust. Please remember that anything you put into a pastry must be cool to the touch. Gently pour in the cream mixture.

Bake 15 minutes. Turn oven to 325 degrees and bake for another 35 minutes or until a knife inserted in the center comes out clean.

For other variations of quiche, try using cheddar cheese and pre-blanched vegetables (cooled).

Heavenly Bananas

Serves: 2

½ cup sour cream
2 tablespoon sugar
1 tablespoon orange juice
½teaspoon grated orange peel
1 banana for each serving
Granola

The night before serving, mix the sour cream, sugar, orange juice, and orange peel. Cover tightly and refrigerate. In the morning, slice one banana for each serving on a place. Stir the sour cream mixture. Top each banana with 2 to 3 Tablespoon. sauce. Sprinkle with granola and serve immediately.

Frozen Fruit Slush

Serves: 12

2 cups sugar
3 cups hot water
One 6 ounce can of frozen orange juice concentrate, diluted with 2 cans water
One 20 ounce can crushed pineapple, undrained
8 bananas, sliced
One 15 ounce can fruit cocktail

This will make a fairly large amount. Dissolve sugar in hot water and let cool. Add the remaining ingredients. Cover and freeze. Thaw for several hours to make a slush, then serve. **Tip:** Freeze in smaller, individual servings, which will thaw much faster.

Pizza Dough

Yield: 1 pizza crust

1 cup warm water
2 1/4 teaspoon dry yeast
1 teaspoon sugar
3 cups white flour or wheat flour
2 tablespoons olive oil
1 teaspoon salt
1 1/2 teaspoon Italian seasoning

In a bowl mix the yeast, sugar, and water, stirring to dissolve the yeast. Let it rest 5 minutes.   Add the other ingredients. Knead the dough on a floured board, adding more flour until it's not sticky. Place in a bowl and cover, letting it rise from five minutes to 2 hours, depending on the texture you would like. The longer you let it rise, the more bread-like the dough will become. Put a little oil on your pan and then spread out your dough. Be sure to not over work it. Then put on your favorite sauce, chesses, and toppings. Bake at 375 or 400 degrees till done.

Homemade Rice-a-Roni

Serves: 6

3 tablespoons butter or margarine
2 boneless skinless chicken breasts
(or any meat that is on sale!)
1 large onion, finely chopped
1 cup carrots, shredded
1 cup corn (fresh or frozen)
2 garlic cloves, crushed
1 cup long-grain white rice
2 cups chicken stock
½ teaspoon salt
Fresh or dried cilantro or parsley (optional)

Melt butter in a 2 qt. pan over med-high heat. Add onion, carrots and corn. Cook through until onions are soft (about 5 min). Stir in garlic and rice; stirring constantly, continue cooking until rice begins to brown slightly. Add stock and salt: cover and simmer until rice is tender and liquid is absorbed. (About 20 min) Stir in cilantro or parsley if desired.

This is a great recipe because it is so versatile and super cheap to make. If you start with the rice and stock you can change up the veggies or meats and use whatever you have on hand. Get rid of the meat and you have great side dish! Enjoy!

Chicken Flavored Rice Mix

Serves: 4

1 cup uncooked long-grain rice
1 tablespoon instant chicken bouillon
1 tablespoon parsley flakes
1 teaspoon celery flakes
1 teaspoon dried minced onions
1 teaspoon sugar
1/2 teaspoon salt
1 teaspoon of graded carrots

Combine all ingredients in an airtight container. Decorate as desired. Label with these instructions: "In a saucepan combine the rice mix with 2 cups water and 2 tablespoons butter or margarine. Cover and bring to a boil. Reduce heat and simmer for 15 minutes or until rice is tender. Makes 3 cups. **Note**: Add cooked, cubed chicken for a full-meal deal!"

Homemade Cool Whip

Yield: 2 cups

1 teaspoon of gelatin
2 teaspoons of cold water
3 tablespoons of boiling water
½ cup ice water
½ nonfat dry milk powder
4 tablespoons sugar (or more if desired)
3 tablespoons oil
2 teaspoons vanilla

Chill a small bowl. Soften gelatin with 2 teaspoons of cold water, then add the boiling water, stirring until gelatin is completely dissolved; cool until tepid (almost room temperature). Place ice water and dry milk power in the chilled bowl. Beat at high speed, until mixture forms stiff peaks; add sugar and vanilla, still beating, then oil and gelatin. Place in freezer for about 15 minutes, then transfer to refrigerator until ready to use. Stir just before using, to retain creamy texture. Do not double recipe or the mixture will not thicken. Also 1 teaspoon pure vanilla may be added if desired.

.Marshmallows

Yield: 30

Nonstick cooking spray
3 (1/4-ounce) packages unflavored gelatin
1/2 cup cold water
2 cups granulated sugar
2/3 cup light corn syrup
1/4 teaspoon coarse salt
1 teaspoon pure vanilla extract, plus 1 vanilla bean (slice the bean in half, scraping the seeds off the pod, and using only the seeds)
Confectioners' sugar, sifted, for coating

Lightly spray a 9 x 9 inch baking pan with cooking spray. Line pan with plastic wrap, leaving a 2-inch overhang on all sides; set aside.

In the bowl of an electric mixer fitted with the whisk attachment, sprinkle gelatin over 1/2 cup cold water; let stand for 10 minutes. In a medium saucepan, combine sugar, corn syrup, and 1/4 cup water. Place saucepan over medium-high heat and bring to a boil; boil rapidly for 1 minute. Remove from heat, and, with the mixer on high, slowly pour the boiling syrup down the side of the mixer bowl into gelatin mixture. Add salt and continue mixing for 12 minutes.

Add vanilla extract and vanilla bean seeds; mix until well combined. Spray a rubber spatula or your hands with cooking spray. Spread gelatin mixture evenly into pan using prepared spatula or your hands. Spray a sheet of plastic wrap with cooking spray and place, spray side down, on top of marshmallows. Let stand for 2 hours.

Carefully remove marshmallows from pan. Remove all plastic wrap and discard. Cut marshmallows into 2-inch squares using a sprayed sharp knife. Place confectioners' sugar in a large bowl. Working in batches, add marshmallows to bowl and toss to coat.

Morning Glory Muffins

1/2 cup (2 1/2 ounces) raisins
2 cups (8 1/2 ounces) unbleached all-purpose flour
1 cup (7 ounces) sugar
2 teaspoons baking soda
2 teaspoons cinnamon
1/2 teaspoon ground ginger
1/2 teaspoon salt
2 cups (7 ounces) peeled, grated carrots
1 large apple (a tart variety is best), peeled and chopped
1/2 cup (1 1/2 ounces) sweetened coconut
1/2 cup (2 ounces) sliced almonds or chopped walnuts
1/3 cup (1 1/2 ounces) sunflower seeds or wheat germ (optional)
3 large eggs
2/3 cup (4 5/8 ounces) vegetable oil
2 teaspoons vanilla

Put the raisins in a small bowl, cover them with hot water, and set them aside to soak while you assemble the rest of the recipe.

In a large mixing bowl, whisk together the flour, sugar, baking soda, spices, and salt. Stir in the carrots, apple, coconut, nuts and sunflower seeds or wheat germ, if you're using them. In a separate bowl, beat the eggs, oil, and vanilla. Add this to the flour mixture, and stir until evenly combined. Divide the batter among 12 greased large-sized muffin cups (or 15 medium-sized ones), heaping the cups full. Bake the muffins in a preheated 375°F oven for 20 to 25 minutes, until they're golden brown. Remove them from the oven, and let them cool for 5 minutes before turning them out of the pan to cool completely on a rack. Yield: 12 large muffins, or 15 medium-sized muffins.

Appetizers

Apple Dip

Serves: 8

1 (8 ounce) package cream cheese
1/2 cup brown sugar
1 teaspoon vanilla extract

In a medium-sized mixing bowl, combine cream cheese, brown sugar and vanilla. Mix well until all of the brown sugar has been blended into the cream cheese and vanilla. If the mixture is too runny for your taste, add a small amount of brown sugar to the mixture. If the mixture is too thick for your taste, add a small amount of milk.

Cheddar Cheese Ball

2 ½ cups shredded white cheddar cheese
1/3 cup grated onion (finely diced)
2 tablespoons mayo (use a little more if cheese isn't binding together to your satisfaction)
½ cup red raspberry preserves
Triscuits crackers

Shred white cheddar cheese until you have 2 1/2 cups. Combine cheese, onion and mayo. Form into a ball, then flatten it a bit so that the preserves don't fall off. Spread preserves on top of the ball. Garnish with fresh raspberries. Spread on Triscuit crackers.

Chicken Roll-Ups

1 loaf very fresh sandwich bread
1 can chicken spread
Worchester sauce to taste
1 lb. lean bacon
Pepper to taste

Mix chicken spread, Worchester sauce and pepper together. Trim all crust off bread. Take one slice of bread and flatten it with the palm of your hand, onto the counter. Spread mixture onto slice. Then roll up (in jelly roll fashion) and cut into 3 equal parts. Cut bacon strip in ^{1}/3 (or ½ depending on size) and wrap it around the bread, securing it with a toothpick. Bake in a convection oven or a regular oven at 350 degrees until brown. I also put them on a grilling rack in a pan, so that they do not sit in grease.

Prosciutto & Melon

Serves: 16

You couldn't ask for anything any easier. Cut a fragrant ripe melon into approximately 1-inch pieces. Wrap a piece of prosciutto around each piece and secure with a toothpick. That's it! You could also marinate the melon in your favorite liquor first.

Mini Pizzas

Serves: 8

1 pound sausage
1 pound. ground chuck
1 chopped medium onion
1 pound Velveeta cheese
1 loaf cocktail party rye bread

Sauté onion in a little butter add meat and brown. Add cheese and cook over low heat until the cheese is melted. Spoon onto rye, place on cookie baking sheet and freeze. Then store in bags in freezer until needed.
If not frozen, bake at 400 degrees until hot and brown, about 5 to 7 minutes. If frozen, you may need to bake a little longer. Serve while hot. Teenagers love these!

Crab Rangoon

Yield: 48 pieces (2 per person)

8 ounces cream cheese
8 ounces fresh crab meat or canned crab meat, drained and flaked
1 teaspoon red onion, chopped
1/2 teaspoon Worcestershire sauce
1/2 teaspoon light soy sauce
Freshly ground black pepper, to taste
1 green onion, finely sliced
1 large clove garlic, smashed, peeled, and finely minced
1 package won ton wrappers
1 small bowl water
Oil for deep-frying, as needed

Combine the cream cheese and crab meat. Mix in the remaining six filling ingredients (up to the wonton wrappers) one at a time. On a flat surface, lay out a won ton wrapper in front of you so that it forms 2 triangles (not a square). Wet the edges of the won ton. Add 1 teaspoon of filling to the middle, and spread it out toward the left and right points of the wrapper so that it forms a log or rectangular shape (otherwise the wrapper may break in the middle during deep-frying). Fold over the edges of the wrapper to make a triangle. Wet the edges with water and press together to seal. Keep the completed Crab Rangoon covered with a damp towel or paper towel to keep them from drying out while preparing the remainder. Heat wok and add oil for deep-frying. When oil is ready (the temperature should be between 360 - 375 degrees), carefully slide in the Crab Rangoon, taking care not to overcrowd the wok. Deep-fry until they are golden brown, about 3 minutes, turning once. Remove with a slotted spoon and drain. Serve hot with Sweet and Sour Sauce or Chinese Hot Mustard.

Crostini

Grape Crostini:
Spread toasted baguette slices with goat cheese. Top with chopped seedless red grapes, thinly sliced green onions, minced fresh rosemary, and salt and pepper to taste. Drizzle with store-bought balsamic glaze.

Goat Cheese & Strawberries:
Spread goat cheese on toasted baguette slices. Spread red pepper jelly on top of goat cheese.   Top with sliced strawberries & fresh watercress.

Goat Cheese & Onion Jelly:
Brush olive oil onto your baguette slice and toast. Then spread with goat cheese, and some onion jelly. Yum!

Deviled Eggs

Yield: 24 halves

12 Eggs
1 teaspoon dry mustard
Dash of pepper
1/3 cup mayonnaise
1 tablespoon vinegar
1 teaspoon Worcestershire sauce
Paprika

Place eggs in large saucepan cover eggs with cold water. Bring to a boil. Reduce heat simmer about 12 minutes. Immediately drain run cold water over eggs to stop cooking.

Peel eggs halve lengthwise. Remove yolks place in small bowl. Mash yolks with fork. I sometimes cut a little bit of the white out if there doesn't seem to be enough space to put the yolk back in.

Add all remaining ingredients except paprika mix until fluffy. Spoon or pipe mixture into egg white halves. Sprinkle with paprika.

Optional: you can also add capers, bacon bits, chopped olives, or other mix-ins to the yolk mixture for variety.

Nutrition Information Per Serving: 1 Deviled Egg * Calories: 120 * Calories from Fat: 90 * % Daily Value: Total Fat: 10 g 15% * Saturated Fat: 2 g 10% * Cholesterol: 215 mg 72% * Sodium: 100 mg 4% * Total Carbohydrate: 1 g 1% * Dietary Fiber: 0 g 0% * Sugars: 1 g * Protein: 6 g * Vitamin A: 8% * Vitamin C: 0% * Calcium: 2% * Iron: 4% * Dietary Exchanges: 1 Medium-Fat Meat, 1 Fat

Black Bean Hummus

Serves: 4

1 cup cooked black beans
1 clove minced garlic
2 tablespoons olive oil
2 tablespoons lemon juice
1 tablespoon white wine vinegar
1/2 teaspoon ground cumin
Kosher salt
Pepper
1/2 head iceberg lettuce, cut into wedges

Blend all the ingredients, except the lettuce, in a food process until almost smooth. Let sit for 15 minutes before serving with iceberg lettuce wedges.

Bacon-Wrapped Water Chestnuts

Serves: 6

This is a fancy-looking appetizer that appears to be a lot more expensive than it actually is, especially when you get the bacon and syrup on sale!

1 package Oscar Mayer center-cut bacon
1 (8-ounce) can whole water chestnuts
toothpicks
maple syrup

Preheat oven to 350 degrees. Wrap 1/2 piece of a bacon strip around a whole water chestnut. Then put a toothpick to secure. Cook either in a convection oven or a regular oven. Remove when done and drizzle with maple syrup. Approximately 25-35 minutes to cook (when bacon is done).

Vegetables

Oven Roasted Vegetables

Serves: 4

1 1/2 fresh cauliflower, florets
1 cup fresh broccoli, florets and stalks, cut into 3/4" pieces
3 medium red potatoes, cut into 1" pieces, leave skin on
1 tablespoon olive oil
2 cloves minced garlic
1 teaspoon dried basil
1/4 teaspoon pepper
2 teaspoons grated parmesan cheese

Preheat oven to 375 degrees.

Combine vegetables and 3 tablespoons water in a large bowl toss to coat. Add remaining ingredients except cheese; toss to mix.

Spread vegetable mixture in a 15 x 10 jelly-roll pan sprayed with non-stick cooking spray. Roast vegetables 35 to 40 minutes or until just tender, stirring once or twice. Sprinkle with parmesan and mix lightly.

Roast 5 to 10 minutes more to desired doneness.

Beets in Orange Sauce

Serves: 8

8 whole fresh beets
1/4 cup sugar
2 teaspoons cornstarch
Dash pepper
1 cup orange juice
1 medium navel orange, halved and sliced, optional
1/2 teaspoon grated orange peel

Place beets in a large saucepan and cover with water. Bring to a boil. Reduce heat cover and cook for 25-30 minutes or until tender. Drain and cool slightly. Peel and slice place in a serving bowl and keep warm. In a small saucepan, combine the sugar, cornstarch and pepper stir in orange juice until smooth. Bring to a boil cook and stir for 2 minutes or until thickened. Remove from the heat stir in orange slices if desired and peel. Pour over beets. **Note**: A 15-ounce can of sliced beets may be substituted for the fresh beets. Drain the canned beets and omit the first step of the recipe.

Nutritional Information: 1 cup equals 63 calories, trace fat (trace saturated fat), 0 cholesterol, 39 mg sodium, 15 g carbohydrate, 1 g fiber, 1 g protein.

Carrot Casserole

Serves: 6 to 8

2 pounds carrots, sliced into bite sizes
1 cup Miracle Whip
4 tablespoons diced onions
4 tablespoons prepared horseradish
½ teaspoon salt
Pinch of pepper
¾ cup crushed saltine crackers (about 21)
5 teaspoons melted butter

In a saucepan, cook carrots, covered, in boiling salted water 10 minutes or until tender. Drain. Place in a shallow casserole dish. Combine Miracle Whip, onion, horseradish, salt, and pepper, and spoon over carrots. Mix cracker crumbs and melted butter; sprinkle over mixture. Bake uncovered in a 350 degree oven for 30 minutes or until hot.

Best Ever Creamed Corn

Serves: 4 to 6

1½ tablespoon butter
1½ tablespoon flour
½teaspoon salt
1½ cups whipping cream
2 tablespoons sugar
3 cups fresh, frozen, or canned whole kernel corn

Melt butter in heavy saucepan add flour and salt, stirring to blend. Slowly add whipping cream, stirring constantly until thickened. Add sugar and corn heat.

Au Gratin variation: Place corn in 9 or 10-inch shallow casserole dish. Sprinkle with ¼ cup freshly grated parmesan cheese and brown under broiler.

Green Bean Casserole

Serves: 6

1 (16-ounce) can French-style green bean
1 (2.8-ounce) can French-fried onions
1 10.75 ounce can cream of mushroom soup

Preheat oven to 450 degrees. Mix green beans, cream of mushroom soup, and 1/2 can of french-fried onion together in a 1 1/2 quart casserole. Sprinkle with reminder of onions. Bake uncovered for about 25 minutes or until bubbly around the edges.

Sweet Corn Pudding

Serves: 8

1/2 cup chopped bacon
2 tablespoons butter
1 cup chopped onion
4 ears sweet corn, or one 15 oz can
1 1/2 teaspoon salt
1/4 teaspoon cayenne pepper
6 eggs
2 cups heavy cream
1 cup milk
1/4 teaspoon fresh ground pepper
1/8 teaspoon nutmeg
1/2 cup grated parmesan cheese
1/2 cup yellow cornmeal

Preheat oven to 375 degrees.
In a sauté pan, over a low flame, place the chopped bacon and cook until it's crisp. Remove it from the pan, reserving the fat. Add the butter to it and sauté the onions until translucent. Add the corn kernels, salt, and cayenne pepper and sauté a few minutes more to cook the corn. Remove from the heat. In a bowl, whisk the eggs swell then add the cream and milk and whisk some more until well combined. Add the pepper, nutmeg, Parmesan, and cornmeal and whisk to combine. Stir in the bacon, onion, and corn mixture and pour into a greased 6 cup casserole dish. Bake for 1 hour. Serve immediately.

Red Beans and Rice

Serves: 10
Yield: 1 cup servings

1 pound dried red kidney beans
1/2 pound Andouille smoked sausage, thinly sliced
3 celery ribs, chopped
1 green bell pepper, chopped
1 medium onion, chopped
3 cloves garlic, minced
1 tablespoon Creole seasoning
3 cups uncooked long-grain rice
Garnish:
Sliced green onions

Place beans in a Dutch oven; add water until 2 inches above the beans. Bring to a boil. Boil 1 minute; cover, remove from heat and allow beans to soak 1 hour. Drain.

Sauté sausage, celery, bell pepper and onion in the Dutch oven over medium-high heat for 10 minutes or until sausage is browned. Add garlic; sauté 1 minute more. Add beans, Creole seasoning and 7 cups of water. Bring to a boil; reduce heat to low; and simmer 1 to 1 1/2 hours or until beans are tender.

Meanwhile, cook rice according to package directions. Serve with red bean mixture. Garnish if desired.

Salads

Strawberry Pretzel Jell-O Salad

Serves: 8

2 cups crushed pretzel
3/4 cup melted butter
3 tablespoons plus 3/4 cup sugar
1 (8-ounce) package cream cheese
1 (8-ounce) container whipped topping
2 (3-ounce) packages strawberry gelatin dessert mix
2 cups boiling water , measure after water boils
2 (10-ounce) bags frozen strawberries
1 (8-ounce) can crushed pineapple
Whipped topping to garnish

Hint: If your frozen strawberries are whole, you might try cutting them in half (top to bottom) to make them spread more easily.

You can also make this salad with orange Jell-O and mandarin oranges or lime Jell-O with pineapple and mandarin oranges.

Heat oven to 400 degrees. For the crust, mix the pretzels, butter, and 3 tablespoons of sugar. Press this mixture into a 9 x 13 inch pan and bake for 7 minutes. Set aside and allow to cool. In a mixing bowl, beat together the cream cheese and 3/4 cup of sugar. Fold in the whipped topping and spread over the cooled crust. Refrigerate until well chilled. In a small bowl, dissolve the gelatin in the boiling water, and allow to cool slightly. Add the strawberries and pineapple, and pour over the cream cheese mixture. Refrigerate until serving time.
To serve, cut slices and serve with a dollop of whipped topping.

Watergate Salad

Serves: 8

1 package (4-serving size) Jell-O Pistachio Flavor Instant Pudding & Pie Filling
1 can (20 ounce) crushed pineapple in juice, undrained
1 cup miniature marshmallows
2 cans mandarin oranges
2 cups thawed Cool-Whip

Stir pudding mix, pineapple with juice, marshmallows, and oranges in large bowl until well blended. Gently stir in whipped topping.

Refrigerate for 1 hour or until ready to serve. Garnish as desired.

Note: Do not use fresh or frozen pineapple, kiwi, gingerroot, papaya, figs, or guava in any gelatin salad. An enzyme in these fruits will prevent the gelatin from setting.

Canned Bean Salad

Serves: 8

3/4 cup Pace® Picante Sauce
2 tablespoons chopped fresh cilantro leaves
2 tablespoons red wine vinegar
1 tablespoon vegetable oil
1 large green pepper, diced (about 1 cup)
1 medium red onion, very thinly sliced (about 1/2 cup)
1 can (about 15 ounces) kidney beans, rinsed and drained
1 can (about 15 ounces) pinto beans, rinsed and drained

Stir the picante sauce, cilantro, vinegar, oil, pepper, onion, kidney beans and pinto beans in a medium bowl. Cover and refrigerate for 2 hours, stirring occasionally during chilling time. Garnish with additional cilantro.

Festive Fruit Salad

Serves: 12-16

1   15 ounce can of mandarin oranges, drained
1 ½ cups red seedless grapes, halved
1 ½ cups green grapes, halved
1   10 ounce jar each of red and green maraschino cherries, halved, rinsed and drained
1   8 ounce can of unsweetened pineapple chunks, drained
2 cups miniature marshmallows
1 cup flaked coconut
1 cup of sour cream

In a large bowl, combine all ingredients except sour cream. Just before serving, add sour cream and toss to coat.

Waldorf Chicken Salad with Cantaloupe

Serves: 4

1 cup vanilla yogurt
¼ teaspoon apple pie spice or pumpkin pie spice
Dash of salt
1 cup chopped pear or chopped apple
1 teaspoon lemon juice
2 cups chopped cooked chicken (10 ounce)
1 cup halved seedless red or green grapes
½ cup chopped celery
2 tablespoons sliced green onion
1 small cantaloupe
Red-tip leaf lettuce
¼ cup slivered almonds, toasted

For dressing, in a small mixing bowl combine yogurt, apple pie or pumpkin pie spice, and salt. Set aside. In a medium mixing bowl, toss pear or apple with lemon juice. Stir in chicken, grapes, celery, and green onion. Pour dressing over chicken mixture. Toss lightly to coat. Cover chill for 2 to 24 hours. Serve, cut cantaloupe into 4 wedges. Remove seeds and, if desired, the rind. Place cantaloupe wedges on lettuce-lined salad plates. Stir toasted almonds into turkey mixture. Spoon onto melon wedges.

Mandarin Orange Salad

Serves: 4

1/2 cups slivered almonds
3 tablespoons sugar
1/2 head iceberg lettuce
1/2 head romaine lettuce
1 cup celery , chopped
1 (11-ounce) can mandarin oranges
2 whole green onions, chopped

Salad Dressing:
1/2 teaspoon salt
Dash of pepper
1/4 cup vegetable oil
1 tablespoon chopped parsley (optional)
2 tablespoons sugar
2 tablespoons white vinegar
Dash of Tabasco sauce

In a small pan over medium heat, cook almonds and sugar, stirring constantly, until almonds are coated and sugar is dissolved. Watch carefully as they will easily burn. Cool and store in an airtight container. Mix all dressing ingredients and chill. I make this dressing in quart batches, because it is great on any salad with fruit and greens. If you want to do this, mix 2 cups oil, 1 cup sugar, and 1 cup vinegar. Put it in a glass quart container and shake, shake, shake. Combine lettuces, celery and onions. Just before serving, sprinkle almonds and oranges on top of lettuce and pour on dressing.

Variations include:
Strawberries and feta cheese
Berries and candied walnuts
Bananas, oranges and almonds
Use your imagination and don't be afraid to experiment!

Fruit Salad Dressing

Serves: 8 ¼ cup serving

½ cup sugar
½ teaspoon salt
½ teaspoon dry mustard
½ cup cider vinegar
2 eggs, beaten
2 tablespoons butter or margarine
1 cup whipping cream
½ teaspoon vanilla

Combine sugar, salt, dry mustard, and vinegar in small saucepan. Bring mixture to a boil, stirring occasionally. Slowly pour the hot mixture into the beaten eggs, stirring constantly to prevent curdling. Return the mixture to a saucepan and cook until thickened. Stir in butter. Cool and refrigerate. In a small bowl with electric mixer at medium speed, beat cream until stiff peaks form; fold in vanilla and cooled egg mixture. Cover tightly with plastic wrap and refrigerate.

Soups

Cold Strawberry Soup

Serves: 4

2 pints fresh strawberries, washed and hulled
1½ cups sugar
¾ cup sour cream
1 cup half-and-half
1½ cups dry white wine (preferably Chablis or Moselle)
Whipped cream to garnish (optional)

Reserve 2 or 3 strawberries to garnish.

Puree remaining berries with sugar in a blender or processor. Strain through a fine sieve into a 3-quart bowl. Whisk in the sour cream, then the half-and-half and the wine. Serve in well-chilled cups, garnished with a halved strawberry or whipped cream.

Autumn Chowder

Serves: 4

4 strips bacon, diced
1/2 cup onion, chopped
2 medium red potatoes, cubed
2 small carrots, halved lengthwise and thinly sliced
1 cup water
1 1/2 teaspoon chicken bouillon granules
2 cups milk
1 1/3 cup frozen corn
1/4 teaspoon pepper
1 tablespoon plus 2 teaspoons flour
1/4 cup cold water
1 1/2 shredded cheddar cheese

In a large sauce pan, cook bacon over medium heat until crisp remove to paper towels. Drain reserving 2 teaspoons of drippings. In the drippings, sauté onion until tender. Add the potato, carrots, water and bouillon. Bring to a boil. Reduce heat cover and simmer for 15-20 minutes or until the vegetables are almost tender.

Stir in the milk, corn, and pepper. Cook 5 minutes longer. Combine the flour and cold water, mix until smooth and gradually whisk into soup. Bring to a boil. Reduce heat cook and stir for 1-2 minutes or until thickened. Remove from heat; stir in cheese until melted. Sprinkle with bacon.

Acorn Squash Soup

Serves: 4-6

2 medium acorn squash or butternut squash, about 3 pounds
3 cups chicken broth
3 cups half and half
1/3 cup firmly packed brown sugar
1 teaspoon ground cinnamon
1/4 teaspoon ground nutmeg
1/4 cup creamy peanut butter (optional)

Preheat oven to 350 degrees. Cut each squash in half lengthwise remove and discard seeds and membranes. Place squash halves, cut side down, in 2 lightly greased baking pans. Bake uncovered, 1 hour. Let cool scrape out pulp and discard rind. Position knife blade in food processor bowl add pulp and process 2 minutes or until smooth.

Combine pureed squash, chicken broth, half-and-half, brown sugar, cinnamon and nutmeg in a large Dutch oven stir well. Cook uncovered, over low heat 15 minutes or until mixture is thoroughly heated, stirring occasionally. If desired, whisk peanut butter with 1 cup hot soup in medium bowl until smooth stir peanut butter mixture into soup and cook 5 minutes more.

Apple Pumpkin Soup

Serves: 12

2 finely chopped peeled tart apples
1/2 cup finely chopped onion
2 tablespoons butter
1 tablespoon all-purpose flour
4 cups chicken broth
3 cups canned pumpkin
1/4 cup packed brown sugar
1/2 teaspoon ground cinnamon
1/2 teaspoon ground nutmeg
1/2 teaspoon ground ginger
1 cup unsweetened apple juice
1/2 cup half and half
1/4 teaspoon salt
1/2 teaspoon pepper

In a large saucepan, sauté apples and onion in butter for 3-5 minutes or until tender. Stir in flour until blended. Gradually whisk in broth. Stir in the pumpkin, brown sugar, cinnamon, nutmeg, and ginger. Bring to a boil. Reduce heat cover and simmer for 25 minutes. Cool slightly.

In a blender, cover and process soup in batches until smooth. Pour soup into a bowl cover and refrigerate for 8 hours or overnight.

Just before serving, transfer soup to a large saucepan. Cook over medium heat for 5 to 10 minutes. Stir in the apple juice, cream, salt and pepper, heat through.

Chicken Noodle Soup

Serves: 8
Approximately $1.00 per serving.   Can cut this down further if you only use chicken thighs when on sale.

Stock:
1 (3-4 pound) fryer chicken, cut up
3 1/2 quarts water
1 onion, peeled and diced
1 1/2 to 2 teaspoons Italian seasoning
1 teaspoon lemon-pepper seasoning
3 cloves garlic, minced
3 bay leaves
3 chicken bouillon cubes or chicken base to taste
Kosher salt and freshly ground black pepper

Soup:
2 cups sliced carrots
2 cups sliced celery, with leafy green tops
2 1/2 cups uncooked egg noodles
1 cup sliced mushrooms (optional)
1 cup of small diced onions
3 tablespoons chopped fresh parsley leaves
1/3 cup cooking sherry or wine
2 teaspoons chopped fresh rosemary leaves
Seasoning salt
Freshly ground black pepper

For the stock: add all ingredients to a soup pot. Cook until chicken is tender, about 35 to 45 minutes. Remove chicken from pot and set aside to cool. Remove and discard bay leaves and onion. You should have approximately 3 quarts of stock. When chicken is cool enough to touch, remove meat from bones, discarding bones, skin, and cartilage. Set chicken aside.

For the soup: bring stock back to a boil, add carrots, onion, and cook for 3 minutes. Add celery and continue to cook for 10 minutes. Add egg noodles and cook according to directions on package. When noodles are done, add chicken, mushrooms, parsley, sherry and rosemary.

Optional: Add parmesan and cream (your own personal preference if using) nb. Cook for another 2 minutes. Adjust seasoning, if needed, by adding seasoning salt and pepper. Serve with hot crusty bread.

Fresh Tomato Soup

2 tablespoons olive oil
1 tablespoon butter
2 large onions, chopped
2 garlic cloves
2 celery ribs, chopped
2 tablespoons all-purpose flour
10 large, very ripe tomatoes, coarsely chopped, juice reserved
2-3 teaspoons sugar
1 teaspoon dried basil
¾ teaspoon salt
¼ teaspoon black pepper

Heat oil and butter in a large stockpot over medium heat. Add the onions, garlic and celery. Cook until very soft but not brown, 6 to 8 minutes. Add the flour and cook 1 minute more stirring frequently.

Add tomatoes, reserved tomato juice, sugar, basil, salt, and pepper. Bring to a gentle boil. Skim the surface of the soup and discard any foam. Simmer 10 minutes.

Run the soup through the fine blade of a food mill or press it through a coarse strainer, discarding the solids. Return the soup to the pot to rewarm.

Cream of Tomato Soup

Makes 4 ½ cups

4 tablespoons plus 2 teaspoons unsalted butter
1 medium sweet onion, coarsely chopped
3 cups of peeled, seeded, or cut-up tomatoes (canned or fresh)
2 cups chicken broth
½ cup heavy cream
Salt to taste

Melt 4 tablespoons butter in a large saucepan over medium-high heat until it just start to brown. Add the onion and cook until translucent and starting to brown, about 2 minutes. Put in the tomatoes and cook until soft, about 3 minutes. Add the chicken broth and bring to a soft boil. Turn the heat down and simmer for 5 minutes.

Puree the soup in a food processor fitted with the metal blade or a blender. Return the soup to the pot and bring to a boil.

Add the heavy cream and 2 teaspoons butter continuing to heat until the butter is melted and the soup is hot. Season with salt.

This soup will stay fresh in the refrigerator 3 to 5 days.

Ham & Corn Chowder

Serves: 6
Approximate 75 cents per serving.

1 (10) 3/4-oz can cream of celery soup , undiluted
1 1/2 cup milk
1 (15 1/4-ounce) can whole corn , drained
1 (15-ounce) can creamed-style corn
1/2 cup cubed fully cooked ham
1/3 cup minced onion
2 teaspoons dried parsley
1 (14 1/2-ounce) can diced potato, drained
Sour cream, shredded cheddar cheese or paprika for toppings

In a large saucepan, combine soup and milk. Hear through, stirring frequently. Sauté onion in a skillet with 1 tablespoon of oil till translucent. Stir onion, corn, ham and parsley into soup mixture. Bring to a boil. Reduce heat: Cover & simmer for 5 minutes. Stir in potatoes heat through. Garnish with sour cream, cheese or paprika.

White Chicken Chili

Serves: 8
Approximate 62 cents per serving.

2 pounds boneless, skinless chicken thighs
1 large green bell pepper seeded & chopped
1 small onion, diced
1 (14.5-oz) can chicken broth
1/2 teaspoon ground cumin
1/4 teaspoon black pepper
1 (10-ounce) package frozen corn kernels, thawed
1 Tablespoon dried cilantro

Place chicken thighs in a slow cooker and top with green pepper and onion. In a blender, combine chicken broth, salsa and 1 can of beans (drained & rinsed). Puree until smooth. Add to slow cooker, along with cumin and black pepper. Cover and slow cook to 6 hours on HIGH or 8 hours on LOW. Uncover, and remove chicken thighs to cutting board. Stir in corn, remaining can of beans (drained and rinsed), and cilantro into slow cooker. Shred chicken and return to slow cooker.

Serve with tortilla chips, if desired.

Nutritional Information: 330 Calories; 7 g fat (2 g sat); 33 g protein; 36 g carbohydrate; 9 g fiber; 460 mg sodium, 110 mg cholesterol.

Hearty Bean Soup

Serves: 6

Ingredients
3 cups chopped parsnips
2 cups chopped carrots
1 cup chopped onion
1-1/2 cups dried great northern beans
5 cups water
1-1/2 pounds smoked ham hocks or ham shanks
2 garlic cloves, minced
2 teaspoons salt
1/2 teaspoon pepper
1/8 to 1/4 teaspoon hot pepper sauce

In a 5-qt. slow cooker, place parsnips, carrots and onion. Top with beans. Add water, ham, garlic, salt, pepper and hot pepper sauce. Cover and cook on high for 6-7 hours or until beans are tender.
Remove meat and bones when cool enough to handle. Cut meat into bite-size pieces and return to slow cooker heat through.

Corn Chowder

Serves: 4

2 tablespoons butter
4 scallions, white bulbs and green tops chopped and reserved separately
1 red bell pepper, chopped
2 ribs celery, chopped
1 pound boiling potatoes (about 3), peeled and cut into 1/2-inch dices
4 cups fresh corn kernels (cut from about 8 ears)
1 bay leaf
1 quart canned low-sodium chicken broth or homemade stock
2 teaspoons salt
2 cups milk
1/4 teaspoon fresh-ground black pepper
Sour cream, for topping (optional)

In a large saucepan, melt the butter over moderately low heat. Add the scallion bulbs, bell pepper, and celery and cook, stirring occasionally, until the vegetables start to soften, about 10 minutes. Stir in the potatoes, 2 cups of the corn, the bay leaf, broth, and salt. Bring to a boil. Reduce the heat and simmer, stirring occasionally, for 15 minutes.

In a blender or food processor, puree the remaining 2 cups corn with the milk. Stir the puree into the soup along with the black pepper. Simmer until the soup thickens slightly, 5 to 10 minutes. Remove the bay leaf. Stir in the scallion greens. Top each serving with a dollop of sour cream, if using.

Notes: If you want to use frozen corn, puree two cups of it with the milk as directed above, and add the remaining two cups to the soup along with the puree. Since the corn is already cooked, it could toughen if it goes in earlier. You could add a pinch of sugar, too.

Traditional Gazpacho

Serves: 6

6 to 8 large beefsteak tomatoes or other full-flavored ones
1 small sweet red onion chopped
4 cloves garlic
6 tablespoons red wine vinegar
2 regular cucumbers halved, peeled, seeded and diced
1/2 cup plus 2 tablespoon extra-virgin olive oil
Salt and pepper to taste
3 slices bread slices w/crusts removed & cut into 1" cubes
1 small green bell peppers seeded and finely diced
1/4 cup finely minced red onion

Bring a large saucepan 3/4 full of water to boil over high heat. Have ready a large bowl of ice water. Meanwhile, cut a shallow cross in the blossom end of each tomato and then remove the core. Carefully slip the tomatoes into the boiling water for 30 seconds. Using a slotted spoon, transfer to the ice water to cool. Remove from the water and peel immediately. Cut the tomatoes in half crosswise and squeeze out the seeds. In a blender or food processor, puree 3 of the tomatoes until liquefied and transfer to a large bowl. Reserve the remaining tomatoes.

Put the onion in the blender or food processor. Chop 3 of the garlic cloves and add them as well. Puree, adding a bit of the vinegar if needed for a smooth consistency. Add to the bowl with the tomato puree. Add the cucumbers with a little of the vinegar to the blender or processor and pulse until they are coarsely chopped. Add to the bowl as well. Chop the remaining tomatoes coarsely in the blender or processor. Add to the bowl. Whisk in the 1/2 cup olive oil and the remaining vinegar, and season with salt and pepper. Serve immediately, or cover and refrigerate until well chilled, about 2 hours.

Just before serving the soup, in a large fry pan over medium heat, warm the 2 tablespoons of olive oil. Crush the remaining garlic clove, add to the pan and cook to release its fragrance, 1 to 2 minutes. Add the bread cubes and stir and toss until golden brown, about 5 minutes. Transfer to paper towels to drain; keep warm.

Taste the soup and adjust the seasonings with salt. Ladle into chilled bowls and garnish each serving with the diced bell pepper and the minced red onion. Float the croutons on the top and serve.

Home-style Potato Soup

Serves: 7 (1 cup soup and 1 tablespoon cheese)

4 cups peeled baking potato
1 cup chopped onion
1 cup thinly sliced celery
3/4 cup thinly sliced carrot
3 tablespoons butter, cut into small pieces
1 1/4 teaspoon salt
1/2 teaspoon black pepper
1 14 ounce can chicken broth
3 minced cloves of garlic
1/4 cup all-purpose flour
1 1/2 cup 2% reduced-fat milk (or cream)
7 tablespoons shredded sharp cheddar cheese

Cheddar cheese's sharpness contrasts well with the mild potato soup, making it an ideal topping. The sharper the cheese, the better, since you can use less of it for the same amount of flavor. When you're shredding Cheddar, use the largest holes of a box grater to get long shreds.

Place the first 9 ingredients in a 4 1/4 quart electric slow cooker; stir well. Cover and cook on LOW 6 to 7 hours or until vegetables are tender. Increase heat to HIGH. Lightly spoon flour into a dry measuring cup; level with a knife. Place flour in a bowl; gradually add milk, stirring with a whisk until well blended. Stir into soup; heat through. Ladle soup into individual bowls, and sprinkle with cheese and additional pepper if desired.

Sausage & Bean Soup

Serves: 5

2 strips diced bacon
1/2 cup chopped onion
1 cup thinly sliced and halved fresh carrots
1 cup cubed peeled potato
3 cups water
8 ounces Polish sausage, halved & thinly sliced
2 cups frozen cut green beans, thawed
1 (15-ounce) can white kidney beans or cannellini beans, rinsed & drained
1/4 cup dried parsley
3/4 teaspoon salt
1/2 teaspoon pepper
1/8 teaspoon dried marjoram

In a large saucepan, cook bacon over medium heat until crisp. Using a slotted spoon, remove to paper towels to drain. Sauté the onion in bacon drippings until tender. Stir in carrots and potatoes; cook for 2 minutes. Add water and bring to a boil. Reduce heat cover and simmer for 9 to 12 minutes or until the vegetables are tender. Stir in sausage, green beans, kidney beans, parsley, salt, pepper, and marjoram heat thoroughly. Sprinkle with reserved bacon.

Cream of Chicken Soup

Serves: 4 to 6

½ cup unsalted butter
1 medium onion, chopped
2 stalks of celery (with leaves), chopped
3 medium carrots, chopped
½ cup plus 1 tablespoon flour
7 cups chicken broth
2 teaspoons dried parsley
1 teaspoon dried thyme
1 bay leaf
2 ¾ cups cooked, diced chicken
½ cup heavy cream
2 ½ teaspoons dry sherry
1 tablespoon kosher salt
Pepper to taste

Melt the butter in a large soup pot over medium heat. Add the onion, celery, and carrots and cook, covered, stirring occasionally until soft, about 12 minutes. Add the flour and cook, stirring with a wooden spoon, for 2 minutes more. Pour in the broth and bring to a boil while whisking constantly. Add the seasoning, lower the heat, and simmer for 15 minutes. Stir in the chicken and bring to a boil. Remove from the heat. Whisk the heavy cream, sherry and salt into the soup and season with pepper to taste. Divide among soup bowls and serve immediately.

Roasted Pumpkin Apple Soup

Serves: 6

4 pounds pie pumpkin or butternut squash, peeled, seeded and cut into 2-inch chunks
4 large sweet-tart apples, unpeeled, cored and cut into eighths
1/4 cup extra virgin olive oil
1 teaspoon freshly ground pepper
1 teaspoon salt
1 tablespoon chopped fresh sage
6 cups reduced-sodium chicken broth or vegetable broth
1/3 cup chopped hazelnuts, toasted
2 tablespoons hazelnut oil

Preheat the oven to 450 degrees F.

Toss pumpkin or squash, apples, olive oil, 1 teaspoon salt and pepper in a large bowl. Spread evenly on a large rimmed baking sheet. Roast stirring once, for 30 minutes. Stir in sage and continue roasting until very tender and starting to brown, 15-20 minutes more.

Put about one-third of the pumpkin (or squash) and apples to a blender along with 2 cups broth. Puree until smooth. Transfer to a Dutch oven and repeat for two more batches. Season with the remaining 1/4 teaspoon salt and heat over medium-low heat, stirring constantly to prevent splattering, for about 6 minutes.

Garnish with hazelnuts and a drizzle of hazelnut oil.

Beans, Rice, and Pasta

Perfect Black Beans

Serves: 4

1/2 pound dried black beans
1 medium onion, roughly chopped
3 cloves fresh garlic, pressed
1/2 teaspoon dried oregano
1/2 teaspoon ground cumin
pinch of red pepper flakes
2 teaspoons sugar
2 tablespoons white wine vinegar
Salt and pepper to taste
Chopped scallions for garnish

The night before soak the black beans in a large pot of water.

The next day, rinse the beans, cover with 3 cups of fresh water and bring to a boil over high heat. Reduce the heat and simmer covered for 30 minutes, skimming off any foam. Stir in the onion and simmer for 30 minutes more. Add the garlic, oregano, cumin, and red pepper flakes, and simmer uncovered for 30 minutes, stirring occasionally.

Stir in sugar and vinegar, and taste before seasoning with salt and pepper. Turn out into a large serving bowl and garnish with chopped scallions.

Creamy Fettuccine Alfredo

Serves: 4
Approximately $1.85 per serving

2 sticks softened butter
2 cups whipping cream
2 cups grated parmesan cheese
1 pound box fettuccine pasta
1/8 teaspoon salt
1/8 teaspoon pepper
Fresh basil leaves

Place the butter in a large heatproof bowl. Using a wooden spoon or an electric mixer set on low speed, beat until smooth. Add the cream and parmesan cheese. Stir until well blended; set aside.

Bring a large saucepan of lightly salted water to a boil. Add the pasta and cook according to package directions. Drain well and immediately add the hot pasta to the butter mixture in the large bowl. Using two forks, toss the fettuccine in the butter mixture to coat well. Add the salt and pepper.

Divide the pasta between 4 serving plates. Quickly slice the basil into shreds to equal 1/4 cup. Sprinkle shredded basil over each serving. Serve immediately.

Homemade Fried Rice

Serves: 4
Approximately $1.00 per serving

Salt
1 1/3 cups long-grain un-cooked rice
3 tablespoons of vegetable oil
2 large eggs
1 large chopped onion (about 1 cup)
1 large green bell pepper
8 ounces button mushrooms
3 cloves garlic, minced
¼ cup apple juice or dry sherry
3 tablespoons of soy sauce
1 to 2 bunches scallions (about ¾ cup chopped)
1 cup frozen green peas
1 ½ tablespoons toasted sesame oil

Bring 2 2/3 cups lightly salted water to a boil in a covered medium-size saucepan over high heat. Add the rice, stir, and reduce the heat to low. Cover the pan and simmer until the rice is tender, about 20 minutes.

Meanwhile, heat 1 tablespoon of oil in an extra-deep 12 inch skillet over medium heat. Beat the eggs lightly, pour them into the skillet and cook without stirring (as you would an omelet) until they are almost dry, 2 to 3 minutes.

While the eggs cook, peel and coarsely chop the onion and set it aside. When the eggs are ready, transfer them to a plate and set aside. (Do not wash or wipe skillet.)

Heat the remaining oil in the same skillet used for the eggs over medium heat. Add the onion and cook, stirring occasionally, until it just begins to soften, 2 to 3 minutes.

Meanwhile, stem, seed and cut the bell pepper into bite-size pieces and add them to the skillet. Rinse, pat dry, and coarsely chop the mushrooms, discarding any tough stems. Add the mushrooms and garlic to the skillet. Cook, stirring for 2 minutes.

Add the apple juice or sherry, soy sauce, and cooked rice. Stir occasionally while you slice the scallions, using the white and enough of the tender green tops to make ¾ cup. Add them to the skillet and stir well.

Add the peas and sesame oil. Cut the eggs into thin strips, add them to the pan, and stir. Stir-fry to heat the peas and mix in the sesame oil, 1 minute. Serve at once, passing extra soy sauce at the table, if desired.

Casseroles & Slow Cookers

Slow-Cooked Pot Roast

Serves: 4

1 tablespoon vegetable oil
1 tablespoon all-purpose flour
1/2 teaspoon ground black pepper
1 pound boneless beef chuck roast, well- trimmed, cut into large pieces
2 medium red-skinned potatoes, cut into 2-inch pieces
1 cup sliced carrots
1/2 cup onion, chopped
2 teaspoons minced garlic
1/2 cup lower sodium beef broth
2 tablespoons Worcestershire sauce
1 can (14.5 ounce each stewed tomatoes, undrained
5 tablespoons tomato paste
1/2 teaspoon granulated sugar

Heat oil in large non-stick skillet over medium-high heat. Combine flour and pepper in shallow dish coat meat with mixture. Place meat in skillet and brown all sides transfer to 4-quart slow cooker. Add potatoes, carrots, onion and garlic. Stir together broth, Worcestershire sauce, undrained tomatoes, tomato paste and sugar in medium bowl. Pour over meat and vegetables. Cook on LOW 8 hours or HIGH 4 hours.

Johnny Marzetti

Serves: 6
Approximately $1.50 per serving with everything on sale.

1 box elbow macaroni pasta
2 large jars spaghetti sauce
1 pound ground beef
1 medium onion, chopped
1 medium green bell pepper, chopped
1 teaspoon chopped garlic
Salt & pepper to taste
1 (12-ounce) package mozzarella cheese

Put a large pan of salted water on to boil. Then cook pasta 8 to 10 minutes. Sauté onion and bell pepper. When the onions are translucent, add ground beef, garlic, salt & pepper and cook till beef is browned. Drain off grease. Add this meat mixture to 1 to 2 large jars of spaghetti sauce. Mix with pasta and cover with shredded mozzarella cheese. Put in appropriate baking pan and bake at 350 degrees until cheese has melted and is bubbly around the edges.

Slow-Cook English Roast Sandwiches

Serves:8 to 12

3 pounds English Roast
1 bottle chili sauce
1 envelope dry onion soup mix
12 ounces of your favorite cola
12 fresh buns

Place the unseasoned roast in a crock pot. Pour chili sauce over beef, then sprinkle with the onion soup mix; pour in the cola. Cover and cook on low for 8 to 10 hours. The aroma will drive you crazy, but resist the temptation to lift the lid! Shred cooked beef and serve on buns

Tuscan White Beans

Serves: 8

1 pound dried white cannellini beans (or navy beans)
1/4 cup olive oil
4 cups chopped fennel, stalks, fronds, & core removed (2 large)
2 cups chopped carrots (4 carrots)
1 tablespoon minced garlic (3 cloves)
1 cup chicken stock
1 tablespoon minced fresh sage
1 tablespoon minced rosemary
2 teaspoons kosher salt
1/2 teaspoon black pepper
1/2 cup fresh, grated Pecorino Romano cheese

The night before, soak the beans in a large bowl with water to cover by at least 2 inches. Cover & refrigerate overnight.

The next day, drain the beans, rinse them well, and place them in a large stockpot. Add twice as much water as you have beans, bringing to a boil, then lower the heat and simmer uncovered for about 45 minutes, until the beans are very tender. Skim off any foam that accumulates.

Meanwhile, heat the olive oil in a large pan or Dutch oven over medium heat. Add the fennel and carrots and sauté for 8 to 10 minutes, stirring occasionally, until tender. Add the garlic and cook for 1 minute more. Drain the beans and add them to the vegetables. Add the chicken stock, sage, rosemary, salt, and pepper and simmer, stirring occasionally for 12 to 15 minutes, until creamy. Stir in the Pecorino, season to taste, and serve hot.

French Style Beans with Smoked Sausage

Serves: 8 (1 ¼ cups each)
Approximately 87 cents per serving with meat on sale.

2 pounds smoked sausage, cut into 1 1/2" pieces
1 tablespoon canola oil
1/3 cup minced shallot
3 cloves of garlic, minced
2 cups dried flageolets or 1 pound white cannellini beans (or navy beans)
2 cups water
1 tablespoon dried thyme
1 teaspoon celery seed
1/4 teaspoon black pepper
2 (14-ounce) can chicken broth

Heat a large non-stick skillet over medium heat. Add sausage, sauté 5 minutes or until browned. Remove from pan; place in a 5 quart electric slow cooker. Heat oil in pan over medium heat. Add shallots and garlic; sauté 1 minute.

Sort and wash beans. Add beans, shallot mixture, water and next 4 ingredients to cooker. Cover and cook on high for 8 hours or until beans are tender. Garnish with fresh thyme springs if desired

Cabbage with Polish Sausage & Apples

Serves: 8 to 10
Approximately 75 cents per serving with meat & apples on sale.

2 large apples
1 medium head of cabbage
1 cup apple juice
1 medium/large onion
2 packages of polish sausage
2 tablespoons butter
Salt & pepper to taste

In a large pan over medium heat, sauté onion with 2 tablespoons of butter until they are translucent. Open your sausage packages and cut the sausage into 1 inch pieces and add to skillet. Cook until the meat is lightly browned. Then add 1 cup of apple juice. Cut up your cabbage head and add it. Season with salt and pepper. Cover and let it simmer for 3-5 minutes. Core and slice your apples. When the cabbage is tender add your apples...cover again for 1 minute. Then serve hot.

Southern Classic Red Beans and Rice

Yield: 4 servings (serving size: 1 cup bean mixture, 3/4 cup rice, and 1 tablespoon green onions).
Approximately 75 cents per serving with meat and bell pepper on sale.

3 cups water
1 cup dried red kidney beans
1 cup chopped onion
1 cup chopped green bell peppers
3/4 cup chopped celery
1 teaspoon dried thyme
1 teaspoon paprika
3/4 teaspoon ground red pepper
1/2 teaspoon ground black pepper
1/2 (14-ounce) package sausage
1 bay leaf
5 cloves of garlic, minced
1/2 teaspoon salt
3 cups hot cooked long-grain rice
1/4 cup chopped green onion

Combine the first 12 ingredients in a 2 quart electric slow cooker. Cover and cook on HIGH for 5 hours. Discard the bay leaf; stir in salt. Serve over rice in individual bowls; sprinkle evenly with green onions.

Be sure to add the salt to the dish after it has cooked and just before serving. Add salt to dried beans too early will slow the cooking process and make the beans less tender. Served over rice with a side of slaw, this southern classic is hard to beat.

Saucy Italian Style Chicken Thighs

Serves: 6
Approximately 83 cents per serving.

12 chicken thighs
1 (14.5 ounce) can Italian-style diced tomatoes
1 (6 ounce) can tomato paste
1/2 cup chopped onion
1 tablespoon minced garlic
1 teaspoon dried Italian seasoning
1/4 teaspoon salt
1/4 teaspoon black pepper

Place chicken in a 4-quart electric slow cooker. Combine tomatoes and next 6 ingredients; stir well. Pour sauce over chicken. Cover and cook on High 1 hour. Reduce heat to low and cook 4 to 5 hours or until chicken is tender. Serving size is 2 thighs and 3/4 cup sauce.

Nutritional Information: Calories 202 (24% from fat); Fat 5.4g (sat 1.4g, mono 1.6g, poly 1.4g); Protein 27.8g; Carb 9.6g; fiber 2.1g; chol 109mg; iron 2.3mg; sodium 526mg; calc 35mg

Chicken Enchiladas

Serves: 4
Approximately $1.87 per serving.

21 1/2 ounce cream of chicken soup (2 cans)
4 1/2 ounce jarred chopped green chili pepper, undrained
3 boneless, skinless chicken breasts cooked and shredded
5 flour tortillas (6 inch)
Chopped tomato (optional)
Chopped avocado (optional)

Combine soup, chilies, and chicken in a medium bowl. Coat interior of slow cooker with cooking spray. Spoon 1/5 of soup mixture into slow cooker. Top with 1/3 cup cheese and 1 tortilla. Continue layering in that order 4 more times, and end with remaining cheese on top. Cover and cook on low 4 hours. Top with chopped tomato and avocado, if desired.

Turkey Tetrazzini

Serves: 8

8 ounce uncooked spaghetti
1/4 cup margarine or butter
2 cups sliced fresh mushrooms
3 tablespoons all-purpose flour
2 cups chicken broth
3/4 cup half-and-half
1 to 3 tablespoons dry sherry, if desired
1/4 cup chopped fresh parsley
1 teaspoon salt
1/8 teaspoon nutmeg
Dash pepper
3 cups cubed cooked turkey
1/2 cup grated parmesan cheese
Chopped fresh parsley, if desired

Cook spaghetti as directed on package. Drain. Meanwhile, melt margarine in Dutch oven over medium heat. Add mushrooms; cook 5 minutes or until tender, stirring frequently. Reduce heat to medium-low. Add flour; cook and stir until bubbly. Gradually add broth, stirring constantly, until mixture boils and thickens. Remove from heat; stir in half-and-half, sherry, 1/4 cup parsley, salt, nutmeg and pepper. Add cooked spaghetti and turkey to mushroom mixture; stir gently to mix. Spoon mixture into an ungreased 13x9-inch (3-quart) glass baking dish.

Cover with foil; refrigerate at least 8 hours or overnight.

Preheat oven to 350 degrees. Uncover baking dish sprinkle parmesan cheese over top. Cover; bake 45 to 55 minutes or until thoroughly heated, removing foil during last 10 minutes of baking time. Sprinkle with parsley.

Beef Daube Provencal

Serves: 4

2 teaspoons olive oil
12 cloves of garlic
2 pounds boneless beef chuck roast (choice or prime)
1 1/2 teaspoon salt, divided
1/2 teaspoon pepper, divided
1 cup red wine (or 1 small bottle)
2 cups chopped carrots
1 1/2 cup chopped onion
1/2 cup beef broth
2 tablespoons tomato paste
1/3 teaspoon rosemary
1/3 teaspoon thyme
1 (14.5-oz) can diced tomato, undrained
1 bay leaf
3 cups cooked noodles or rice

Use a 4 quart electric slow cooker, or cook in the oven. Preheat oven to 300 degrees.

Heat oil in a 8 quart Dutch oven over low heat. Add garlic and cook 5 minutes or until garlic is fragrant, stirring occasionally. Remove garlic with a slotted spoon, and set aside. Increase heat to medium-high. Add roast to pan, sprinkle with 1/2 teaspoon salt and 1/4 teaspoon pepper. Cook 5 minutes, browning on all sides. Remove roast from pan. Add wine to pan, bring to a boil, scraping pan to loosen browned bits. Add garlic, roast, remaining 1 teaspoon salt, remaining 1/4 teaspoon pepper, carrot, and next 8 ingredients. Bring to a boil.

Place roast mixture in a 4 quart electric slow cooker. Cover and cook on High for 5 hours. Discard bay leaf. Serve over noodles, rice or mashed potatoes.

Note: If using an oven, rather than placing roast mixture in slow cooker, keep in the Dutch oven. Cover and bake at 300 degrees for 2 ½ hours or until beef is tender.

This classic French stew made with braised beef, red wine, and vegetables is simple and very delicious. It's perfect cold-weather fare, and very versatile. Serve alone for an easy weeknight meal, or try it with a whole-grain baguette and a mixed green salad tossed with your favorite vinaigrette. Serve over mashed potatoes, noodles or rice.

When cubing meat for a stew, cut the pieces to a uniform size to ensure even cooking. Otherwise, smaller pieces of meat will cook too quickly and become overdone, while the larger pieces will need to cook longer. Begin by trimming any visible fat; then cut the roast into 2" thick slices; then cut the slices into 2" cubes.

Serving Size is 3/4 cup stew and 1/2 cup noodles.
Nutritional information: Calories 367 (31% from fat); FAT 12.8g (sat 4.3g, mono 5.8g, poly 0.9g); Protein 29.1g; Carb 33.4g; Fiber 3.9g; Chol 105mg; Iron 4/3mg; Sodium 776mg; Calc 76mg

Baked Eggplant Parmesan

Serves: 4

1/4 cup Italian-style bread crumbs
1 large eggplant, peeled if desired
Non-Stick cooking spray
1 cup shredded part-skim mozzarella cheese
1 can (14.5 oz each) diced tomatoes with basil, garlic and oregano, undrained
1 can (8 oz each) tomato sauce with basil, garlic and oregano

Preheat oven to 42 degrees. Place bread crumbs in shallow dish; set aside. Cut eggplant into 12 slices, about 1/2-inch thick. Spray each side with cooking spray. Coat with bread crumbs on both sides and place on baking sheet. Bake 10 minutes or until tender, turning once. Top slices evenly with cheese; bake 1 minute more or until cheese has softened. Meanwhile, combine undrained tomatoes and sauce in small saucepan. Bring to a boil over medium-high heat. Reduce heat to medium-low; simmer 10 minutes or until slightly thickened. Spoon tomato mixture evenly into 4 shallow bowls. Place 3 eggplant slices over sauce in each bowl.

Nutritional Information: Calories per serving 202, Total fat 6 g, Saturated fat 3 g, Cholesterol 18 mg, Sodium 859 mg, Carbohydrate 27 g, Dietary fiber 6 g, Sugars 9 g, Protein 10 g,

Potato Kielbasa Skillet Recipe

Serves: 4
Approximate 87 cents per serving. Purchase your sausage on sale, then don't forget to use your coupon.

1 pound red potatoes, cubed
3 tablespoons water
¾ pound smoked kielbasa or Polish sausage, cut into ¼ inch slices (or 1 large link)
½ cup chopped sweet onion
1 tablespoon olive oil
½ teaspoon dried thyme
¼ teaspoon pepper
4 bacon strips, cooked and crumbled

Fry bacon until done. Cool and crumble or cut into small pieces. Place potatoes and water in a microwave-safe dish, cover and microwave on high for 4 minutes or until potatoes are tender. Drain. In a large skillet, sauté sausage and onion in oil until onion is translucent. Add potatoes and sauté for 3-5 minutes until potatoes are lightly browned. Sprinkle thyme and pepper over potatoes & sausage and serve while warm.
Optional: Serve with steamed green beans and French bread.

Macaroni and Cheese

Serves 12

8 tablespoons (1 stick) unsalted butter, plus more for dish
6 slices of good white bread, crusts removed, torn into ¼ to ½ inch pieces
5 ½ cups milk
½ cup all-purpose flour
2 teaspoons salt
¼ teaspoon freshly grated nutmeg
¼ teaspoon freshly ground black pepper
4 ½ cups grated sharp cheddar cheese (about 18 ounces)
2 cups grated gruyere cheese (about 8 ounces) or 1 ¼ cups grated pecorino romano cheese (about 5 ounces)
1 pound of elbow macaroni

Heat oven to 375 degrees. Butter a 3 quart casserole dish; set aside. Place bread in a medium bowl. In a small saucepan over medium heat, melt 2 tablespoons butter. Pour butter into a bowl with the bread, and toss. Set aside.

In a medium saucepan set over medium heat, heat the milk. Melt remaining 6 tablespoons butter in a high-sided skillet over medium heat. When butter bubbles, add flour. Cook, whisking for 1 minute.

While continuing to whisk, slowly pour in the hot milk. Continue cooking, whisking constantly until the mixture bubbles and becomes thick. Remove pan from the heat. Stir in salt, nutmeg, black pepper, 3 cups of cheddar cheese, and 1 ½ cups gruyere or 1 cup Pecorino Romano; set cheese sauce aside.

Fill a large saucepan with water; bring to a boil. Add macaroni; cook 2 to 3 minutes less than the manufacturer's directions, until the outside of pasta is cooked and the inside is underdone. Different brands of macaroni cook at different rates so be sure to read the instructions. Transfer the macaroni to a colander, rinse under cold running water, and drain well. Stir macaroni into the reserved cheese sauce.

Pour mixture into prepared dish. Sprinkle remaining 1 ½ cups cheddar cheese, ½ gruyere or ¼ cup pecorino Romano, and breadcrumbs over top. Bake until browned on top, about 30 minutes. Transfer dish to a wire rack to cool for 5 minutes; serve hot.

Spinach-Walnut Penne

Serves: 4

2 cups reduced-sodium vegetable broth
1 can (14.5 oz each) diced tomatoes with basil, garlic & oregano, undrained
2 cups dry multigrain penne pasta, uncooked
2 tablespoons butter
1 package (6 oz each) baby spinach leaves
1/3 cup chopped walnuts
1/2 cup shredded parmesan cheese

Combine broth, undrained tomatoes, pasta and butter in large skillet. Bring to a boil over high heat, stirring occasionally. Cover skillet, reduce heat to medium and cook 15 minutes or just until pasta is tender, stirring occasionally. Stir in spinach and cook 3 to 4 minutes or until spinach is wilted, stirring occasionally. Sprinkle with walnuts and cheese just before serving.

Taco Chili

Serves: 4 to 6

1 pound ground chuck
2 (15-ounce) can seasoned tomato sauce with diced tomatoes
1 (15-ounce) can chili beans with chili gravy
1 (15-ounce) can hominy or whole kernel corn, undrained
1 (1.25 ounce) package of taco seasoning
Sour cream (optional)
Shredded cheddar cheese (optional)

In a large skillet, cook ground chuck over medium heat until brown; drain off fat. In a 3 ½ or 4 quart slow cooker, combine the meat, tomato sauce, beans with chili gravy, undrained hominy, and taco seasoning mix. Cover and cook on low-heat setting for 4 to 6 hours or on high-heat setting for 2 to 3 hours. If desired, top individual serving with sour cream and cheddar cheese.

Meat Dishes

Moist Turkey Breast

Serves: 12

1 bone-in turkey breast (about 7 pounds)
1 teaspoon garlic powder
1/2 teaspoon onion powder
1/2 teaspoon salt
1/4 teaspoon pepper
1-1/2 cups Italian dressing

Place turkey breast in a greased 13 x 9 inch baking dish. Combine the seasonings; sprinkle over turkey. Pour dressing over the top. Cover and bake at 325 degrees for 2 to 2-1/2 hours or until a meat thermometer reads 170°, basting occasionally with pan drippings. Let stand for 10 minutes before slicing.

Tangy Turkey Burgers

Serves: 6

1/2 pound ground turkey
2 green onions
2 tablespoons white wine-and herb chicken marinade
1 teaspoon garlic salt
1/4 teaspoon dried parsley
1 teaspoon pepper
6 hamburger buns
Toppings (optional)
Lettuce, sliced avocado, mayonnaise

Gently combine first 5 ingredients. Shape mixture into 6 (4 inch) patties. Heat cast-iron grill pan over medium high heat. Cook patties in pan 6 to 8 minutes on each side or until done. Serve burgers on buns with desired toppings.

Tomato-Broccoli Chicken

Serves: 4

2 large boneless chicken breasts, skinned
Salt and pepper
¼ cup chopped onion
2 tablespoons butter
10 ounce package of frozen cut broccoli, thawed
1 teaspoon lemon juice
¾ teaspoon salt
1/8 teaspoon pepper
¼ teaspoon dried thyme, crushed
1 plastic container of cherry tomatoes, cut in half
2 cups cooked rice

Cut chicken in bit-size pieces, or strips and sprinkle lightly with salt and pepper. In a medium skillet, cook chicken and onion in butter until chicken is no longer pink. Stir in broccoli, lemon juice, salt, pepper and thyme. Cover and simmer for 6 minutes. Add tomatoes, simmer, covered for 1 minute more. Serve over rice

Roasted Citrus Chicken

Serves: 6

12 chicken thighs, skin on
1 ½ teaspoon salt
1 teaspoon paprika
1 teaspoon pepper
2 tablespoons vegetable oil
1 large lemon, quartered
1 large orange, cut into 8 wedges
3 bay leaves
2 cloves garlic, sliced
2 1/2 tablespoons capers, drained

Preheat oven to 350 degrees. Trim excess fat from chicken thighs. Sprinkle chicken with salt, paprika and pepper. In a large skillet, heat oil over medium-high heat. Add chicken to pan; cook, turning occasionally for 5 minutes, or until browned. Place chicken in a shallow 3 quart baking dish. Squeeze juice from lemon quarters and orange wedges over chicken, and add to dish. Add bay leaves and garlic to dish. Bake 35 to 40 minutes or until chicken is done, adding capers during the last 10 minutes of baking time. Remove and discard bay leaves.

Baked Pineapple Chicken

Serves: 8

3/4 cup all-purpose flour
1 1/2 teaspoons salt
1 teaspoon celery salt
1/2 teaspoon garlic powder
1/4 teaspoon onion powder
1/2 teaspoon ground nutmeg
8 chicken breast halves, skin removed
1/2 cup butter
2 cups pineapple juice, unsweetened
1 tablespoon plus 1 teaspoon soy sauce
1/4 cup granulated sugar

Mix together flour, salt, celery salt, garlic powder, onion powder, and nutmeg; dredge chicken in seasoned flour mixture. In a heavy skillet, brown chicken breasts in melted butter. When chicken is golden brown, transfer to a 13x9x2-inch baking dish. Combine pineapple juice, soy sauce and sugar; mix well and pour over chicken. Cover tightly with foil and bake in 350 degrees oven for 30 minutes. Remove foil and continue baking until chicken is tender, about 30 to 40 minutes longer, basting with pan juices several times. Serve sauce with the chicken, if desired.

Deep Dish Pizza

Serves: 6

Crust:
1 package yeast
2/3 cup warm water, divided
1 3/4 cup (or 2 cups) flour, divided
1 teaspoon oregano
1 teaspoon marjoram
1 teaspoon basil
1/2 teaspoon garlic salt
1/2 teaspoon onion salt
1/4 cup vegetable oil

Filling:
1 pound bulk sausage
1 (28-ounce) can whole tomatoes (you can also substitute pizza sauce)
2 medium green peppers, chopped
2 tablespoons vegetable oil
1 pound shredded mozzarella cheese
1 cup shredded Parmesan cheese
1/2 teaspoon dried basil
1/2 teaspoon dried oregano
1/2 teaspoon dried marjoram
Optional: pepperoni slices

Dissolve yeast in 1/3 cup of warm water with 1 teaspoon sugar. In a mixer bowl, combine proofed yeast mixture, 1 cup of flour and the remaining ingredients. Beat until smooth. By hand, stir in additional flour until the dough is no longer sticky. Turn out onto a floured surface and knead until smooth, about 5 minutes. Place in a greased bowl, turning to grease the top. Cover and let rise at room temperature for about 1 hour. Meanwhile, prepare the filling.

Cook the sausage in a frying pan, breaking the meat into small pieces. Drain and set aside. Drain and seed tomatoes, coarsely chop, then drain well again. Sauté onion and green pepper in oil until tender.

Thoroughly grease the bottom and sides of a 10 or 12 inch cast iron skillet.

Punch down dough and roll out on a flour-dusted surface to a 15 inch circle. Fit into skillet, letting the edges drape slightly over pan. Brush lightly with oil.

Sprinkle 1/4 of the mozzarella over the crust. Layer in 1/2 of each of the filling ingredients, except the pepperoni, in this order: onion/pepper mixture, parmesan, seasonings, sausage, and tomatoes. Sprinkle 1/2 of the remaining mozzarella over the filling. Repeat layers. Trim excess crust, if necessary, to within about 1 inch of the filling and fold crust over filling to form an edge.

Bake at 400 degrees for 20 minutes. Remove from oven and sprinkle on remaining mozzarella and, if desired, pepperoni. Return to oven and bake an additional 10 to 15 minutes or until crust is brown. Let stand 10 minutes before cutting into wedges to serve.

Buttermilk Pecan Chicken

Serves: 8

1 cup buttermilk
1 large egg
1 cup all-purpose flour
1 tablespoon salt
1 tablespoon paprika
1/8 teaspoon pepper
1 cup ground pecans
¼ cup sesame seeds
16 chicken thighs
½ cup corn oil
¼ cup finely chopped pecans

Stir together buttermilk and egg in a small bowl until blended. Stir together flour and next 5 ingredients in a small bowl. Dip chicken pieces in buttermilk mixture and then dredge in flour mixture. Quickly dip in oil and drain. Place skin side up in a large roasting pan; sprinkle with chopped pecans. Bake at 350 degrees for 1 hour and 30 minutes.

Chicken Bryan

Serves: 4
Approximately $1.75 per serving with meat on sale.

4 boneless chicken breasts
Salt
Pepper
Olive oil
2 ounce goat cheese , sliced from a log
10-12 pieces of sun dried tomatoes, or chopped fresh tomato if preferred
1 tablespoon fresh basil, chopped

Lemon butter Sauce:
1 teaspoon butter
2 teaspoons finely chopped garlic
2 teaspoons finely chopped onion
2 tablespoons white wine (you can purchase individual bottles for cooking)
2 tablespoons lemon juice
Kosher salt
Pinch of white pepper
1 stick (1/4 pound) butter, cold cut into small cubes

Season chicken on both sides with salt and pepper. Dab with olive oil. Grill chicken until cooked to a minimum internal temperature of 165 degrees. Then place one slice of goat cheese on top of chicken and continue to cook until warm.
Lemon butter instructions:
Place butter, garlic and onion in a pot over medium heat and sauté until garlic and onion are soft and transparent. Do not let garlic and onion burn. Add white wine, lemon juice, kosher salt and white pepper, bring to a boil, then set heat to medium and let it reduce. After liquids have reduced and you have about 1/4 of what you started with, reduce heat to low and gradually add cold butter, beating with wire whisk to allow to blend and melt into a creamy sauce.

Chicken Piccata

Serves: 4

Approximately $1.00 per serving with meat on sale.

2 chicken breasts, boneless, or 4 chicken cutlets
2 tablespoons vegetable oil
1/4 cup dry white wine
1 teaspoon minced garlic
1/2 cup chicken broth
2 tablespoons fresh lemon juice
1 teaspoon capers, drained
2 tablespoons unsalted butter
Fresh lemon slices
Fresh chopped parsley

Pound out chicken breasts between wax paper. Season with salt and pepper; then dust with flour. Coat a sauté pan with a non-stick spray. Add 2 tablespoons of vegetable oil, and heat over medium heat. Sauté chicken for 2 to 3 minutes on one side. Flip chicken over and sauté the other side for 1 to 2 minutes. Transfer cutlets to a warm plate and pour off fat from the pan. Deglaze pan with wine and add minced garlic. Cook until garlic is slightly browned and liquid is nearly evaporated, about 2 minutes. Add broth, lemon juice, and capers. Return cutlets to pan and cook on each side for 1 minute. Transfer to a warm plate. Finish sauce with butter and lemons. Once butter melts pour sauce over cutlets. Garnish with fresh chopped parsley and serve.

Thai-Spiced Chicken Kabobs

Serves: 4

2/3 cup sweet and sour sauce
2 tablespoons snipped fresh basil
1 teaspoon Thai seasoning or five-spice powder
1 clove of garlic, minced
1 small fresh pineapple (3 to 3 ½ pounds)
Non-stick cooking spray
1 pound skinless, boneless chicken breast halves, cut into 1-inch pieces
1 tablespoon melted butter

For sauce, combine sweet and sour sauce, basil, Thai seasoning, and garlic. Reserve ¼ cup sauce to brush on kabobs. Set remaining sauce aside. Cut off pineapple ends. Halve pineapple lengthwise; cut each half crosswise into 4 slices. Lightly coat pineapple slices with cooking spray; set aside. If using wooden skewers, soak in water ½ hour before using. Then thread chicken pieces onto 4 long skewers, leaving a ¼ inch space between pieces. For a charcoal grill, grill skewers on the rack of an uncovered grill directly over medium heat for 7 minutes. Turn skewers; brush with reserved sauce. Discard any remaining brush-on sauce. Arrange pineapple slices on grill rack directly over medium heat. Grill chicken and pineapple for 6 to 8 minutes or until chicken is no longer pink and pineapple is heated through, turning once. In a small bowl, combine remaining sauce and melted butter; serve with chicken and pineapple.

1-2-3 Chicken Cacciatore

Serves: 6
Approximate 50 cents per serving with chicken on sale.

1 tablespoon olive oil
2 pounds chicken legs and thighs
1 jar (1 pound 10 ounce) pasta sauce
3 cups hot cooked rice

Heat oil in 12-inch skillet over medium-high heat and brown chicken.

Stir in Pasta Sauce. Bring to a boil over high heat. Reduce heat to low and simmer covered 45 minutes or until chicken is thoroughly cooked.

Serve with hot rice.

Nutritional Information per serving: Calories 410, Calories From Fat 100, Total Fat 11g, Trans Fat 0g, Cholesterol 125mg, Sodium 620mg, Dietary Fiber 3g, Sugars 12g, Protein 34g, Vitamin A 10%, Vitamin C 8%, Calcium 6%, Iron 20%

Lemon Ginger Chicken Thighs

Serves: 4

1 lemon
1 tablespoon grated fresh ginger
1/2 teaspoon salt
2 tablespoons honey
1 tablespoon reduced-sodium soy sauce
8 chicken thighs, with bone & skin removed
2 teaspoons vegetable oil
Optional:
Sliced green onions
Wedges of lemon

Finely grate peel from lemon and then juice the lemon. In bowl combine the lemon peel, ginger, and salt. In another bowl combine lemon juice, honey, soy sauce, and 2 tablespoons of water. Rub lemon peel mixture under the skin of the chicken thighs. In a 12-inch skillet, heat oil over medium-high heat. Place chicken, skin side down, in the hot oil. Cook 7 minutes or until well-browned. Turn chicken and add lemon juice mixture. Reduce heat cover and cook 14-18 minutes longer or until no pink remains (180 degrees). Transfer chicken to plates. Skim fat from pan juices, if desired. Top with green onion and lemon wedges or slices.

Nutritional information: Each serving: 459 calories (2 thighs), 31 g fat, 158 mg chol, 5567 mg sodium, 12 g carbo, 1 g fiber, 33 g protein

Spinach-Stuffed Chicken Breasts

Serves: 6

4 slices bacon, chopped
1 medium onion, chopped (1/2 cup)
2 cloves garlic, finely chopped
1 box (9 oz) frozen spinach, thawed and squeezed to drain
1 egg, slightly beaten
1/2 teaspoon dried thyme leaves
1 cup shredded Italian cheese blend (4 oz)
6 boneless skinless chicken breasts (4 oz each)
1/2 teaspoon pepper
2 tablespoons olive or vegetable oil
Hot cooked rice or rice pilaf, if desired

In 12-inch skillet, cook bacon over medium heat 5 to 8 minutes, stirring occasionally, until crisp. Remove bacon from skillet, reserving fat in skillet. Drain bacon on paper towels; crumble and set aside. In same skillet, cook onion and garlic in bacon fat over medium-high heat 2 to 3 minutes, stirring frequently, until onion is tender. Remove skillet from heat; set aside. In medium bowl, mix spinach, egg, thyme and cheese. Stir in onion mixture and bacon. In thick side of each chicken breast, cut 3-inch-long pocket to within 1/4 inch of opposite side of breast. Spoon about 1/4 cup spinach mixture into pocket of each chicken breast. Sprinkle pepper over chicken.
In same skillet, heat oil over medium-high heat. Add chicken; cook uncovered 8 to 10 minutes, turning once, until light brown on all sides. Reduce heat to low. Cover; cook 10 to 20 minutes longer, turning if necessary, until chicken is no longer pink in center (170 degrees). Serve immediately with rice.

Pork Piccata

Serves: 4
Approximately $1.25 per serving when you purchase a pork loin at $1.89 per pound.

8 think boneless pork cutlets (about 1 ½ to 2 pounds total of a pork loin)
¼ teaspoon salt
¼ teaspoon black pepper
½ cup all-purpose flour
2 tablespoons olive oil
1 cup chicken broth
3 tablespoons capers
2 tablespoons lemon juice
1 tablespoon butter

Season both sides of pork with salt and pepper. Dredge in flour and shake off excess. Discard remaining flour. Heat oil in a large skillet over medium-high heat. Add pork and sauté for 2 minutes per side. Remove pork to a plate and keep warm. Add broth and simmer for 2 minutes, scraping up any browned bits from the bottom of the skillet. Stir in the capers and lemon juice. Return the pork to the skillet and simmer gently for about 1 to 2 minutes, until pork is heated through. Whisk in the butter. This would be a great meat dish served with mashed potatoes and green beans with lemon slices and chopped parsley for an optional garnish.

Nutritional information: 366 calories: 21 g fat (7 g sat.), 35 g protein; 7 g carbohydrate; 0 g fiber; 582 mg sodium; 101 mg cholesterol.

Maple Pork and Apples

Serves: 4
Approximately $1.50 per serving with Pork Loin being on sale @ $1.89 per pound.

4 pork loin chops, cut ½ inch thick (about 1 ¾ pounds)
Salt and ground black pepper to taste
2 tablespoons butter
12 baby carrots with tops, halved lengthwise
1 medium apple, sliced crosswise and seeds removed
1/3 cup maple syrup

Sprinkle chops with salt and pepper. In a large skillet, melt butter over medium heat; add chops. Cook for 2 minutes, turning once. Reduce heat to medium low. Add carrots, apples and maple syrup. Cover and simmer for about 8 minutes or until chops are done. Using a slotted spoon, transfer chops, carrots and apple slices to a platter. Bring syrup mixture to boiling. Boil gently, uncovered for 1 to 2 minutes or until thickened. Pour over chops.

Dijon Crusted Pork Chops

Serves: 4

4 ¾ inch thick pork chops
2 tablespoons Dijon style mustard
3/4 cup seasoned dried bread crumbs
1 tablespoon vegetable oil
8 ounce wide egg noodles
1 1/4 cup frozen mixed vegetables
1 tablespoon butter
1/4 teaspoon each salt and pepper

Heat oven to 350 degrees. Place a sheet of foil on your kitchen counter. Measure mustard and bread crumbs separately onto foil. Coat pork chops with mustard, then coat with bread crumbs. Heat oil in a large non-stick skillet, over medium-high heat. Add chops and cook 2 to 3 minutes on each side, until bread crumbs are browned. Transfer to a foil-lined baking pan and bake 5 minutes or until cooked through. Don't overcook or they will be tough. Pork can be eaten while slightly pink. Meanwhile, in a large saucepan, heat 4 quarts water to a rapid boil over high heat. Add noodles and cook according to package directions. Add vegetables in the last 5 minutes of cooking. Drain and toss with butter, pepper and salt serve with pork chops.

Nutritional information: 577 calories per serving, 33g protein, 57g carb, 4g fiber, 23g fate (8g sat fat), 108mg chol, 795mg sodium

Succulent Braised Pork

Serves: 4

2 pounds pork shoulder, cut into 6 large chunks
Salt and freshly ground black pepper to taste
2 tablespoons olive oil
1 onion, chopped
2 celery stalks, chopped
1 carrot, chopped
1 clove garlic, roughly chopped
2 tablespoons tomato paste
2 tablespoons all-purpose flour
1 cup red wine
1 1/2 cups beef stock or broth
1 bunch parsley stems, tied with string
2 bay leaves
1 cup water

Preheat the oven to 325 degrees. Pat the pork dry with paper towels and season with salt and pepper.
In a large Dutch oven, heat the olive oil over medium-high heat. Working in batches brown the meat on all sides until a golden crust forms. Transfer the pork to a plate. To the pan add the onion, celery, and carrot and sweat until softened, 5 to 7 minutes. Add the garlic and sweat another 2 minutes. Stir in the tomato paste and cook for 3 minutes to cook off the raw flavor and caramelize it. Sprinkle with the flour and cook another 2 minutes to cook off its raw flavor. Whisk in the wine and reduce it by half. Return the pork to the Dutch oven, then stir in the beef stock, parsley stems, and bay leaves. Add the water if liquid does not come up to the top of the pork.
Do not cover the pork with liquid. Cover the pan and place it in the oven to braise until the meat is fork tender, about 3 hours. Taste and season with more salt and pepper, if needed. Transfer to a serving platter and serve.

Sausage and Beans

Serves: 8

2 pounds sausage cut into 1 1/2 inch pieces
1 tablespoon vegetable oil
1/3 cup minced sweet onion
2 cups dried navy beans (approx. 1 pound)
2 cups water
1 tablespoon dried thyme
1 teaspoon dried celery seed
1/4 teaspoon dried ground black pepper
2 (14 ounce) cans chicken broth
3 cloves garlic, minced

Heat a large non-stick skillet over medium heat. Add sausage; sauté 5 minutes or until browned. Remove from pan, and place in a 5 quart electric slow cooker. Heat oil in pan over medium heat. Add onion and garlic; sauté 1 minute. Sort and wash beans. Add beans, onion mixture, water, thyme, celery seeds, pepper and chicken broth to cooker. Cover and cook on HIGH for 8 hours or more until the beans are tender. Garnish with thyme springs, if desired.

Nutritional Information: 366 calories; FAT 13.6 g; PROTEIN 27.3g; CARB 34.9g; FIBER 0.3g; CHOL 75mg; IRON 4.4mg; SODIUM 1.362mg; CALC 92mg

Pork Roast with Apples & Sage

Serves: 8

4 teaspoons chopped fresh sage
1 tablespoon minced garlic
1 teaspoon kosher salt
1/2 teaspoon freshly ground pepper
2 3/4 pound boneless pork loin roast
1 jar pork gravy
4 medium gala apples

Mix sage, garlic, salt and pepper in a small cup. Spread over top of pork. Place gravy in a 4 quart or larger slow cooker. Core 2 apples and coarsely chop add to gravy. Place pork on top. Cover and cook on low 5 to 7 hours. Core and cut remaining 2 apples into 8 wedges each add to slow cooker for the last hour of cooking.
Remove pork and apple wedges to a tray let stand. Remove chopped apple with a slotted spoon to a food processor puree. Add 1 cup of cooking liquid to apple puree warm. Slice pork serve with apple wedges and apple gravy. **Leftovers**: Make a grilled sandwich with thin slices of pork, cooked apple wedges, sliced gruyere or Swiss and Dijon-coated rye or pumpernickel.   Cut pork roast into thin strips. Toss with cooked pumpkin ravioli and a little melted butter.   Or add chopped pork and apple to mixed greens along with dried cranberries, walnuts and crumbled blue cheese. Toss with vinaigrette.

Nutritional Information: Calories per serving 288, 36g protein, 15g carb, 2g fiber, 9g fat (3g sat fat), 102mg chol, 542mg sodium.

Smothered Pork Chops

Serves: 4

5 pork chops, about 1 1/4 to 1 1/2 pounds
Salt and freshly ground pepper to taste
2 tablespoons canola oil, divided
1 medium onion, chopped
1 cup sliced mushrooms
1/4 cup all-purpose flour
1 teaspoon ground cumin
1 can chicken broth 14.5-ounce
2 tablespoons spicy mustard
2 tablespoons freshly chopped parsley leaves

Pre-heat an ovenproof skillet over high heat. Season the pork chops with salt and pepper to taste. Add 1 tablespoon of canola oil to the pan. Add the pork chops and sear on both sides until golden brown. Remove from skillet and set aside. In same skillet over medium heat, add the remaining canola oil, onions and mushrooms and sauté until slightly softened. Add the flour and cumin and cook until lightly golden in color. Stir in the chicken broth and mustard add bring to a boil. Reduce the heat to a simmer, add the parsley and return the chops to the pan. Season with salt and pepper; spoon gravy over pork chops. Simmer for 5 minutes or until pork chops are cooked thoroughly.

Iceberg Wedge Salad with Warm Bacon Dressing

1 head iceberg lettuce
4 slices bacon
2 teaspoons brown sugar
1/4 cup red wine vinegar
Salt and pepper to taste
1 hard-boiled egg, finely chopped

Remove the core from the lettuce and cut into 4 quarters. Arrange on serving plates and set aside. In a small skillet, sauté bacon until crisp.

Remove from skillet to a plate lined with a paper bag or paper towels. Once cooled, chop into small pieces and add to a small bowl. In the skillet over low heat, add the brown sugar, vinegar and salt and pepper to taste.

Whisk together until combined and sugar is completely dissolved. Stir in the egg and bacon and season with salt and pepper to taste. Pour over the top of the iceberg wedges and serve immediately.

Classic Cabbage Rolls

Serves: 4
Approximately $1.80 per serving.

1 medium head of cabbage, cored
1 ½ cups chopped onion, divided
1 tablespoon butter
2 14.5 ounce cans of Italian stewed tomatoes
4 cloves of garlic, minced
2 tablespoon of brown sugar
1 ½ teaspoon salt, divided
1 cup cooked rice
¼ cup ketchup
2 tablespoons Worcestershire sauce
¼ teaspoon pepper
1 pound ground beef
¼ pound sausage
½ cup V-8 juice, optional

In a Dutch oven, cook the cabbage in boiling water for 10 minutes or until the outer leaves are tender; drain. Rinse in cold water; drain. Remove eight large outer leaves (refrigerate remaining cabbage for another use); set aside. In a saucepan, sauté 1 cup onions in butter until tender. Add tomatoes, garlic, brown sugar and ½ teaspoon salt. Simmer for 15 minutes, stirring occasionally. Meanwhile, in a bowl, combine rice, ketchup, Worcestershire sauce, pepper and remaining onion and salt. Add beef and sausage; mix well. Remove thick vein from cabbage leaves for easier rolling. Place about ½ cup meat mixture on each leaf; fold in sides. Starting at an unfolded edge; roll up leaf to completely enclose filling. Place seam side down in a skillet. Top with sauce. Cover and cook over medium-low heat for 1 hour. Add V-8 juice if desired. Reduce heat to low; cook 20 minutes longer or until rolls are heated through and meat is no longer pink.

Cabbage Rolls

Serves: 10

1 head green cabbage
1 cup cooked rice
1 lb. lean pork sausage
1/2 pound ground beef
1/2 cup diced onions
2 teaspoon Italian herb seasoning
1 teaspoon garlic powder
1 teaspoon each of salt and ground pepper
1 large jar of pasta sauce
2 cans of diced tomatoes

Preparation: In large Dutch oven, bring 4 quarts of water to a boil. Core cabbage and submerge in boiling water boil 10 minutes and drain. When cool enough to handle, separate leaves. In bowl, combine rice, sausage, ground beef, onions and 1/2 teaspoon. of each seasoning. Drain one can of tomatoes, reserving liquid. Add tomatoes and 1/2 jar of pasta sauce to rice mixture. Divide mixture and place on 10-12 cabbage leaves. Fold in ends and roll up. Place cabbage rolls in greased glass baking dish. In bowl, combine other can of tomatoes, reserved tomato liquid, 1/2 jar of pasta sauce, and 1/2 teaspoon. of each seasoning. Pour over cabbage rolls. Cover tightly with foil. Bake at 375 degrees for 1 hour.

Best Meatloaf

Serves: 6-8

3/4 cup ketchup
2 large eggs
1/2 cup milk
2 tablespoons Worcestershire sauce
1 teaspoon salt
1/4 teaspoon pepper
2 pounds meatloaf mix 50% beef, 25% pork, 25% veal
1/2 cup chopped scallion or onion
1/2 cup chopped green bell peppers
1 cup crushed saltine crackers (approx. 24)
1 tablespoon minced garlic
1 tablespoon packed brown sugar

Pre-heat oven to 425 degrees. Line a rimmed baking sheet with nonstick foil. Stir together 1/2 cup ketchup and the next 5 ingredients in a large bowl. Add meatloaf meats, onions, bell pepper, saltines and garlic. Mix well with hands or a wooden spoon. Place on baking sheet and pat into an 11 x 5-inch oval loaf. Mix remaining 1/4 cup ketchup and the brown sugar. Spread over loaf. Bake 50 minutes, or until a meat thermometer inserted in center registers 160 degrees. Let rest 5 minutes before slicing. Leftovers make great sandwiches.

Nutritional Information: 499 calories per serving, 31g fat, 12g saturated fat, 194mg cholesterol, 1094mg sodium, 22g carbohydrates, 1g fiber, 31g protein

Make-Ahead Italian Meatballs

Serves: 6

1 pound lean ground beef
1 medium onion, chopped (1/2 cup)
1/3 cup dry bread crumbs (any flavor)
1/4 cup milk
1 egg
1 teaspoon salt
1/8 teaspoon pepper
1 cup chili sauce
1/2 cup cold water
1 jar (12 ounces) tomato pasta sauce (any variety)
1 teaspoon yellow mustard

Preheat oven to 400ºF.

Mix ground beef, onion, bread crumbs, milk, egg, salt and pepper. Shape mixture into thirty 1-inch balls. Place in ungreased rectangular pan, 13x9x2 inches. Bake uncovered about 15 minutes or until no longer pink in center and juices are clear. Place meatballs on ungreased cookie sheet. Freeze uncovered about 20 minutes or until firm. Place partially frozen meatballs in heavy plastic bag or freezer container. Seal, label and freeze no longer than 3 months. About 25 minutes before serving, mix chili sauce, water, pasta sauce and mustard in 2-quart saucepan. Add meatballs. Heat to boiling, stirring occasionally. Reduce heat. Cover and simmer about 20 minutes or until meatballs are hot.

Spaghetti Sauce

Makes 5 to 6 quarts

1 large diced sweet onion
1 large green bell pepper, diced
4 tablespoon of olive oil
1 ½ pound ground chuck
½ pound ground sausage
8 cloves of garlic, minced
1/3 cup of dried parsley
2 tablespoon of dried basil
1 ½ tablespoon of dried oregano
1 teaspoon of sugar
Salt and pepper to taste
3 (28-ounce) cans of whole tomatoes with juice.
1 (28-ounce) can of tomato sauce
1 (28-ounce) can of crushed tomatoes
1 (6-ounce) can of tomato paste

This is a very special recipe that I have refined over 40 years. Enjoy!

Put olive oil in a large 10 quart stock pot. Add sweet onions and bell peppers and simmer until iridescent. Then add ground chuck and sausage in very small pieces and cook it till no longer pink. While cooking open up all of your cans. Remove the stems from each tomato, and any tomato along with any skins you find. Then squish the tomatoes between your fingers until you have broken them down into small pieces. Add this to your meat mixture along with the tomato sauce, crushed tomatoes, garlic and herbs. Cook this for 1 hour, stirring at least every 5 minutes so that it doesn't stick to the bottom of the pan. If it does, scrap it with a metal spatula and gently lift it out of the sauce, and wipe off the spatula so that none of burnt sauce gets into the sauce. If the sauce seem thin, add one six-ounce can of tomato paste to thicken. Cook for another ½ hour. 1 quart of sauce will usually serve 3 people. You can freeze the leftovers for other Italian dishes.

Dessert Recipes

Bourbon Brownies

Serves: 24 or more

1 cup butter or margarine
2/3 cup cocoa
2 cups sugar
4 eggs
1 cup all-purpose flour
½ teaspoon salt
2 teaspoon vanilla extract
¾ cup chopped nuts
¼ cup bourbon

White Icing:
2 cups powdered sugar
½ cup butter, softened
1 to 4 tablespoon bourbon

Chocolate Glaze:
1 cup (6 ounce) semi-sweet chocolate morsels
3 tablespoon butter, softened

Preheat oven to 350 degrees. Melt butter in saucepan over low heat. Add cocoa mix well with a wooden spoon. Stir in sugar. Add eggs one at a time, beating well after each addition. Stir in flour, salt, and vanilla. Mix just until combined, Do not over-mix. Stir in nuts. Spread mixture in a greased and floured 13 x 9-inch pan. Bake for 30 to 35 minutes or until toothpick inserted in center comes out clean. Sprinkle bourbon over brownies while still hot. Cool completely. Spread with white icing. Spread thin layer of chocolate glaze over icing. Cut into diamonds. **White Icing preparation**: Beat sugar, butter, and bourbon in small bowl with electric mixer until creamy. **Chocolate Glaze preparation**: Melt chocolate and butter in a small saucepan over low heat, stirring constantly. **Note:** I always make extra chocolate glaze.

Passover Brownies

5 bittersweet chocolate bars (1½ ounce each)
4 eggs
1 cup butter
2 cups sugar
½ teaspoon salt
2 tablespoons instant coffee powder
1 cup matzo cake meal
1 cup chopped nuts (optional)

Melt chocolate and butter. Allow to cool. Beat together eggs and sugar. Blend in chocolate mix. Stir in dry ingredients. Fold in the nuts, if desired. Pour into a greased 9 x 13 pan. Bake at 325 degrees for 30 minutes. Cut while still warm.

Rum-Doused Lemon Poppy Seed Cake

Serves: 12-16

1 cup (2 sticks) butter, softened
4 ounces cream cheese, softened
1¾ cups sugar
3 large eggs
1 tablespoon grated lemon rind
1½ cups all-purpose flour
1 teaspoon baking powder
2 tablespoons fresh poppy seeds
¼ cup light rum

Preheat oven to 375 degrees. Grease a 10- inch tube or Bundt pan very well.

In a large mixing bowl, beat together the butter and cream cheese until well-blended. Then beat in the sugar, eggs, and lemon rind, beating until the mixture is light and fluffy. In a separate bowl, sift together the flour and baking powder, then beat this into the butter mixture. Stir in the poppy seeds.

Spoon the batter into the prepared pan and bake until the cake is a light golden brown and springs back firmly when pressed, 55 to 60 minutes. Cool for 15 minutes in the pan, then invert onto a wire rack to cool. Drizzle the rum over the cake a little at a time, allowing it to be absorbed by the cake before drizzling on more. Transfer to a cake plate or stand, cover, and let stand 2 to 3 hours before serving.

For added garnishment, sift some powdered sugar over cake, or put a few fresh flowers or holly around the base.

Grilled Pineapple

Serves: 8

1 fresh pineapple, peeled, cored and cut into 1"
rings
1/4 teaspoon honey
3 tablespoons melted butter
1 dash hot pepper sauce
Salt to taste

Place pineapple in a large re-sealable plastic bag. Add honey, butter, hot pepper sauce, and salt. Seal bag, and shake to coat evenly. Marinate for at least 30 minutes, or preferably overnight.
Pre-heat an outdoor grill for high heat, and lightly oil grate. Grill pineapple for 2 to 3 minutes per side, or until heated through and grill marks appear.

Coffee Granita

Serves: 6

2 cups lukewarm espresso or strong black coffee
1/2 cup sugar
2 tablespoons coffee flavored liqueur
1 teaspoon orange or lemon zest

Combine all ingredients and stir until sugar melts. Pour mixture into 9 by 13-inch metal pan and place on level shelf in freezer for half an hour. (Mixture should come only about 1/4-inch up the side of the pan.) Remove and use a dinner fork to scrape any ice crystals that have formed on the side or bottom of the pan. Return to freezer and repeat scraping every 20 to 30 minutes for 3 to 4 hours. Once mixture is thoroughly frozen, fluff with a fork and allow flakes to "dry" in freezer another half hour before serving. When served, the granita should look like a fluffy pile of dry brown crystals. Scoop into goblets and top with barely sweetened whipped cream; add additional citrus zest if desired.

Mango Granita

Serves: 6

1/3 cup sugar
1 juice from one lime
3 mangoes, peeled and cut into 1" pieces
1/2 cup mango juice (such as Dole Mango Lime Fiesta)
Lime slices or mint leaves for garnish (optional)

Place 1/2 cup cold water and the sugar in a small saucepan and bring to a simmer over medium heat. Stir until sugar dissolves, about 3 minutes. Remove from heat and pour into a large bowl and allow to cool. Stir in lime juice. Place mangoes and mango juice into a blender and puree. Add to sugar syrup and stir. Pour into a shallow metal pan and freeze for 3 to 4 hours. Stir mixture every hour, spooning ice crystals from side of pan into middle. When mixture is frozen, place in food processor and pulse for about 5 seconds until you get a snow-like consistency. **To serve**, spoon into dessert dishes and garnish with lime slices and mint if desired.

Classic Chocolate Chip Cookies

1 cup brown sugar
1 cup granulated sugar
2 sticks butter
1 ½ teaspoon vanilla
2 eggs
2 ¼ cups flour
1 teaspoon baking soda
½ teaspoon salt
2 cups chocolate chips (or any combination of nuts & chips)

Cream both sugars and butter until fluffy. Add vanilla and eggs and beat until smooth. Add flour, baking soda, and salt and beat until smooth. Add chocolate chips. Drop from teaspoon onto greased cooking sheet and bake in a 375 degree oven for 10-12 minutes per batch.

Oatmeal Raisin Cookies

12 tablespoons butter (1 ½ sticks), room temperature
1 cup packed brown sugar
½ cup granulated sugar
1 egg
2 tablespoons + ½ teaspoon warm water
2 teaspoons vanilla
2/3 cup flour
1 teaspoon cinnamon
½ teaspoon salt
½ teaspoon baking soda
3 ¼ cups quick cooking oats
1 cup moist raisins

Preheat oven to 350 degrees. Cream both sugars and butter together in a mixer. Add egg, water and vanilla and blend. Add dry ingredients and mix well. Add oats and raisins and mix with a wooden spoon. Drop by spoonfuls onto a greased baking sheet and bake for 15 minutes.

Presidential Sweet Cookies

Makes: 48

1 cup (2 sticks) butter
3 1/2 cups brown sugar
1 1/2 teaspoon espresso powder
5 eggs
1 1/2 teaspoon vanilla extract
4 cups flour
1 1/2 teaspoon baking soda
1 1/2 teaspoon baking powder
1 1/2 teaspoon salt
1 1/2 cup oatmeal or rice
1 1/2 cup raisins
3/4 cup pecan pieces
1 cup chocolate pieces

Preheat oven to 325 degrees. Cream butter and sugar. Add espresso powder and mix. Add eggs and vanilla in 3 stages, and cream well after each addition. Combine flour, baking soda, baking powder, and salt. Then add the flour mixture to the creamed mixture and mix until smooth. Add remaining ingredients and mix until well combined. Drop by heaping tablespoon onto a cool greased baking sheet. Bake for 10 - 12 minutes.

Bananas Foster

Serve: 4

1 pint vanilla ice cream
4 large bananas
¼ cup banana liqueur or water
½ cup dark rum
6 tablespoons unsalted butter
¼ cup packed light brown sugar
½ teaspoon ground cinnamon

Cover a small rimmed baking sheet (that will fit in the freezer) with parchment paper and place in the freezer for 10 minutes. When chilled, remove pan from the freezer. Quickly scoop ice cream into 12 small balls and place on chilled parchment-lined sheet. Keep in freezer until firm and ready to serve, at least 1 hour and up to 1 day in advance.

When ready to serve, peel bananas and quarter them, cutting lengthwise, then crosswise set aside. Pour banana liqueur and dark rum into separate glass measuring cups and set aside. Heat 3 Tablespoon butter in a large skillet over medium heat. Sprinkle sugar and cinnamon over butter, and cook until sugar is dissolved. Remove pan from heat and carefully stir in banana liqueur. Add bananas, flat side down, and cook until softened and lightly browned on the bottom. Remove pan from heat and add rum. Return to heat and cook about 10 seconds to allow rum to

heat up. If using a gas stove, carefully tip the pan away from you until the vapors from the rum ignite. (Alternatively, you can light the rum with a long match.) When the flames have subsided, remove pan from heat and gently stir in remaining 3 tablespoon butter.

Place 3 scoops of ice cream in each of four serving bowls. Spoon the banana mixture and the sauce over each. Serve immediately.

Note: The key to maintaining the contrasting textures and temperatures of this dish is to prepare all the ingredients before making the sauce. So be sure to measure out the liqueur, rum, butter, brown sugar, and cinnamon, and keep the individual scoops of ice cream in the freezer, before you ever begin to make the sauce to ensure everything turns out as it should.

Chocolate Butter Sweets

Makes: 24

1 cup butter
1 cup confectioner's sugar
½ teaspoon salt
2 teaspoon vanilla
2 cups flour

Preheat oven to 350°. Cream butter, sugar, vanilla, and salt add flour little by little. The more flour you add to this recipe, the tougher (not as delicate) the cookies will be. Shape a teaspoonful into a ball and place on an ungreased cookie sheet, making a thumb imprint into each.

Bake for 12 to 15 minutes until delicately browned. Fill with about 1 teaspoon or so of cream coconut filling while slightly warm, then drizzle a teaspoon of chocolate frosting over the cookies.

Cream Coconut Filling:
Soften 6 ounce of cream cheese and blend with 2 cups of confectioners' sugar, 4 tablespoon of flour, and 2 teaspoon of vanilla. Cream well. Stir in ½ cup flaked coconut.

Chocolate Frosting:
Melt 1 cup semi-sweet chocolate morsels and 4 tablespoons butter with 4 tablespoons water over low heat, stirring occasionally. Add 1 cup sifted confectioners' sugar and beat until smooth.

Butterscotch Pudding

Serves: 6

3 cups milk
1/2 cup granulated sugar
1/2 cup packed dark-brown sugar
3 tablespoons cornstarch
1/4 teaspoon ground nutmeg
3 egg yolks
1/4 teaspoon salt
2 tablespoons unsalted butter, cut into pieces
2 teaspoons vanilla extract
Whipped cream to garnish

Stir together 2 1/2 cup of the milk and the granulated sugar in a large saucepan. Heat until just steaming. Remove from heat set aside. Meanwhile, in a medium-sized bowl, mix together the dark-brown sugar, cornstarch and nutmeg until evenly blended. Whisk in the egg yolks, and the remaining 1/2 cup milk and salt. Stir a little of the hot milk mixture into the brown sugar mixture to warm egg yolks, then stir brown sugar mixture back into milk mixture in saucepan.

Cook, stirring constantly with wooden spoon, over medium-low heat until thickened and it registers 160 degrees on an instant-read thermometer, about 20 minutes. Remove from heat. Add butter and vanilla; stir until smooth. Pour mixture through strainer into six dishes. Cool 10 minutes. Cover surface directly with plastic; refrigerate at least 2 hours. Garnish with whipped cream.

Nutritional Information: 313 calories per serving, 13g fat (7g sat), 5g protein 44g carbohydrate 0g fiber 161mg sodium 135mg cholesterol

Rice Pudding w/Raisins

Serves: 8

4 cups milk
1 cup long-grain white rice
2/3 cup sugar
1/4 teaspoon salt
3/4 cup raisins
1/4 teaspoon ground allspice

In a heavy-bottomed saucepan, mix milk, rice, sugar, and salt. Bring to a simmer over high heat. Reduce heat to low; cover and simmer, stirring occasionally, for 20 minutes. Add raisins and allspice. Continue to cook, covered, stirring occasionally, for about 25 minutes, until rice and raisins are tender. Divide pudding among 8 dishes, about 1/2 cup each. Top with a sprinkling of allspice, serve warm.

Nutritional information per serving: 271 calories 4g fat (2g sat) 6g protein, 53g carbohydrate 1g fiber 124mg sodium 12mg cholesterol

Yesterday's Rice, Today's Rice Pudding

Serve 6

Butter for pan
1 cup cooked medium or long-grain rice
½ cup raisins (optional)
3 large eggs
½ cup sugar
2 cups whole or 2% milk
1 teaspoon vanilla
½ teaspoon ground cinnamon

Preheat the oven to 325 degrees. Lightly butter an 8" square glass baking dish. Set it aside. Combine the rice and raisins in a 2 quart or larger saucepan, add 1 cup water, and heat over medium heat until the rice is rehydrated, about 10 minutes. Drain, if necessary, and set aside.

Meanwhile whisk the eggs, sugar, milk, vanilla and cinnamon together in a medium-sized bowl. Add the drained plumped rice and raisins to the mixture. Stir well and pour into the prepared baking dish. Bake the pudding, uncovered, until the center is almost set and a knife inserted within1 inch of the side of the dish comes out clean, about 45 minutes.

Serve warm, at room temperature, or chilled with whipped cream as a garnish.

Old Fashioned Rice Pudding

Serves: 6

1 to 2 tablespoons unsalted butter
1 large egg
1 cup half-and-half
3 cups milk
½ cup sugar
¼ cup long grain wild rice
1 cup raisins or currants
1 teaspoon vanilla
Ground cinnamon and ground nutmeg, for garnish heavy cream for topping

Preheat oven to 300º. Lightly butter a shallow 1½ quart glass baking dish. Lightly beat the egg and half-and-half in a 2 quart bowl. Add the milk, sugar, rice, raisins, and vanilla. Mix well and pour into the baking dish. Stirring occasionally, bake for 2½ to 3 hours or until the liquid is absorbed and the pudding is set. Sprinkle the top with cinnamon and nutmeg. Serve warm or chilled with cold heavy cream.

Pumpkin Dessert Bars

Serves: 15

1-3/4 cups graham cracker crumbs
1-1/3 cups sugar, divided
1/2 cup butter, melted
1 package (8 ounces) cream cheese, softened
5 eggs
1 can (15 ounces) solid-pack pumpkin
1/2 cup packed brown sugar
1/2 cup milk
1/2 teaspoon salt
1/2 teaspoon ground cinnamon
1 envelope unflavored gelatin
1/4 cup cold water
Whipped topping and ground nutmeg, optional

In a small bowl, combine graham cracker crumbs and 1/3 cup sugar; stir in butter. Press into a greased 13 x 9 inch baking dish. In a small bowl, beat cream cheese and 2/3 cup sugar until smooth. Beat in 2 eggs just until blended. Pour over crust. Bake at 350 degrees for 20-25 minutes or until set. Cool on a wire rack. Meanwhile, separate remaining eggs and set whites aside. In a large saucepan, combine the yolks, pumpkin, brown sugar, milk, salt and cinnamon. Cook and stir over low heat for 10-12 minutes or until mixture is thickened and reaches 160 degrees. Remove from the heat. In a small saucepan, sprinkle gelatin over cold water; let stand for 1 minute. Heat over low heat, stirring until gelatin is completely dissolved. Stir into pumpkin mixture; set aside. In a large heavy saucepan, combine reserved egg whites and remaining sugar. With a portable mixer, beat on low speed for 1 minute. Continue beating over low heat until mixture reaches 160 degrees, about 12 minutes. Remove from the heat; beat until stiff glossy peaks form and sugar is dissolved. Fold into pumpkin mixture; spread evenly over cream cheese layer. Cover and refrigerate for 4 hours or until set. Garnish with whipped topping and nutmeg if desired.

Nutrition Information: 1 bar (calculated without whipped topping) equals 284 calories, 14 g fat (8 g saturated fat), 104 mg cholesterol, 257 mg sodium, 36 g carbohydrate, 2 g fiber, 5 g protein

New York Style Cheesecake

Serves: 16

Graham Cracker Crust:
1/2 cup butter
2 tablespoon sugar
1 1/4 cup graham cracker pie crust
Filling:
6 (8-ounce) packages cream cheese
2 cups sugar
7 large eggs
Juice of one lemon
4 tablespoons heavy cream
1 tablespoon pure vanilla extract

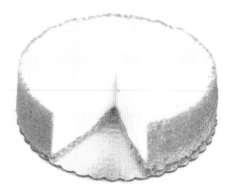

Preheat oven to 325 degrees. Melt butter; mix in graham cracker crumbs and sugar, then press firmly onto bottom of a 9 inch spring-form pan. Put in freezer for 15 minutes. Cut up cream cheese bars and put into food processor. Turn on and slowly add 2 cups of sugar. Then add eggs one at a time, mixing well after each addition. Mix in lemon juice, followed by cream and vanilla extract. Scrape bowl down and mix again. Pour into spring-form pan (lined with graham cracker crust). Bake approximately 90 minutes or until set. Then leave the oven door open and cool down for one hour. Then put in the refrigerator. Cheesecake will taste better if you can make the day before serving.

Pumpkin Pie

Serves: 8

1 large pie crust
1/2 cup granulated sugar
1/2 cup brown sugar
1 tablespoon all-purpose Flour
1/2 teaspoon salt
1 teaspoon ground ginger
1 teaspoon ground cinnamon
1/2 teaspoon nutmeg
1/8 teaspoon ground cloves
1/8 teaspoon freshly ground black pepper
(optional)
3 large eggs, beaten
2 cups (or one 15 ounce can) pumpkin
1 1/4 cups light cream or evaporated milk

pumpkin pie ▸

In a large measuring cup, beat together the eggs, pumpkin, and cream or evaporated milk. Whisk into the dry ingredients. For best flavor, cover and refrigerate the filling overnight before baking. Lightly grease a 9" pie pan that's at least 1 1/2" deep. Roll the pie dough out to a 13" circle, and transfer to the pan. Crimp the edges above the rim; this will give you a little extra headroom to hold the filling when it expands in the oven. Refrigerate the crust while the oven preheats to 400 degrees. Or you may use a ready-made pie crust. When the oven is hot, place the pie pan on a baking sheet to catch any drips. Pour the filling into the unbaked pie shell. Bake for 45 to 50 minutes, until the filling is set 2" in from the edge. The center should still be wobbly. Remove the pie from the oven and cool on a rack; the center will finish cooking through as the pie sits.

Rum Pudding with Raspberry Sauce

Serves: 8

6 egg yolks
½ cup plus 4 tablespoon sugar
4 tablespoons 151 rum
2 teaspoon vanilla
½ teaspoon salt
2 packages (envelopes) unflavored gelatin 1½ cup cold water
2 cups whipping cream

Raspberry sauce:
2 packages (16 ounce) frozen raspberries
1 cup sugar
2 tablespoons cornstarch

Beat yolks in a medium-sized mixing bowl until thick and lemon-colored. Gradually add sugar, beating well. Add rum, vanilla, and salt, beating well. In a saucepan, soften gelatin in cold water. Bring to a boil, stirring until gelatin dissolves. Cool slightly. Slowly pour gelatin into rum mixture, beating constantly. Cool completely, but do not allow mixture to set. Beat whipping cream until soft peaks form. Fold into rum mixture. Pour into a lightly oiled 5 or 6 cup mold and chill until set. Unmold pudding onto a serving platter. Spoon sauce over pudding or ladle on plate. Add fresh berries, if desired.

Sauce: Combine berries and sugar in a saucepan bring to a boil and boil 5 minutes. Process mixture through a food mill. Combine a small amount of mixture and cornstarch stir into remaining berry mixture. Cook over low heat, stirring constantly until smooth and thickened. Yield about 1¾ cups.

Apricot Bars

Makes: 3 dozen

¾ cup softened butter
1 cup sugar
½ teaspoon vanilla
1 egg
2 cups all-purpose flour
1/3 teaspoon baking powder
1 1/3 cups flaked coconut
½ cup chopped walnuts
1 jar (10 to 12 ounces) apricot preserves.

In a large bowl, cream butter, sugar and vanilla. Add egg; mix well. Combine flour and baking powder. Gradually add to creamed mixture. Fold in coconut and walnuts.

Press two-thirds of dough into a greased 13 x 9 inch baking pan. Spread with preserves; crumble remaining dough over preserves. Bake at 350 degrees for 30-35 minutes or until golden brown. Cool in pan on wire rack. Cut into bars.

Chapter 15

Understanding Some of the Foods We Use

Cooking Lean Cuts of Beef

These beef cuts have the least amount of fat. In many cases, moist-heat cooking methods are best for tenderizing them.

Cut of Beef	Best Cooking Method
Bottom Round Roast	Roast or braise large pieces Broil or pan-grill steaks
Brisket	Braise
Chuck Roast	Braise or stew or have ground 80/20
Eye of Round	Roast large pieces Braise chunks Broil or pan-grill steaks
Flank Steak	Broil or pan-grill
Round Tip	Roast or braise large pieces Broil or pan-grill steaks Sauté thick strips
Shank Cross Cuts	Braise
Sirloin Steak	Broil or pan-grill (whole or cubed)
Top Round	Roast large pieces Broil or pan-grill marinated steaks

Gelatin and Other Thickeners

Gelatin is developed from collagen, a naturally occurring protein obtained from meat by-products. Most gelatin available commercially is derived from pig skin. The collagen is cleaned and processed, which results in the yellow dry powder we know as gelatin. Alone it is odorless and tasteless, used as a thickening agent for molded desserts and salads, as well as for thickening cold soups.

When gelatin is dissolved in hot water, then cooled, it creates a jelly. Most unsweetened gelatin is sold in granulated form. Leaf or sheet gelatin is also available, though it is not as common as granulated. We are all familiar with the sweetened form of granulated gelatin, often referred to as the brand name "Jell-O."

Professional chefs often use leaf gelatin, as do many European recipes. You can, however, substitute granulated gelatin in any recipe for leaf gelatin. One envelope (1 tablespoon) of granulated gelatin is the equivalent to four sheets of leaf gelatin.

Those who wish a vegan substitute to gelatin to use as thickener have many choices. Agar-agar is the most common. It is derived from seaweed and is usually sold in strands, powder or blocks. Arrowroot, guar gum, xanthan gum, pectin, and kudzu are other vegan thickeners.

Doneness Tests and Temperatures

For the most accurate doneness test, use an instant-read thermometer to get a temperature reading. Insert the thermometer into the center or thickest portion of the meat. After roasting meats, let the roast rest 10 minutes before carving to allow the juices to seep back into the meat.

This Food…	Is done when…
BEEF	
Ground (Loose)	No Longer pink
Ground (in loaf or patties)	160 degrees Fahrenheit, no longer pink
Roasts, steaks	145 degree Fahrenheit (medium-rare) 160 degree Fahrenheit (medium) 165 degree Fahrenheit (well-done)
Long-cooking pot roasts	Fork-tender
Cutlets	No longer pink
Calf's liver, sliced ¼" thick	Just pink in the center
Veal, roasts	145 degrees (medium-rare) 155 degrees (medium) 165 degrees (well-done)
PORK	
Chops, ribs	160 degrees, juices run clear
Roasts, tenderloin	155 degrees, juices run clear
Ham, country	160 degrees
Ham, precooked	140 degrees
LAMB	
Chops	160 degrees, juices run clear
Roasts, leg steaks	145 degrees (medium-rare) 155 degrees (medium) 165 degrees (well-done)
CHICKEN AND CORNISH GAME HEN	
Boneless breasts	160 degrees, juices run clear
Bone-in parts	170 degrees, juices run clear
Whole or butterflied	180 degrees for breast, juices run clear, 165 degree , for stuffing
Ground (loose)	No longer pink
Ground (in loaf or patties)	165 degree, no longer pink
Cutlets	No longer pink, juices run clear

This Food...	Is done when...
TURKEY	
Breasts	170 degrees, juices run clear
Whole	180 degrees for breast, juices run clear, 165 degrees, for stuffing
Ground (loose)	No Longer pink
Ground (in loaf patties)	165 degrees, no longer pink
DUCK AND GOOSE	
Whole	175 degrees, 180 degrees for thigh
Breast	Still slightly pink
GAME MEATS	
Bison tenderloin steaks	145 degrees (medium-rare) 155 degrees (medium) 165 degrees (well-done)
Emu Steaks	145 degrees (medium-rare)
Venison Chops	145 degrees (medium-rare)
VARIOUS CUT-UP MEATS	
Cubed or crumbled meats	No longer pink
Long-cooking stew and other meats	Fork-tender
FISH	
Fillets (salmon)	Fish is opaque
Fillets (other)	Fish just flakes easily
Steaks	Fish is just opaque
SHELLFISH AND MOLLUSKS	
Clams, mussels, oysters	Shells open (discard any unopened shells)
Shrimp, scallops, lobster, crabs	Flesh is opaque
Octopus	Until tender
Squid	Until tender

Grits

Old-fashioned stone-ground grits are as American as can be. They are very popular in the South and are often served for breakfast, either sweetened like hot cereal or cooked with savory flavorings such as cheese and beer. Many cooks make creamy grits by cooking them in milk and cream until tender.

Polenta

Polenta is an Italian food that can be used as side dish or a main dish, depending on what you choose to top it with. Typically it can be high in fat if made with butter and cheeses. The polenta that you find is the store is in a tube and pre-cooked. It is economical and can be bought with or without herbs. It is easy to prepare; it requires only slicing, a little frying and adding a topping of your choice. Just follow the instructions on the package.

Polenta is made from cornmeal, water and butter. You can buy a corn flour called Polenta but it is still just cornmeal and will be more expensive.

If you like a smooth texture, use a fine cornmeal. A fine cornmeal will produce more lumps. Add the cornmeal slowly to the liquid, whisking as it cooks to prevent a lumping problem. If you like a heavy, grainy texture uses course cornmeal.

If you make homemade polenta, you will probably use a loaf pan that measures 8 1/2 inches by 4 1/2 inches. Spray the loaf pan with cooking spray and then pour in hot polenta, cover with plastic wrap and refrigerate. When completely chilled, cut into 1-inch slices and sauté in 1 tablespoon butter or oil until lightly browned.

Polenta can also be served as soon as you make it. Spoon it while still hot onto a plate and garnish as desired. Polenta plates up nicely with a piece of grilled chicken or fish. It looks nice when topped with vegetables and/or sauces.

Rice, Pasta, and Dried Beans

Rice, beans, and pasta are staples of cuisines worldwide. And for very good reason. They are nutritious, easy to prepare, adaptable and inexpensive. They can be added to many dishes as extenders without concern that you are diluting the nutrition or the flavor of the meal. (Just be certain that the dish you are extending has plenty of liquid or sauce, as these starches will continue to absorb liquid after cooking.) When added to soups, they add bulk and substance. They can transform a soup into a hearty stew.

Since these starches are such an important part of the diet of the frugal and nutrition-conscious cook and are frequently interchangeable in recipes, it is worthwhile to do a comparison of the nutritional profiles. Pasta and rice are nutritionally similar, though pasta is slightly higher in both protein and fiber. In a one cup serving, spaghetti has 221 calories, 8.12g of protein, 43.2g of carbohydrates, and 2.5g of fiber. Rice has 242 calories, 4.43g of protein, 53.18g of carbohydrates and .6g of fiber in a one cup serving. Making the switch to brown rice or whole-wheat pasta further increases the nutrients and fiber. Whole wheat spaghetti contains 12.6g of fiber versus 5.0g in white spaghetti. Brown rice contains 7.0g of fiber versus 1.2g in white rice. Brown rice is slightly higher in vitamins and minerals than whole wheat spaghetti.

When preparing dried rice and pasta, adding the starch to *salted* water is important, unless there are low sodium diet restrictions. Adding 1 or 2 tablespoons of salt (preferably sea salt for a more complex flavor than table salt) to a large pot of boiling water for pasta seasons the pasta internally as it absorbs the liquid. Not only is the pasta itself more flavorful, but the dish overall may require less salt as a result. **Another tip:** do not add oil to the water. Contrary to popular belief, it does not keep the pasta separate as it cooks. It just wastes oil. To keep the pasta from sticking together, be certain that you stir it well during the first two minutes of boiling.

Many varieties of beans are available, and all are nutritious and better sources of protein than rice or pasta. Two examples are red beans and Great Northern beans. Red beans contain 254 calories and have 18g of protein, 56 mg of calcium and 6mg of iron for each 1 cup serving. Great Northern beans contain 236 calories and have 16g of protein, 136mg of calcium and 4mg of iron.

There are many kinds of beans available. The older the bean, the drier it will be, and the more water it will require to tenderize. The following is for 1 pound of beans.

Bean Type	Soak	Water	Cooking Time	Yield
Black beans	Yes	About 6 cups	1 ½ hours	6 ½ cups beans and broth
Black-eyed peas	Yes	About 6 cups	2 hours	7 cups beans and broth
Chickpeas	Yes	About 7 cups	2 ½ hours	7 to 8 cups beans and broth
Lentils	Not req'd	5 cups	30-40 minutes	6 cups beans and broth
Pinto beans	Yes	About 6 cups	2 hours	7 cups beans and broth
Red beans	Yes	About 6 ½ cups	2 ¼ hours	7 cups beans and broth

Are dried beans worth it? Those who are not accustomed to cooking often assume that buying dried beans are too much of a hassle. But consider this: dried beans are often about 1/3 the cost of canned beans. And they are not as much of a hassle as you may think. Most of the soaking required can be done either overnight or while you are at work.

Most dried beans should be soaked before cooking. Use about 3 times as much cold water as beans. Although most kinds of beans will not absorb more water after four hours of soaking, some varieties—fava, gigandes, and soybeans—need 12 hours soaking time. However, soaking for longer will not harm the beans. If you do not have time for that much soaking, you can instead boil beans for 2 minutes, remove them from heat, and allow them to continue soaking while covered for one hour.

An essential point when cooking from dried beans: Do not use the soaking water to continue cooking the bean recipe. Drain off the liquid when the beans are hydrated, as the liquid contains most of the gas-causing, indigestible complex sugars in the outer coating of the beans. Even more importantly, draining and rinsing the beans removes the remaining residues (dirt, pesticides, other chemicals) from the beans. That is why it is also essential to rinse beans before hydrating them. Dried beans cannot be washed before they are packaged, as that step would cause them to start sprouting and becoming moldy.

While individual recipes will vary, the basic method for cooking beans is to cover beans with two inches of fresh water (no more, as it will only slow the cooking process), bring to a boil, then cook, covered, at a very low simmer. Keeping the simmer low will prevent beans from bursting. Do not add salt to the beans until they have become tender, as it will prevent them from becoming so. As an extra preventative measure against splitting, take beans off heat ten minutes before they will be done and allow them to cool in their cooking water.

Small beans like black-eyed peas need about 2 hours to cook; pintos and kidneys, about 2 and a half hours; and lima and larger beans, about 3 hours. <u>Fresher beans take less time to cook</u>. If you want to add more flavor to beans and ensure tenderness, try soaking them in a saltwater solution. Do so overnight, and they'll be ready to cook the next day. Better still, soak them overnight in salt water, then freeze them in plastic bags. The beans will be ready to cook whenever you want them!

Make using beans even more convenient by preparing a big pot of beans every few weeks. Let them cool, then divide them into plastic bags for freezing. Now beans will be ready whenever you wish to use already-cooked beans in a recipe. This is more economical than using canned beans, and with a little prep work, you can make it just as convenient.

Beans from Scratch

1. Pour 1 pound of dried beans into a colander and rinse well under cool water, running your fingers through the beans to find and rinse away any clumps of dirt.
2. For a quick soak, place the beans in a Dutch oven or soup pot and add water to cover by 2 inches. Place pot over high heat, cover, and bring to a boil. Then remove from the heat and let the beans soak for 1 hour. For an overnight soak, place the beans in a Dutch oven or soup pot. Cover the beans with water by 2 inches and cover pot. Let the beans soak for 8 to 12 hours.
3. Drain the beans, discarding the soaking water. Return the beans to the pot and add 6 cups water. Place the pot over high heat, cover, and bring to a boil. Uncover, reduce the heat to low, and simmer the beans until they reach the desired tenderness (see chart above for cooking times). Add more water if necessary to keep beans covered during cooking time.
4. Remove the beans from the heat and set aside to cook or to use in a recipe. The beans can be covered and refrigerated for up to 4 days or frozen in 1 cup batches for up to a month.

Reasons to eat more beans:

1. The fiber in beans helps you feel full faster, which means a little goes a long way.
2. Beans are an excellent and inexpensive source of protein.
3. They can help lower your cholesterol and reduce your risk of a heart attack.
4. They have a positive effect on blood sugar and provide you with long-lasting energy.
5. They help protect against some forms of cancer.

Some may be concerned that only a diet low in carbohydrates (including starches such as pasta, rice, and beans) will promote weight loss or health. Remember that the healthiest diet is a balanced one based on fruits, vegetables, whole grains and lean sources of proteins, not rigid lists of "good" and "bad" foods.

Cooking Time for Grains

Most grains are incredibly easy to cook. For those listed below, measure the water into a saucepan and bring to a boil (unless otherwise indicated). Add ¼ teaspoon salt and/or 1 tablespoon butter or oil if you like. Then, stir in the grain and return to a boil. Reduce the heat to medium-low, cover, and simmer until tender. If necessary, drain off any excess liquid.

Grain	Amt in Cups	Water in cups	Cooking Directions	Yield in cups
Barley, pearl	¾	3	Simmer 45 minutes	3
Barley, quick-cooking	1 ¼	2	Simmer 10-12 minutes	3
Barley, whole (with hull)	¾	4	Soak overnight in the 4 cups water; do not drain; bring to a boil, reduce heat, cover, and simmer 55 min.	3
Buckwheat groats (kasha)	2/3	1 ½	Add to cold water; bring to a boil; cover and simmer 10-12 min	3
Bulgur	1	2	Add to cold water; bring to a boil; cover and simmer 12-15 min	3
Cornmeal	1	2 ¾	Combine cornmeal and 1 cup cold water; add to the 2 ¾ cup boiling water; cover & simmer 10 min	3 1/2
Farina, quick cooking	¾	3 ½	Simmer 2-3 min; stir constantly	3
Hominy grits, quick-cooking	¾	3	Simmer 5 minutes	3
Millet	¾	2	Simmer 15-20 min; let stand, covered, 5 minutes	3
Oats, rolled quick-cooking				
Oats, rolled, quick-cooking	1 ½	3	Simmer 5-7 min; let stand, covered 3 minutes	3
Oats, steel cut	1	2 ½	Simmer 20-25 minutes	2 1/2
Quinoa	¾	1 ½	Rinse thoroughly; simmer 12-15 minutes	2 3/4
Rice, brown	1	2 ½	Simmer 35-45 minutes, let stand covered 5 min.	3
Rice, white	1	2	Simmer 15 minutes, let stand, covered 5 min.	3
Rye berries	¾	2 ½	Soak overnight in the 2 ½ cup water; do not drain; bring to a boil, reduce heat, cover and simmer for 30 minutes	2
Wheat, cracked	2/3	1 ½	Add to cold water; bring to a boil, cover and simmer 12-15 minutes; let stand covered 5 min.	2
Wheat berries	¾	2 ½	Soak overnight in the 2 ½ cup water; do not drain; bring to a boil, reduce heat cover and simmer 30 minutes	2
Wild rice	1	2	Simmer 45-55 minutes	2 2/3

Salt

Use coarse salt crystals in cooking water or to sprinkle onto or into foods for seasoning. Fine-grained or table salts are preferred for most baking because they measure and dissolve evenly.

Measure for measure 1 teaspoon of kosher salt contains less salt than the same amount of table or iodized salt.

Sea salt is available in both fine and coarse grains and is more expensive than kosher salt.

Stale Bread

Perhaps you have purchased extra bread because there was a great sale, or you were given bread from a food pantry. The problem is, you have no more room in the freezer and more bread than you can use.

What can you do with stale bread, besides feeding the birds? The good news is that stale bread has many uses. You can make:

- Bread crumbs in the food processor. Use to coat meats for sautéing or baking, or as a topping for roasted vegetables and casseroles
- Croutons can be made in different sizes or flavors to top a salad. Just cut bread into pieces, toss with some oil and kosher salt, and arrange in a single layer on a baking sheet and bake in a 350 degree oven for 25 to 30 minutes. Before baking you can add herbs (parsley, thyme, rosemary), spices (paprika, ground cumin, cayenne pepper) or cheese (Parmesan – but be sure to use these croutons within a week!)
- French toast – can be made in individual slices or in a French toast casserole
- Strata (either savory or sweet)
- Bread pudding (either savory or sweet)
- Stuffing – can be used for pinwheel meats as well as Cornish hens and turkeys

Tips for Better Tea

Many tea purists insist on china pots and cups. Buy tea in small batches. Store it in a cool place in a tightly sealed container.

Tea bags tend to contain more powder than good-quality loose tea. Loose tea needs a little longer to brew, but the flavor is superior.

Start with cold, fresh water. The flavor of the water affects tea more than coffee, so you may wish to use bottled or filtered water if your tap water is a heavy taste.

Pre-warm the teapot by filling it with hot tap water. Empty it just before adding the dry tea and boiling water.

Use two or three tea bags or two to three teaspoons of loose tea per pot, depending on the size of the pot and how strong you like your tea. Put the tea in the pot and add water.

Remove the kettle from the heat just as the water comes to a full rolling boil. Pour immediately over the tea.

Let the tea steep until it reaches the desired strength remove tea bags before serving. Do not squeeze the tea bags into the pot squeezing releases tannin, which can make the brew bitter.

Keep the tea warm with a British-style cozy (an insulated or quilted fabric cover) or improvise by covering the pot with one or two kitchen towels.

Tips for Perfect Coffee

Start with clean equipment. Coffee gets its flavor from essential oils in the beans. These oils, however, can cause a stale flavor if they build up. Scrub all coffee equipment, especially metal pots and parts, in hot, soapy water after each use.

Use fresh coffee. Store whole beans and ground coffee in an airtight container in the refrigerator or freezer. Unopened cans of vacuum-packed coffee and jars of instant coffee will keep one year at room temperature in a cool, dry place. Once opened, coffee stays fresh for two to three weeks in a cool place, eight weeks in the refrigerator and six months in the freezer.

Use high-quality or gold filters for the best flavor. Poor-quality filters can add an "off" flavor.

Serve coffee immediately after brewing. Use an insulated carafe or thermos rather than keeping the pot on a warmer.

How to Purchase the Freshest Foods

Shopping at warehouse clubs, or getting a great price on fresh produce or meat, is a great time to stock up and save money; but not if half of it ends up going bad before you can eat it. According to a new study the average American wastes more than 200 pounds of food each year.

If you want to know when the fish came into the store, when the peaches arrived, or how to interpret the expiration dates on products, make friends with the staff in the store, and ask them. Every time I go shopping I make sure I say hi to everyone as I go up and down the aisles.

Produce

Apples

There are so many different varieties of apples to choose from. Some are better for eating and others for baking. New Zealand also exports many wonderful tasting apples into our country that rival the famous Honey Crisp apple. These are very firm, tart but with a sweet underlying taste and keep well in the refrigerator for a couple of months. I usually eat them well before they go bad because they are so good. In a few years I will expect our country will start growing them. The more expensive apples run around $1.99 a pound. However, if you get to the store after they have sorted out the bruised and damaged ones, you can often get them for 40 cents a pound. If they are really bad I use them to make apple sauce or chutney, or if the slices are good enough, an apple pie. I always leave a bowl of apples out on my counter for anyone to enjoy.

Berries

When selecting berries do not be afraid to open up the container and see how fresh they are or if there is any mold. If they look fresh and only one berry is molded, I have been known to ask them to mark down the price, and they usually oblige me. When selecting blueberries always select the container that has the hardest berries; these stay fresh longer. I also vacuum seal berries in a wide-mouth quart canning jar with my vacuum sealer. They will usually stay fresh up to 10 days this way. Do not wash them until you are ready to eat them.

Broccoli

Look for firm stalks and firm, tightly bunched heads. Avoid any that have tiny yellow buds on the head. You can also check the bottom of the stalk to see when it was harvested. Older stalks will look dried up and will start turning brown.

Citrus Fruits

They will usually stay fresh in your refrigerator for up to 3 weeks. Be sure to keep them separate from other produce, because the gases they give off will affect other fruits. Make sure citrus fruits are ripe when you purchase them as they will not continue to ripen once they have been harvested.

Cantaloupe and Honeydew

Avoid melons with stems; ripe ones pull easily from the vine, so an attached stem is a sure sign that the melon is under ripe. Weigh melons in your hands; the sweet ones are heavy for their size. Sniff at the stem. It should smell sweet. Cantaloupe should have no green on them if you are going to eat them right away. If they do, leave them on your counter for a few days until they develop a soft spot and the green disappears. Then refrigerate, and when cold, enjoy.

Celery

When purchasing celery look for light colored full stalks, with a mild smell. These will taste the best. If the strings on the stalks bother you, you can always peel them off. Use the leaves in your salads, as a garnish, or to feed to your birds.

Corn

Fresh corn is best purchased from the farmer. But that is not to say that you cannot get good corn from your local grocery store. There are many varieties of sweet corn with cute sounding names. However, I have always found that the sweetest corn has smaller kernels, and tend to be iridescent or pearly looking. Avoid tough, milky looking kernels. Also look at the green leaves surrounding them; they should look fresh.

Cabbage

Look for the heaviest heads with bright, firm leaves. Check the stem end. If it is dry and shows signs of cracking, it may have been on the shelf for a while. Dry stems could also indicate that the cabbage grew in dry weather and may have a sharp, unpleasant flavor.

Garlic, Onions and Potatoes

Do not purchase any that have started sprouting, which causes spoiling. These items should be stored separately in a cool dark area, and not in the refrigerator, as flavors could be altered. Avoid storing potatoes next to onions as they shorten each other's shelf life. The green color on a potato is chlorophyll developing in the skin. Along with this change, increased quantities of solanin are formed. Solanin is part of the flavoring compound that gives the potato its taste and could give you a bellyache. This is concentrated close to the potatoes' surface and is easily removed when peeled. Only if the potato has prolonged exposure to light will the bitter taste and color penetrate deeper into the potato. We recommend that you don't purchase potatoes that have started to turn green.

For baking, mashing or frying, look for a high-starch potato, such as a russet, Idaho, or a Burbank. For roasting or using in au gratin, look for a medium-starch, all-purpose potato such as a white, blue or purple, or one of the golden-fleshed potatoes such as a Yellow Finn or a Yukon Gold. For salads use a low-starch potato such as a red-skinned potato or a white California potato.

Ginger

Choose the hardest, smoothest pieces you can find. Avoid any that have mold or wrinkled skins. If you only need a small amount, break off one of the knobs. If the ginger is fresh, it will break with a clean snap. You can wrap it in a paper towel, seal it in a plastic bag, and refrigerate for 2 to 3 weeks.

Grapes

When shopping for table grapes, look for full, plump clusters with no bruises or soft spots. Check the stem; it should be green and very pliable. Refrigerate in a loosely closed plastic bag.

Leafy Greens

Purchase only the most vibrant greens with no discolorations or brown on the cut stems. If you are buying a head/bunch of lettuce look at where it was cut when harvested. If it is dark brown it is probably 3-5 days old already. When storing, store either in a vacuum-sealed container (where it will then last approximately 2 ½ weeks), or in a plastic bag on a refrigerator shelf. Some people have told me that if you put a folded damp paper towel in the plastic bag, they will keep better. Do not clean until you are ready to use.

Peaches, Plums, and Nectarines

To see how sweet a peach or nectarine is, use the sniff test on room temperature produce. It does not work if they are cold. If they smell sweet but are still firm, they are okay. You can then take them home and put them in a brown paper bag; check them every day. Once they yield to gentle pressure they are ready to eat. I keep the bag on my kitchen counter until they are ripe, then I put them in the refrigerator.

Tomatoes

Once again there are many varieties to choose from. Tomato plants vary in size from small cherry tomatoes to elongated plum tomatoes. Heirloom tomatoes are also becoming increasingly popular among home gardeners and organic producers. Heirloom tomatoes tend to be more disease resistant and produce very tasty, interesting fruits. Tomatoes should not be stored in the refrigerator, as this will alter their taste and texture. Just leave them on the counter away from sunlight.

Watermelon

It would be great if we could see the inside of a watermelon before we bought it. Everyone seems to have a different way of telling if it is good or not. I have had people tell me to look for a whitish/yellow spot on the bottom of the watermelon; look for pin holes where insects have left a mark; or measure the weight of two the same size, and then purchase the heaviest one. Try to avoid purchasing cut melon if you can, as you will pay twice as much. However, if you need only a little and do not have enough refrigerator room for a whole melon, make sure that the flesh seems firm, is not shrinking back from the seeds, and is dark red in color.

Vegetable Cooking Times

Vegetable	Amount	Microwave, High (min)	Steamer (Min)	Pressure Cooker (min)
Artichokes	4 medium	20-25	30-35	9-11
Asparagus	1 lb, trimmed	5-6	6-7	1-2
Broccoli	1 lb, cut into florets	8-12	5-7	2-3
Brussels sprouts	1 lb	7-11	11-12	4-5
Cabbage	1 medium, cut into wedges	9-13	12-15	3-4
Carrots	1 lb, sliced	8-10	7-10	4-5
Cauliflower	1 lb, cut into florets	4-7	8-10	2-3
Corn on the cob	4 ears	10-14	10-12	3-4
Eggplant	1 medium, cubed	7-10	5-7	3-4
Green beans	1 lb	10-12	7-9	2-3
Kale	1 lb, 2" pieces	8-10	5-6	3-4
Leeks	1 lb; ½" slices	4-6	8-10	2-3
Mushrooms	1 lb, sliced	6-8	3-4	1-2
Onion, small whole	1 lb	6-8	15-20	4-5
Peas, green	1 lb, shelled	5-7	8-10	Not recommended
Peas, snap	1 lb	6-10	8-10	Not recommended
Potatoes, small whole	1 lb; pricked with fork	9-11	25-30	6-7
Spinach	1 lb	5-7	3-4	2-3
Squash, spaghetti	3 lb, halved and seeded	7-9	25-35	14-17
Squash, summer	1 lb, sliced	4-6	8-10	2-3
Squash, winter	1 medium, halved and seeded	8-10	25-30	6-7
Sweet potatoes	2 lb, pricked with fork	13	30-35	8-10
Turnips	1 lb, peeled and cut	7-9	10-12	3-4
Zucchini	1 lb, sliced	4-6	8-10	2-3

Vegetable Roasting Times

Almost any vegetable can be roasted, even greens. Winter squash takes on a wonderful flavor because the high heat enhances the vegetable's natural sugar. To roast any of the following vegetables, prepare them as necessary and roast on a lightly oiled, rimmed baking sheet in the lower third of a 450 degree oven for the specified time. Toss any cut vegetables with olive or canola oil, then sprinkle with salt and pepper. Cut them the same size so that they will cook in the same amount of time. Make sure that vegetables are in a single layer on the roasting pan. The amounts are calculated for about 4 servings.

Vegetable	Amount	Preparation	Roasting Time
Acorn Squash	1-2	Cut in half and seed; place, cut side up on pan	50 minutes
Asparagus	1 lb.	Trim	10-15 minutes
Beets	2 lb.	If small leave whole and scrub well. If larger cut in half or quarter. Remove skins after cooking when cool enough to handle. Be sure to wear gloves.	35-40 minutes
Bell Peppers	3	Cut in thin strips	12 minutes; stir halfway through cooking
Buttercup Squash	1	Peel and cut into 1" chunks; cover with foil on pan	10-12 minutes
Carrots	1 lb.	Cut into 1" sections or ½" sticks	18 to 32 minutes depending on size
Corn	4 ears	Clean	8 to 10 minutes
Eggplant	1 medium	Cut into ½" slices and brush with olive oil	20 minutes; turn slices over halfway through cooking and brush again
Green Beans	1 lb.	Trim	12 minutes; stir halfway through cooking
Potatoes	2 lb.	Cut into wedges or ½" slices	30-35 minutes; turn halfway through cooking
Red onions	2	Leave unpeeled; halve; place cut side down on pan; cover with foil	25-30 minutes
Shallots	1 lb.	Peel, leave whole	Rotate and turn over halfway through
Sweet Potatoes	2	Peel and cut into ¼" slices; cover with foil	20 minutes; uncover and roast 10 minutes more
Tomatoes	2 lb.	Use whole plum tomatoes	20-25 minutes; turn halfway through cooking
Zucchini	2 lb.	Halve lengthwise and cut into 1 ½" chunks	20 minutes; stir halfway through cooking

Guide to Grilling Vegetables

Vegetable	Preparation	Type of Heat
Artichokes	Trim, blanch and cut in half	Direct
Asparagus	Cut off tough ends	Direct
Baby Carrots	Wash but don't peel; blanch	Direct
Beets	Blanch and cut into wedges	Indirect
Bell Pepper, sliced	Core, seed and cut into strips	Direct
Corn	Grill whole; peel back husk and silk after cooking	Direct
Eggplant, sliced	Cut into ½" thick slices; slice Japanese eggplant lengthwise	Direct
Eggplant, whole	Pierce in several places with a fork	Indirect
Fennel	Trim tops and peel fibrous strings; cut into wedges	Direct
Garlic	Slice off top of head	Indirect
Leeks	Trim, rinse and remove tough outer leaves, halve lengthwise; blanch large leeks	Direct
New Potatoes	Blanch; cut in half or quarters	Direct
Onions	Slice; secure slices with soaked toothpicks	Direct
Portobello Mushrooms	Wipe clean and remove stems and gills, grill caps gill side up	Indirect
Scallions	Trim root ends	Direct
Zucchini	Trim and slice lengthwise	Direct

Dairy Department

Eggs

There is no difference in taste or nutritional value between white and brown eggs. The color of the egg shell just depends on the breed of the chicken. Freshness, however, does affect taste so always purchase the freshest eggs available. At a grocery store, the month's expiration date is stamped on the carton. Eggs stored in their original carton will stay fresher and protect the eggs from absorbing other food odors.

Free range eggs are richer and healthier for you, and free range farms house chickens more humanely. I love to drive into the country and watch the chickens follow Diane all over the yard, even ignoring the dog, to purchase my eggs. And when I eat the eggs I have purchased from her, I know where my food has come from.

If you want to check for an egg's freshness, a simple test will tell you. Place the egg in a small bowl of water. A fresh egg will stand straight up and float. Alternately, you can crack open the egg. With an older egg, the albumin (the white of the egg) will be runny.

When a recipe calls for 2 eggs, what this really means is 2 large eggs. So if you use another size—for instance, medium or extra-large, you will need to adjust the amount you are putting into the recipe.

Skip the bagel this morning. Eggs, which are full of protein will help you feel fuller longer. A multicenter study of 30 overweight or obese woman found that those who ate two scrambled eggs (with two slices of toast and a reduced-calorie fruit spread) consumed less for the next 36 hours than women who had a bagel breakfast or equal calories.   Other research has shown that protein may also prevent spikes in blood sugar, which can lead to food cravings.

Evaporated Milk

Evaporated milk is simply milk that has been boiled until 60% of the water has evaporated away. It is available in full, non- and low-fat varieties. Recipes call for it to add richness; it is about the same consistency as cream.

Do *not* confuse evaporated milk with sweetened condensed milk. They are not the same! Sweetened condensed milk, as the name implies, has been artificially sweetened, while evaporated milk is not sweet. It has only the kind of sugar found naturally in milk. In a pinch, you can add ½ cup of water to a can of evaporated milk to turn it into regular milk.

Yogurt and Milk

Always check the best-by date; the later the better. Refrigerated dairy foods last at least a week after opening. Light and heat destroy vitamins in milk, so return it to the fridge as soon as you are finished using it. Yogurt is very economical and easy to make at home, with a savings up to 80%.

Frozen Foods

Ice Cream

Do not purchase ice cream package that is dented, leaky, or covered in frost, which could indicate that it thawed and was refrozen. Reach into the back of the case for the coldest containers. Once you have taken out what you want to eat, put it back in the freezer.

Frozen Vegetables

Cut-up vegetables are individually quick frozen, which means that each piece should remain separate. Feel the package; if it is in chunks or one big block, it might have been stored improperly. Purchase reusable insulated bags in the frozen-food department to help keep things frozen until you get home (up to 3 hours). For extra insurance, pack all of your frozen food together in one or two bags or a cooler.

Meat and Seafood

Meat

Use your eyes and nose to judge meat. To save money, purchase only meat that is on sale. Look at the expiration or sell-buy dates and purchase the freshest one. Ground beef should be sold in one day from the store, so if it is marked differently, ask them to mark it down then repackage and freeze it at home. Regular packaging will last 3 months while vacuum sealing will last a year or two. Whenever I can get chuck roast on sale at a really good price, I even can it. This makes fantastic sandwiches when heated and served on French bread, with sautéed onions and provolone cheese. In warm months I always put an ice cooler in the car for my refrigerated food purchases.

Lean Beef

It's what's for dinner, or should be, if you're trying to shed pounds. The amino acid leucine, which is abundant in proteins like meat and fish as well as in dairy products, can help you pare down while maintaining calorie-burning muscle. That's what it did for 24 overweight middle-aged women in a study at the University of Illinois at Urbana-Champaign. Eating anywhere from nine to ten ounces of beef a day on a roughly 1,700 calorie diet helped the women lose more weight, more fat, and less muscle mass than a control group consuming the same number of calories, but less protein. The beef eaters also had fewer hunger pangs.

Shellfish

Pick the freshest lobster, oysters, and crabs which are sold alive and should react immediately to prodding. Clams or mussels should stay closed when you tap the shells. Shellfish should be packed in breathable mesh or paper bags rather than plastic. Live shellfish can't stand too-cold temperatures, so cook it the same day or store it in a cooler at about 40 degrees surrounded by damp newspaper as insulation from the cold.

Fish

When choosing fresh fish, look for flesh that is bright white or rosy (depending on the type of fish), without gaps between muscle layers. Eyes should be bright not cloudy. Sniff it to make sure it has a clean, briny scent. Store it right away in your refrigerator and cook it that day or the next. If not cooking it until the next day, store it on crushed ice.

Nuts

Once the package has been opened you should vacuum seal nuts to enjoy at a later date. Some nuts can also be frozen, but I have had better luck with vacuum sealing them.

Deli Department

Cheese

All cheeses, especially soft ripened types, dry out and lose flavor quickly, so buy only what can be eaten in a few days. If possible, cheese should be cut as it's needed. Cheese in plastic wrap or vacuum-packed should be free of moisture or a white powdery bloom, signs that the cheese is beginning to grow mold and is going downhill. The best way to store cheese is wrapped in butcher or waxed paper. Cheese needs to breathe.

Deli Meat

Cold cuts should be sliced to order so that you do not overbuy. Meats will normally last 2 weeks. However, if in doubt do not eat it. For the freshest deli meats, shop at a store that is busy in their deli department.

Canned and Dry Foods

Canned Goods

Look at the expiration date on the can. Never buy cans that do not look fresh, i.e., with dust on the cans, bulges, dents, or rust. You can normally keep cans 2 years beyond their expiration date without any effect on color or texture.

Flour, Dried Pasta, Cookies, Crackers and Cereal

To keep flour fresh, if you have the space, put a plastic bag around the paper bag of flour and put it in your freezer. Be sure to mark a date on the bag. After you open a package of crackers or cookies, vacuum seal them in a large wide-mouth jar to keep them fresh. Vacuum seal everything that you can to keep them as fresh as possible and to protect against flour moths.

I store my cereal and oats in a 2 quart canning jars. Clear jars make my food look so enticing.

Bread and Pastry

Bread, Rolls, Pastry

Do not refrigerate bread, as it will go stale faster. Store commercial loaves in their original wrappings on the counter or freeze (up to a month) and use it as you need it. Bakery bread will normally stay fresh only for 1-3 days. If you enjoy the smell of fresh bread, but do not know how to make it, you might want to invest in a bread machine. You can then have fresh bread under 50 cents a loaf.

Chapter 16

Homemade Cleaning Supplies

Why use homemade cleaners? There are many reasons why an economically and health-minded family may want to use cleaners whipped up at home, rather than purchased at a store.

1. **Peace of mind.** Ever read the ingredient list on a commercial cleaner? If not, try it some time. You may be surprised to find that you do not recognize over half of the items listed! Knowledge is power, and when you use a cleaner filled with chemicals you do not recognize, you also do not know what kind of harm it could do. But when you make your own cleaner, you know exactly what you put into it, and you can decide what you are comfortable using in your own home.

2. **Savings.** For you, dear reader, this may be the biggest incentive to making your own cleaners. Just how much you can save will, of course, depend on the ingredients you use. But the more you replace commercial detergents and soaps with your own, the more you will save!

3. **Safety.** The chemicals found in many commercial cleaners are not safe for pets or children. Using your own homemade cleaners can allow you to keep those chemicals out of your home and make it a little safer for your loved ones (both furry and otherwise).

4. **Ecology.** Commercial cleaning products can impact the environment in negative ways. Harsh chemicals that go down the drain can affect the water supply; plastic containers can end up in a dump and stay there for decades, if not centuries! Using your own cleaners prevents such negative impacts on the environment and makes your own atmosphere a little healthier, too.

5. **Effectiveness.** Of course none of these would matter much if homemade cleaners did not work. But they do! Commercial cleaners may get the job done quicker, but homemade cleaners are friendlier all around, and they work very well. You may find that certain formulas work better than others for your purposes; feel free to experiment. There are many different kinds of formulas for many different kinds of jobs!

The following cleaning formulas have been tested and have found to be effective. They can be used together without fear of causing dangerous chemical reactions (such as those caused by mixing bleach and ammonia or vinegar and bleach).

While the following cleaners are safe for children to use, be aware that borax is not safe to ingest. If you find that a child has accidentally ingested borax, call Poison Control (911).

Colors & Labeling: You may want to use a drop of food coloring to each formula; this helps differentiate them from one another. Many formulas tend to look like plain water without some sort of coloring. Some like to use blue for window cleaners, green or orange for all-purpose cleaners (depending on their scents), or red for floor cleaner, for example.

Of course all cleaner bottles should be clearly labeled. To make your containers easier to refill, you may want to include the cleaner's formula on its label. And do not forget instructions on how to use the cleaner.

Containers: Spray containers can easily be found at dollar stores and other discount stores. Nearly any leftover plastic containers can be used for cleaners that are not sprayed, such as dishwashing detergent. You could use empty food containers or empty commercial cleaner bottles; just be sure you wash and rinse them thoroughly before re-using them.

Wiping: The best wipes are not paper towels, but surgical hock towels. They are not easy to find in stores, but enter "surgical hock towels" into a search engine, and you will find about a dozen or so outlet shops that sell them. They are lint-free and fantastic for cleaning glass and dusting.

For other cleaning needs, microfiber cloths have amazing dust attracting qualities. They grab dirt like other towels and rags simply cannot. Sam's Club is rumored to have the best quality and price for these, so if you have a friend who is a member, great! If not, you are bound to find them elsewhere, as they are becoming increasingly popular.

Our Favorite Homemade Formulas

Citrus-Infused Vinegar
Total Cost: 8 cents

Orange oil smells wonderful and has fantastic cleaning abilities. Soak orange peels in vinegar, which will absorb the orange oils as well as its pigment. Vinegar, of course, is also renowned for its cleaning prowess, and together, these two are a tough cleaning combination.

The best time to make this is when you're already eating oranges, which should be during the winter because that's when oranges are in season. Try to make enough during the winter to last until next year.

Take the peels of 4 to 6 oranges and place into a glass quart canning jar. Cover the peels with vinegar and screw the lid shut. Keep sealed for 1 to 2 weeks, shaking the jar ever once in a while. After this time has passed, strain the peelings. The vinegar should now be a dark orange color.

An alternate method is to place orange peels in a jar with vinegar as you eat them. So start with one orange peel in a jar of vinegar, then add more peels over time. Be sure to leave enough room in the jar for additional peels when you add the vinegar.

Use this vinegar in place of white vinegar in any of the formulas below, as you desire.

Alternately, you may use another citrus fruit other than oranges. You could use lemons, limes, grapefruits, or tangerines - any will work.

Organic Disinfecting All-Purpose Spray
Total Cost: 59 cents

This recipe uses castile soap and a bit of borax, which disinfects without becoming toxic. You can give it a different scent either with a few drops of essential oil or by using castile soap that already is scented with essential oils.

1/4 cup vinegar (white or citrus-infused)
2 teaspoon borax
1/4 cup liquid castile soap (Dr. Bronner's is a great brand. Shop around online for the best price. Any scent will work.)
2 cups hot water
1 drop food coloring (optional)

Shake all ingredients together in a spray bottle. Shake before each use. Spray and wipe. Ideal for countertops, table tops, stove tops, high chair trays, etc.

Basic Cleaner Spray
½ teaspoon baking soda or washing soda
2 teaspoons borax
½ teaspoon liquid soap or detergent
2 cups hot water

Combine all ingredients in a spray bottle and shake well. The washing or baking soda works wonders for cutting grease. This formula makes about 2 cups.

Heavy-Duty Cleaner
1 tablespoon ammonia
1 tablespoon liquid laundry detergent
2 cups water

Combine all ingredients and pour into a spray bottle.

Window/Glass Cleaner - Version 1
Total cost: less than 5 cent

4 cups water
2 drops Joy brand concentrated dish detergent (other brands may or may not work)

1 drop blue food coloring (optional)

Combine in a spray bottle and shake. Use as you would any glass cleaner.

Window/Glass Cleaner - version 2

½ cup vinegar plus 1 gallon of water (or 2 tablespoons to a quart)
or
½ cup sudsy ammonia to 1 gallon of water (or 2 tablespoons to a quart)
or
½ cup sudsy ammonia
2 cups rubbing alcohol
1 teaspoon liquid dishwashing detergent
1 gallon water

Combine all ingredients in a large-enough container to hold the entire solution. This cleaner is less likely to freeze in cold weather.

Automatic Dishwasher Detergent
Total cost for 75 ounces: $2.27

People with hard water may need to increase the amount of this cleaner, as well as add vinegar to the rinse compartment of the dishwasher.

1 cup salt
2 cups baking soda
2 cups borax

Combine all ingredients; store in an airtight jar.

Use 1 tablespoon in each compartment; run dishwasher as you normally would.

Laundry Booster
Add any of the following to your washing machine's wash cycle improve a laundry detergent's performance:

½ cup baking soda
¼ cup vinegar
¼ cup borax
½ cup washing soda

Adding any of these to your washing machine's rinse cycle will guard against graying, too.

Bleaching Agents for Laundry
Add any of the following to your washing machine's wash cycle to brighten clothes:
¼ cup washing soda
¼ cup borax
¼ cup lemon juice

Another natural clothing brightener is sunlight -- just hang your clothes in the sunshine. If you put ¼ cup lemon juice in your washing machine's rinse cycle *and* then hang your clothes in the sunshine, you'll get a double brightening boost!

Fabric Softener
Add any of the following to your washing machine's wash cycle:

¼ cup baking soda
¼ cup vinegar
¼ cup borax

To prevent static cling, you can also add ¼ cup vinegar to the washing machine's rinse cycle.

Dusting Spray & Wood Polish

Total Cost: 4 cents

While this is a perfect wood floor cleaner, it can be used for vinyl floors as well. It's a great duster when sprayed onto a surgical huck cloth. Add a few drops of olive or linseed oil to a dusting cloth along with this spray, and it makes a great wood polish.

Essential oil will help mask that vinegary scent that some people may not care for.

2 cups water
1 cup vinegar (white or orange)
5 drops essential oil (optional)

Mix in a spray bottle and use as you would a commercial cleaner.

Cleaning with a Commercial Floor Cleaner (for less)

Total Cost: 6 cents

If you like the way a certain brand of floor cleaner works, you can continue to use it and save money doing it. Most people use a commercial cleaner by adding ¼ cup to a gallon of water. A 32-oz bottle of cleaner will therefore give you about 16 cleanings.

A better (and cheaper) way: Fill a spray bottle with 4 cups of water and 1 tablespoon of cleaner. Wet a microfiber cloth, spray the cleaner, and wipe the floor. Rinse the cloth periodically, either in the sink or in a bucket of water. If you have a mop that uses disposable cleaning cloths, you may be able to pinch in a microfiber cleaning cloth and refill the cleaner container with this formula of 4 cups water to 1 tablespoon cleaner.

Microwave Cleaner

Total Cost: Nearly free!

Fill a glass measuring cup with water and a pinch of salt (which prevents the water from exploding from the cup). Microwave on high for 2 minutes. Keep the door shut for another 5 to 10 minutes. Then open the door and wipe out the microwave. Everything will wipe out very easily - even the heavily baked-on debris!

Homemade Cream Scrubber
Total cost: 80 cents

This is a great non-abrasive scrub for stove and range tops. Create a paste from baking soda and dish detergent; rub in with a stiff brush or non-scratching pad. Rinse with water (but only at the end - do not dilute the paste with water).

Tub & Shower Cleaner
Total Cost: 4 cents

Combine 1 cup of water with ¼ cup of vinegar; this removes soap scum and hard water deposits. It's good for maintenance cleaning; if it's been years since you've cleaned your shower, this won't be much help - you'll need a more heavy-duty cleaner for that job.

Baking soda is a good tub cleaner as well - it's gritty and can help remove soap scum and hard water buildup. To remove the baking soda afterward, spray with some vinegar to rinse. The vinegar will dissolve away the baking soda.

Toilet Cleaner 1
Total cost: 27 cents

Sprinkle a cup of borax into the toilet bowl and allow it to sit overnight. Be sure to keep any pets and children out of the bathroom. Scrub with a brush in the morning and flush. That's it!

Toilet Cleaner 2
Pour a cup of bleach into the toilet bowl and do the same as you did with the borax. Be *very* careful not let it splash onto your clothing, though, or else you'll wind up with ruined clothes!

The Magic of Baking Soda

Baking soda has been renowned for its cleaning power for over a century and a half. It is not only affordable, but it is environmentally friendly as well. It is also safe around young children and pets. In addition to its many uses as a cleaning agent, baking soda has many other uses around the household as well. Below are just some of the many ways in which you can use this powerful, versatile substance!

1. Used regularly, baking soda is very effective at keeping drains clear and fresh. Just sprinkle some down your drain while running hot water.

2. You can also sprinkle baking soda on a damp sponge and easily wipe away soap scum from tubs, tiles, and sinks. (The sponge should be damp, but not soaking wet; too much water negates the mild abrasive effect that allows baking soda to be so effective at this task.)

3. Vinyl shower curtains coated with grime and soap scum? Sprinkle some baking soda onto a damp sponge, wipe down the curtains, rinse, and allow to dry.

4. To clean your tile floors, mix a bucket of warm water with ½ cup of baking soda. Mop the floor with this solution, then rinse. Baking soda can also be used to buff away scuffmarks when sprinkled onto a damp sponge.

5. Sprinkle baking soda onto your carpets, allow to sit for a few minutes, then vacuum to make your carpets smell fresher.

6. Freshen clothing and linens by adding ½ cup of baking soda to your washing machine's rinse cycle.

7. You probably already know to place an open box of baking soda in your refrigerator and freezer to help eliminate odors. But did you know it also works for closets? Use it the same way. Just place an open box on a shelf, and remember to replace it every month. Of course I would want to know what was causing the odor and eliminate it instead.

The Magic of Vinegar

Clean Pet Bowls: When your pet's water dish gets coated with lime, soak it in vinegar and water until the lime is loosened and rinses out.

Electric Iron Cleaner: To remove dark or burned spots on the bottom of an iron, rub with vinegar then wipe off with a clean, wet cloth.

Coffee maker cleaner: To eliminate unpleasant lime deposits that can build up and clog a coffee maker, once a month fill the coffee maker with 2 cups of white vinegar and one cup of water; then run through the brew cycle. Rinse two more pots of water through to rinse.

Thermos bottle cleaner: Add ¼ cup of vinegar and fill with warm water. Soak overnight and rinse well.

Water spot remover: Add ½ cup of vinegar to final rinse in dishwasher to remove spots on glasses.

Remove sticky remains of tags and decals: Apply full strength vinegar directly on top and around stickers, let soak and gently scape with fingernail or old plastic credit card to remove.

Remove Mildew: Use vinegar full strength for heavy mildew or mixed with water for light mildew. Works for clothing, furniture, bathroom fixtures, shower curtains, painted surfaces, among others.

Absorb odors: Inside old box, foot locker, or car trunk smells, moisten a piece of bread with vinegar and leave it inside overnight to absorb the odors.

Remove furniture polish buildup: Buildup on wood, mix ½ cup vinegar and ½ cup of water. Dip in solution and wring out well, rub wood well then immediately with another soft cloth.

Clean Plastic stains for storage bowls: Soak in full strength vinegar for thirty minutes, then rinse with water and wash with soap and water. Even removes spaghetti sauce stains!

Chapter 17

Recipes for Pets

Dogs

Leaping Liver Dog Cookie

1 pound sliced beef liver (save the juice)
1/4 cup water
1 small box corn bread and muffin mix

Preheat oven to 350 degrees. Spray an 8 1/2 x 11 inch baking pan with cooking spray. Grind the liver in a food processor one slice at a time. Add a little water with each slice so you end up with a liquid. Thoroughly combine the muffin mix and the liver liquid in a large bowl. Pour the liver mix into the prepared pan. Bake until the middle springs back at your touch, 20 to 25 minutes. Cool and cut into small cubes. (Organ meat, while good for your dog, is too rich to give in large amounts.) Use for an occasional treat. Can be stored in the freezer for as long as 3 months.

Delectable Dog Biscuits

Yield: 16 pieces

2 pound calcium-rich dog food or canned dog food
1/4 cup whole wheat flour
3/4 cup oat bran
1 cup rolled oats
1/4 cup shredded Parmesan or cheddar cheese (optional)
1/2 cup vegetable oil

Preheat oven to 250 degrees Mix dog food, flour, bran, rolled oats, vitamin, and cheese. Add oil gradually, mixing dough to a consistency that can be rolled out and cut with a cookie cutter. Roll and cut, or mold into biscuits. Place on ungreased baking sheet. Bake for 3 1/2 hours or until hard. Allow to cool and store in a covered container in refrigerator for one week or freezer for up to one month.

Cats

Wholesome Kitty Dinner

2/3 cup ground chicken or beef
1 jar mixed vegetable baby food
1 pet vitamin, crushed
1/3 cup plain dry bread crumbs

In a small saucepan over medium heat, poach the ground meat in a small amount of water until medium rare. Remove from heat and allow to cool.

Stir together the meat with its juices, baby food, and vitamin. Form into bite-sized balls and roll in bread crumbs.

Serve as much as your cat will eat in one sitting. Store the rest in a covered container in the refrigerator for up to three days.

Heavenly Kitty Hash

3 or 4 servings

1 cup water
1/3 cup uncooked brown rice
2 teaspoon vegetable oil
2/3 cup lean ground turkey
2 tablespoon chopped liver

In a medium saucepan, bring the water to a boil. Stir in the rice and oil and reduce the heat to low and allow the mixture to simmer for 20 minutes covered.

Add the ground turkey and chopped liver. Stir frequently and simmer for 20 more minutes.

Equivalents, Substitutions and Recipe Index

Recipes for Pets